VOLLEYBALL
Systems
& Strategies

USA *Volleyball*

Human Kinetics

Library of Congress Cataloging-in-Publication Data

Volleyball systems & strategies / USA Volleyball.
    p. cm.
  Includes bibliographical references and index.
  ISBN-13: 978-0-7360-7495-7 (soft cover)
  ISBN-10: 0-7360-7495-3 (soft cover)
  1. Volleyball. I. USA Volleyball (Organization) II. Title: Volleyball systems and strategies.
  GV1015.3.V66 2009
  796.325--dc22

                                2008050283

ISBN-10: 0-7360-7495-3
ISBN-13: 978-0-7360-7495-7

Acquisitions Editor: Laurel Plotzke; **Developmental Editor:** Kevin Matz; **Assistant Editor:** Elizabeth Watson; **Copyeditor:** John Wentworth; **Proofreader:** Coree Clark; **Permission Manager:** Martha Gullo; **Graphic Designer:** Fred Starbird; **Graphic Artist:** Francine Hamerski; **Cover Designer:** Keith Blomberg; **Photographer (cover):** Kazuhiro Nogi; **Photos (interior):** © Human Kinetics, unless otherwise noted; **Photo Asset Manager:** Laura Fitch; **Visual Production Assistant:** Joyce Brumfield; **Photo Production Manager:** Jason Allen; **Art Manager:** Kelly Hendren; **Associate Art Manager:** Alan L. Wilborn; **Printer:** United Graphics

Human Kinetics books are available at special discounts for bulk purchase. Special editions or book excerpts can also be created to specification. For details, contact the Special Sales Manager at Human Kinetics.

Printed in the United States of America   10 9 8 7 6 5 4 3 2 1

Human Kinetics
Web site: www.HumanKinetics.com

United States: Human Kinetics
P.O. Box 5076
Champaign, IL 61825-5076
800-747-4457
e-mail: humank@hkusa.com

Canada: Human Kinetics
475 Devonshire Road Unit 100
Windsor, ON N8Y 2L5
800-465-7301 (in Canada only)
e-mail: info@hkcanada.com

Europe: Human Kinetics
107 Bradford Road
Stanningley
Leeds LS28 6AT, United Kingdom
+44 (0) 113 255 5665
e-mail: hk@hkeurope.com

Australia: Human Kinetics
57A Price Avenue
Lower Mitcham, South Australia 5062
08 8372 0999
e-mail: info@hkaustralia.com

New Zealand: Human Kinetics
Division of Sports Distributors NZ Ltd.
P.O. Box 300 226 Albany
North Shore City
Auckland
0064 9 448 1207
e-mail: info@humankinetics.co.nz

VOLLEYBALL
Systems
& Strategies

Contents

DVD Contents   vi

Preface   vii

Key to Diagrams   ix

 PART I **Serve, Transition, and Serve-Receive**   1

CHAPTER 1   **Serve and Transition**   3

CHAPTER 2   **Five-Player Serve-Receive System**   11

CHAPTER 3   **Four-Player Serve-Receive System**   17

CHAPTER 4   **Three-Player Serve-Receive System**   23

CHAPTER 5   **Serve-Receive Drills**   29

 PART II **Defensive Systems**   43

CHAPTER 6   **Player-Back System**   45

CHAPTER 7   **Player-Up System**   55

CHAPTER 8   **Two-Blocker System**   65

CHAPTER 9   **One-Blocker System**   73

CHAPTER 10   **Defensive System Drills**   79

PART III **Defensive Strategies**   97

CHAPTER 11   **Block the Line and Dig Inside Strategy**   99

CHAPTER 12   **Block Inside and Dig the Line Strategy**   105

CHAPTER 13   **Middle-Block Strategies**   111

CHAPTER 14   **Defensive Strategy Drills**   121

PART IV Offensive Systems   135

CHAPTER 15 5-1 System   137

CHAPTER 16 6-2 System   143

CHAPTER 17 International 4-2 System   149

CHAPTER 18 Offensive System Drills   155

PART V Offensive Strategies   169

CHAPTER 19 Spread Strategy   171

CHAPTER 20 Fast-Tempo Strategy   177

CHAPTER 21 Multiple Tempos With
            Combination Plays Strategy   185

CHAPTER 22 Swing Strategy   193

CHAPTER 23 Offensive Strategy Drills   201

PART VI Systems, Strategies, and the Team   219

CHAPTER 24 Practicing Team Tactics   221

CHAPTER 25 Match Coaching Tactics   229

Appendix: The Ranking System   236
About USA Volleyball   237

DVD Contents

Serve-Receive Systems

Five-Player Serve-Receive System

Four-Player Serve-Receive System

Three-Player Serve-Receive System

Serve-Receive Drills

Defensive Systems

Player-Back System

Player-Up System

Two-Blocker System

One-Blocker System

Defensive System Drills

Defensive Strategies

Block the Line and Dig the Angle Strategy

Block the Angle and Dig the Line Strategy

Middle-Block Strategies

Defensive Strategy Drills

Offensive Systems

5-1 System

6-2 System

International 4-2 System

Offensive System Drills

Offensive Strategies

Spread Strategy

Fast-Tempo Strategy

Multiple Tempos With Combination Plays Strategy

Swing Strategy

Offensive Strategy Drills

Preface

The *Volleyball Systems & Strategies* book and DVD package offers coaches at the high school and college levels the information they need for devising the optimal tactical approaches for their teams. It was written to present an insider's view of the best approaches to both the offensive and defensive aspects of volleyball. Coaches and players alike will find valuable guidance on the movements, tactics, and options in the most effective offensive and defensive systems used in the game. The book also compares the systems and strategies—based on alignment and execution, personnel requirements, and unique advantages and disadvantages—so that coaches can match them up to make the best use of their team's talents, fit specific opponents, situations, or player combinations.

Whether coaching players at the highest levels of the sport or coaching beginners who know virtually nothing about the sport, coaches must develop sound principles in order to give their teams opportunities to succeed. *Volleyball Systems & Strategies* focuses on team systems, but coaches must remember that at the heart of any successful team is the ability to master the individual skills of volleyball. *Volleyball Systems & Strategies* offers advice on which systems will nurture and develop players' skills. The package also outlines which skills are most important in running a given system or strategy most effectively. For more advanced teams, it provides coaches with the information needed to determine the best systems and strategies for their team based on the team's existing player strengths and weaknesses. This book and DVD package also offers valuable advice for players: It helps them understand the demands of the game and their roles within the specific systems and strategies that coaches ask them to perform on the court.

Volleyball Systems & Strategies is divided into six parts. The various types of offensive and defensive systems and strategies are organized in a way that follows a team through the flow of the game, from serve and serve-receive to defense to the transition into offense. This setup allows for a logical progression of learning. Part I covers serving, transitioning, and five-player, four-player, and three-player serve-receive systems. Part II covers the player-back, player-up, two-blocker, and one-blocker defensive systems. Part III addresses the block the line and dig inside, block inside and dig the line, and various middle-block strategies. Part IV provides all the information needed to succeed using the 5-1, 6-2, and International 4-2 offensive systems. Part V covers how to run the spread offense, fast-tempo offenses, offenses with multiple tempos and combination plays, and the swing strategy. Additionally, each of these parts contains a chapter of drills to help teams learn to execute these systems and strategies effectively. And part VI gives coaches everything they'll need for practicing the tactics in the book and coaching the strategies in matches.

Volleyball Systems & Strategies also includes a companion DVD which puts the instruction from the book into motion. Featuring demonstrations by the gold medal-winning men's national team and collegiate women's players, the DVD brings the book's instruction to life. It shows alignment and execution of the systems and strategies, along with the accompanying match-play drills. Chapters 1 through 23 are covered in depth on the DVD, with explanations of how to run the system or strategy, its advantages and disadvantages, as well as special coaching concerns for each system and strategy. The DVD Contents, included on page vi of the book, outlines all of the topics covered on the DVD for easy reference.

The DVD also contains many drills designed to develop the skills needed to run each system and strategy. Throughout the book's drill chapters (chapters 5, 10, 14, 18, and 23), look for the 🔾 icon next to specific drills to indicate which are demonstrated on the DVD.

In this package are strategies based on the experiences and best practices of coaches associated with USA Volleyball and the Coaching Accreditation Program (CAP) at all levels of the game. Designed to be a comprehensive guide to maximizing results for every aspect of the game, the *Volleyball Systems & Strategies* book and DVD package can be used by any coach in developing great players and a gold medal–caliber system of play.

Key to Diagrams

⟶	Player movement
- - ⟶	Pass
B	Blocker
D	Digger
H	Hitter
P	Passer
S	Setter
SV	Server
T	Target
TS	Tosser
X	Defender
LB	Left back
MB	Middle back
PB	Right back
LF	Left front
MF	Middle front
RF	Right front
LFB	Left-front blocker
MFB	Middle-front blocker
RFB	Right-front blocker
MH	Middle hitter

Serve, Transition, and Serve-Receive

Serve and Transition

EXPLANATION OF TACTIC

There's much more to the volleyball serve than simply putting the ball into play. Serving is the only skill in the game in which success is determined solely by a single player: the server. When putting the ball into play, the server's goal should be one of several desirable outcomes: an ace that cannot be returned by the opponent; a serve delivered in such a way to disallow the opponent mounting any kind of effective attack; or a serve that takes away at least one of the opponent's offensive options, while giving their own blockers and backcourt defenders a better chance of handling the return. Depending on the server, the skills of the opponents, and the circumstances, these three outcomes can be accomplished via several kinds of overhand serves: a standing float serve, a standing topspin serve, a jump float serve, or a jump topspin serve.

1. Standing float serve: This serve has no spin as it floats through the air in unpredictable movement patterns, making it difficult for the opposing team to read its flight and thus presenting problems for their passers. An effective float serve can result in a service ace or can at least limit what the receiving team can do offensively. Of course servers going for an ace must serve the ball close to the top of the net and at greater speed than usual, which leads to a higher risk for error.

2. Standing topspin serve: In this serve, the server makes contact with the hand and wrist rolling up and over the top of the ball, creating topspin as the ball travels over the net, and causing the ball to drop to the ground more quickly. The toss is higher than for a float serve and in line with the hitting shoulder. This serve has decreased in popularity over the years, giving way to the traditional jump topspin serve, which many coaches feel is more effective in generating service aces and putting opponents at a disadvantage. However, a good athlete having trouble making consistent tosses for jump serves might have better success with a standing topspin serve because the toss is easier to execute.

3. Jump float serve: This serve resembles the standing float serve, but here the server contacts the ball while the server's body is in the air, so the ball is struck from a higher point than in a standing serve. The jump float serve is more difficult to master than the standing float serve because the toss and approach are harder to execute effectively. Once a server masters a consistently effective toss, the jump float serve can be very successful because opponents are expecting the ball to have spin (because the server contacts the ball after jumping and it starts out looking like the more traditional jump topspin serve).

4. Jump topspin serve: Again, the server makes contact rolling the hand and wrist over the top of the ball to create topspin, but now the ball is hit from a higher point, creating more difficult angles for opposing passers to deal with. The toss here is more complex than for the standing topspin serve. The server must toss the ball with topspin high enough and far enough out in front to leave plenty of room and time to approach, gain momentum, and generate significant topspin on contact. Once these components are mastered, the jump serve is an extremely effective weapon. Even though the path of the ball is more predictable than with a float serve, the speed with which the ball drops to the floor causes great problems for opposing passers.

PERSONNEL REQUIREMENTS

Coaches should allow servers to experiment to discover which serve works best for them as well as which hand to toss with. They should also learn how the circumstances of a match might determine the best choice of serve.

Let's look at the physical attributes and technical skills that maximize performance for each of the four types of serves.

Standing float serve

▶ Moderate arm speed. Of course fast arm speed comes in handy regardless of the type of serve, but servers with only moderate arm speed can have success with a standing float serve.

▶ Consistently low lift. Because the standing float serve is contacted at a point as high as the server's extended arm, the ball should be lifted (without spin), rather than tossed to that position, allowing for greater control. The toss is generally made with the non-hitting hand.

▶ Minimal foot movement. Servers most effective with standing float serves have minimal movement of their feet. This allows the server to focus on the toss, serving arm preparation, and contact. Many servers execute this serve without taking any steps. Other servers use one step with the lead foot to generate greater weight transfer, power, and distance, and this is still considered minimal foot movement. Servers who lack upper body strength find it helpful to take a step to generate enough power for the ball to clear the net.

▶ Consistent contact point. Servers using the standing float serve should be able to consistently strike the ball directly on the center back point, well out in front of and in line with the hitting shoulder, making contact with the lower part of the stiff serving hand (palm and heel). The wrist should be kept stiff throughout contact.

Standing topspin serve

▶ Fast arm speed. The faster the arm swing, the deeper the serve can travel, and the faster the ball drops to the ground. Players with moderate arm speed will have less success with this serve because the ball travels too slowly over the net and usually in a higher arc, allowing passers more time to react.

▶ High and consistent toss. Being able to consistently toss slightly out in front and in line with the hitting shoulder is an important technical skill for the execution of this serve. Servers who toss consistently in front of the hitting shoulder have the momentum of their entire body to help them generate greater speed on the ball. This momentum is important because only minimal momentum can be generated by the feet (because servers generally take only one step). The ball is typically tossed with the nonhitting arm, but may be tossed with the hitting arm with topspin.

▶ Strong upper body. Because the majority of power for this serve is generated by the upper body and minimal force is provided by the feet, players need a good deal of upper body strength to use this serve.

Jump float serve

▶ Fast to moderate arm speed. Fast-twitched players (players with fast-twitch muscles) have the greatest success in serving a low fast jump float serve, but servers with only moderate arm speed can also disadvantage opponents. A slow-twitched player will have less success because the ball travels more slowly over the net and may not reach into the deeper zones of the court.

▶ Consistent toss. Because the ball is contacted out in front of the body, servers must be able to consistently lift the ball without spin to the same spot slightly out in front and in line with their hitting shoulder. The toss is generally made with the nonhitting hand or even with two hands—whichever is most comfortable, consistent, and controllable.

▶ Consistent footwork pattern. Traditionally, the jump float server finishes with a right–left step (for right-handed servers). Servers who don't perform this footwork pattern consistently tend to have trouble executing the jump float serve. A player who uses backward feet (i.e., finishes L-R for a right-handed player) has great difficulty in making this serve.

Jump topspin serve

▶ Fast arm speed. Fast-twitch muscles are required for serving an effective jump topspin serve. For this traditional jump serve, moderate arm speed is generally not enough. A jump serve struck with moderate arm speed is similar to a down ball attack, which opposing teams can handle with good success because they have had many opportunities to practice defending that ball. The faster the arm swing, the flatter and faster the ball will travel across the net, and the sooner it will drop to the floor, giving opponents less time to respond.

▶ Fast feet, fast approach. Because the objective of the jump serve is to create topspin, servers must generate momentum with their approach; ideally, this momentum then transfers to a fast arm in flight. Fast feet tend to make for a fast arm.

▶ High and consistent toss. The height of the toss for the serve will always vary from server to server based on several factors (server's height, feet quickness, fast- or slow-twitch muscles), but for the jump topspin serve you generally want what's considered a high toss. A high toss gives the server time to generate speed on the approach and gain enough time to get through a two-, three-, or four-step approach to the contact point. Because the toss is farther out in front of the body than in other serves, consistency is difficult with this type of serve and requires much practice. Also, the toss must be tossed with topspin, giving the server a head start in adding heavy topspin when contacting the ball. Finally, servers using this serve should take their last two steps right to left (for right-handed servers). Left-handed servers take their last two steps left to right. Unlike the previous types of serves, this ball is generally tossed with the hitting arm, since it is easier to toss straight out in front of the hitting shoulder on the approach. Some players, however, find it more comfortable and consistent to toss with their nonhitting arm (as in the standing serves), or even with two hands. Again whatever is comfortable, consistent, and controllable.

▶ Overall ball control. Because of the toss difficulty, players with good ball control typically have better luck executing this serve. Ball control is defined as the ability to consistently place the ball in the spot and at the height desired for success. Servers with good ball control can do this while generating topspin on the toss. If the toss doesn't have topspin, less spin is generated on contact, making the ball easier for the opponents to receive.

▶ Height. Because taller players can strike the ball at a higher point than shorter players can, it makes sense to have taller athletes work on this serve. They can create even more downward movement with the ball, making it that much more difficult for opponents to pass.

ADVANTAGES AND DISADVANTAGES

By incorporating all the serves described in this chapter your team creates opportunities to keep opposing players off balance. Opponents who must try to pass a jump float from one server and then face an aggressive standing float serve from the next will find it difficult to maintain rhythm because different adjustments are required based on the kind of serve being received. When a team uses different kinds of serves, everyone must understand the technical and tactical demands of each serve so errors in mechanics and performance can be recognized and corrected. It's better not to use a certain type of serve if players and coaches don't understand how and when to use it properly. Let's look at the specific technical and tactical advantages and disadvantages of each of the serves we've discussed.

Standing Float Serve Advantages

- Players at most levels can master an effective standing float serve—a definite advantage in choosing this type of serve.
- The toss for this serve is a low compact toss (or lift) that's easily controlled.
- Servers can prepare prior to the toss. Much can be done to get ready to serve before the toss is initiated. Servers can preload the serving arm and extend the tossing arm in front of the hitting shoulder well before they lift the toss, increasing consistency and effectiveness.
- Unpredictable movement of the ball makes this serve hard to read for receivers.

Standing Float Serve Disadvantages

- The ball might not float as expected. Servers might execute all the technical skills associated with this serve perfectly and still not have the ball move whatsoever because of factors beyond their control, such as air movement or humidity levels in the gym.
- Receivers might be more comfortable passing these serves. The standing float serve is widely popular, giving opposing passers many opportunities and repetitions to become adept at receiving it.
- If the server is serving short (inside the three-meter line), it can be difficult to achieve the unpredictable ball movement this serve is known for.

Jump Float Serve Advantages

- This serve is contacted while high off the ground, allowing for greater force and creating more difficult angles for receivers to deal with.
- Serving the ball while jumping in the air gives the receiver less time to read where the serve is going and less time to react.
- This serve is relatively easy on the serving shoulder, but can still be hit with great force, flat across the net, which adds to greater ball movement.
- This serve can be deceptive. Once they see the server approach to jump serve, many passers take a step or two forward, anticipating a ball with traditional topspin that's going to drop to the ground in a hurry. Once the passer moves forward, the server gains a tactical advantage, especially when the jump float serve dances , moves around, and may even float up into a passer's chest or face if they have stepped forward.

Jump Float Serve Disadvantages

- Because this serve is contacted in flight and must be struck directly in the middle of the back of the ball to achieve the desired float, mis-hits are common. A mis-hit often results in an easily passed ball for the opponent.
- The server risks accuracy in serve placement because the ball is contacted while in flight.
- Tossing the ball with two hands can hinder ball control because the toss is from the midline of the body and must cross over to the hitting shoulder.
- It can be difficult to disguise this short serve because servers tend to toss the ball slightly behind them, or may drop their hitting elbow, in order to place the serve inside the three-meter line.
- If hit deep with some power, the ball may float out of bounds long.

Standing Topspin Serve Advantages

- A consistent toss is easier to generate than the traditional jump serve toss.
- The ball travels to the floor faster than with a float serve and can be hit deep with tremendous speed and power, yet still drop into the court.
- The server can more easily force the opposing team's poorest passer to receive aggressive serves.
- Servers can more easily direct the serve between passers, promoting breakdowns in communication.

Standing Topspin Serve Disadvantages

- This serve can cause wear and tear on the server's hitting shoulder because of the speed and forces generated.

- The serve is relatively easy for opponents to read, because it travels in one direction; passers may not have to make many position adjustments.

Jump Topspin Serve Advantages

- The ball is contacted high and at fast speed. This serve is the equivalent to a fastball in baseball and can have the same effect when executed well. Even when they see it coming, receivers have difficulty reacting quickly enough. The topspin jumper can be hit with tremendous speed and power to simply blow the ball by an opponent.

- This serve can change the dynamics of a match by forcing the opposing team's setter to set high and outside because the pass won't often be good enough to run a middle or other quick attack.

Jump Topspin Serve Disadvantages

- This serve is relatively risky because the toss is difficult to execute with consistency. Many a great athlete can't jump serve because of difficulty in developing a consistent toss that's far enough in front to generate a fast aggressive approach.

- This serve is physically demanding and might cause fatigue during a long match, and fatigue can effect placement, speed, and power.

- The server might not be able to accurately control the placement of the serve.

- If a team has several jump topspin servers, opponents will be able to prepare for the serve and establish a passing rhythm.

- Because this is a high-risk serve (with a higher error to ace ratio than other serves) there's a greater chance for a server to have a bad night and miss a lot of serves, causing a momentum shift and loss of server and team confidence.

OPTIONS

Once players can execute at least one kind of serve with consistent accuracy, they should work toward developing greater skill in a second kind of serve. This allows them to mix up their serves to catch receivers off guard. They'll also have a backup serve to resort to when their preferred serve isn't working for them.

Servers should also master serving their primary serve to many different areas of the court as well as from different areas along the end line. A standing float server, for example, can cause problems for opponents if he or she can consistently serve to all areas of the court, including short, deep, crosscourt, and line serves. This effect is multiplied if servers can hit that same zone when serving from the right, the middle, and the left areas of their end line, since passers who may get good at receiving serves from one angle may not be quite so successful if they have to receive a serve from the opposite side of the end line. Servers who can vary their type of serve, their serve placement, and their location on the end line are rare and extremely valuable. Forcing opponents to deal with a wide variety of trajectories, speeds, and angles gains the serving team a significant advantage.

COACHING POINTS

Motor learning texts suggest that for learning and transfer to occur, athletes must practice the skills of volleyball in gamelike ways. Very rarely does a server in competition get to serve repeatedly for five minutes, yet inexperienced coaches often ask their players to do just this during practice. If coaches want each server to have five minutes of serving in a given practice, they should instead break the time up into 30- or 60-second blocks, which is much more gamelike. Fifty serves in sets of 1 to 4 serves at a time presents a far more effective learning opportunity than two sets of 25 serves in a row.

When determining which kind of serve best suits a particular server, coaches must be clear on what they want that server to accomplish. Depending on their skills, some servers will be asked to generate aces, whereas others will be asked to serve aggressively enough to limit opponents to fewer offensive options. If a server is serving for aces, the coach must be willing to accept serving errors as part of this strategy. Opposing teams will not be aced if the server simply puts the ball into play. Servers wanting an ace must serve the ball closer to the top of the net and, in most cases, with more speed than usual, which can lead to a greater number of serving errors.

Many coaches believe that the jump serve is riskier than all other serves. You might consider the jump serve your "high risk, high return" serve—when properly executed this serve can take opponents out of their system, making your team's defensive adjustments simpler and more effective. However, the jump serve becomes an easy ball to receive if the server hasn't generated enough speed with the arm and feet to get good velocity on the ball. Plus the toss for the jump serve is the most difficult to master because the server must toss the ball with topspin and get it high enough and far enough out in front to leave room and time to approach, gain momentum, and generate significant topspin on contact. The key to mastering these components is giving servers many opportunities to develop the jump serve in practice. Remember that all components must be practiced together (as opposed to breaking them down into parts) to promote effective transfer from practice to games.

Regardless of what kind of serve your players are practicing, they should be required to transition at gamelike speed to their defensive positions after each serve. In games, servers never get to stand back and admire their serve, so why allow them to do so in practice? Servers should always serve *and* transition or even serve, transition, and dig before serving again.

© Nick Laham/Getty Images

Five-Player Serve-Receive System

EXPLANATION OF TACTIC

Some teams, particularly young or inexperienced teams whose coaches want to expose players to all parts of the game, might opt for the five-player serve-receive. This strategy gives everyone opportunities to develop their skills as forearm passers, without placing undue pressure on any one passer. In the five-player serve-receive pattern, all players except the designated setter are placed in a W formation (figure 2.1).

As you see in the figure, three players position nearer the net, on or near the three-meter line, whereas the two deeper passers are positioned closer to the end line. The strategy of this alignment is to hold all passers accountable for effectively handling a serve in their area of the court. Notice that the two deepest passers split the court down the middle, giving each of them equal responsibility in receiving serves that go behind the three-meter line. Passers stationed nearer the three-meter line are responsible for receiving serves that fall on or inside the line (short serves).

Though the entire W serve-receive pattern can be adjusted deeper or shallower in the court to place passers in the areas served most frequently by the opponent, passers who are closer to the backcourt typically have responsibility for the deeper hard-driven serves. The two players in the backcourt portion of the W also usually get more opportunities to receive serves (because most serves land behind the three-meter line and in the middle of the court), but as long as everyone gets a chance to rotate into and pass from these positions all players can practice their receiving skills.

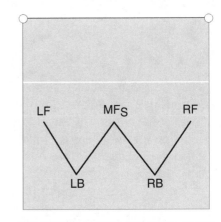

Figure 2.1   Five-player W serve-receive pattern.

PERSONNEL REQUIREMENTS

Because one major reason for incorporating a five-player serve-receive is to give all players an opportunity to develop the skill of receiving serves, there are no strict personnel requirements. That said, as players work on developing their receiving skills in this system, they should have at least an average amount of ball control. If they don't, they will have only minimal chances to practice passing an "in system" ball, which of course undercuts the primary reason for using the five-player pattern to begin with. Average ball control means being able to put the ball—in this case with a forearm or overhead pass—to the desired target 70 percent of the time (90 percent of the time indicates outstanding ball control).

The decision to use the W serve-receive formation to help players develop their passing skills should be applauded, however you also don't want to put your team at a technical and tactical disadvantage to the point of crippling your offense. Disadvantages will always be present when passers of varying skill levels are receiving serves, so it's up to each team to balance the benefits of developing skills with the desire to compete.

ADVANTAGES AND DISADVANTAGES

It's easy to recognize the main disadvantage of the five-player serve-receive. As you can see in figure 2.1, multiple seams exist between players, both front to back and side to side (seams are the spaces between each of the back-row passers, between each of the front-row passers, as well as between back-row and front-row passers), which present opportunities for good servers to serve between two or even three receivers. Whenever two or more potential receivers are wondering if a ball is theirs to receive, the serving team gains a tactical advantage. In such a case, receivers must communicate well; if they don't, many balls will be passed ineffectively, drop between passers, or cause passers to collide

A second disadvantage of the W formation is that with so many players potentially receiving serve there's a much greater likelihood for inconsistent serve-receive, making it difficult for an offense to establish any rhythm. Some serves easily passed by one player (or from one position in the W) might be a challenge for another, causing disruption for players receiving the passes.

Finally, assuming all players are receiving serve from each of the five positions, it becomes difficult for them to become consistently effective because they're passing from various parts of the court. For instance, a passer passing from a back-row position has different angles and demands than a passer passing from a front-row position. If players must play all positions, they will take much longer to hone their skills because there are so many more skills (and angles) to learn. On the other hand, a formation that promotes some specialization of skills allows players to become adept at the skills required of their position; unfortunately, the W serve-receive is not such a formation.

There are of course some advantages to the five-player serve-receive, or else no team would choose to use it. As mentioned, this formation promotes all players developing proficiency in a variety of passing skills, which makes the formation beneficial for young or less experienced teams that are building skills for the future. This formation can help coaches determine which players have skills in certain areas and which do not.

Another advantage is that a five-player serve-receive makes it difficult for opponents to pick on any one passer since a struggling passer can be moved slightly out of an area or have their area of responsibility limited a bit if he or she is having trouble handling serves.

It's also difficult to wear down a particular passer in this formation because five players are taking responsibility for receiving serve as opposed to only three or four. In a more specialized passing system (using three or four passers; see chapters 3 and 4), it's easier to cause one of the primary passers to struggle because they are forced to receive all serves, whether they play in the front or back row.

OPTIONS

As previously mentioned, because each player is passing all five serve-receive positions in the W pattern, it's difficult for any player to become proficient in any one area. One way to help players gain proficiency of skills in a single area within the W formation is to create serve-receive patterns in which players get to pass from one or more positions in more than one rotation. You'll need to keep in mind the overlap rule, which regulates the positioning of adjacent players before the serve is contacted. For example, the overlap rule would apply to the left-back and middle-back players; before contact of the serve the left-back player's closest foot to the left sideline must be closer than the middle back's closest foot to the left sideline. The rule also pertains to an adjacent player directly in front of or behind another player. For instance, the middle-front player is adjacent to the middle-back player, so the middle-front player's closest foot to the center line must be closer than the middle back's closest foot to the center line.

Coaches can devise a serve-receive pattern for their team that adheres to the overlapping rule but which also manipulates the player start positions to allow players to pass from one location within the W in more than one rotation. In this way, even though a team is not specializing in the traditional sense, they are allowing passers to get comfortable and confident from at least one and maybe two positions in the reception pattern. It's quite simple to have the same passer in the right-back or middle-back position pass while positioned in the deep part of the W on the right side of the court in two or more rotations.

Although the five-player W is a nonspecialized strategy, allowing passers to pass from the same position within the W pattern twice or more gives them greater confidence and ability in receiving any serve. Also, within the five-player serve-receive, coaches can identify either as a general rule or by specific rotations who they would like to handle the majority of the opposing team's serves. This creates opportunities to improve overall ball control by giving more leeway and discretion to your better passers to handle more serves. So although it looks to the opponent as if five people are responsible for passing the serve, the players on your team know that one or two players have been given greater responsibility for balls behind, in front, and to the side of them.

COACHING POINTS

As explained earlier, because the five-player serve-receive creates lots of seams between players, coaches must clarify who's responsible for each of the seams. Who takes the ball that will otherwise drop between the two passers closest to the end line? Who takes the serve that will land between the passer stationed near the left-front position and the passer stationed near the left-back position?

Coaches must also determine where they want the passers at the top part of the W to position prior to the serve. The closer they are to the three-meter line (or the further they are in front of it) indicates that the passers at the bottom of the W will handle more of the serves, because passers are generally better when their movement can be primarily forward. Conversely, if the passers on the top of the W are stationed considerably behind the three-meter line, this indicates that the front-row passers will assume more of the responsibility for receiving serve because they're positioned farther back from the net.

Regardless of where a coach ends up positioning passers, a team should generally follow two simple rules of thumb: First, the passer who can move forward (as opposed to backward) should pass the ball, and second, when two passers are both moving forward to a ball that will fall between them, whichever player is moving more to the right (toward the setter) should assume responsibility for the pass. It's easier to pass a ball to a target that you're moving toward rather than away from.

You may not see the five-player serve-receive used frequently, but that doesn't mean it can't be effective for some teams. If a coach believes this system allows all players to develop some reception skills, and that he or she can train passer responsibilities with confidence within this system, there's no reason not to give it a try.

© Mike Hewitt/Getty Images

Four-Player Serve-Receive System

EXPLANATION OF TACTIC

The four-player serve-receive pattern can be considered the beginning of specialization within a serve-receive system because one third of your team has no part in receiving the serve in any single rotation (one of these players is the designated setter). There are two basic strategies regarding the four-player serve-receive pattern. The first strategy, which is the most common, designates the same four players to pass in every rotation. Whether these players are front or back row, and whether the serve is deep or short, jumping or standing, one of these four players is responsible to receive every serve. This strategy gives a team a greater chance to successfully pass the serve to its desired target. In the second strategy, similar to the five-player W described in chapter 2, all players but the designated setter take a turn passing from each of the positions within the four-player reception pattern. This still allows five out of six players the chance to develop their passing skills within the parameters of this more specialized system.

Whichever strategy your team employs, the basic formation of the four-player serve-receive is U shaped (figure 3.1). Two passers who represent the top part of the U are positioned 4 to 5 feet (1.2-1.5 meters) inside the sideline—one near the right sideline and one near the left sideline, as shown—and about 12 to 15 feet (3.6-4.5 meters) from the net. The remaining two passers split the deep backcourt midway between their sideline and the middle of the court. This puts each deep passer at the bottom of the U about 10 feet (3 meters) from their closest sideline. In relation to the end line,

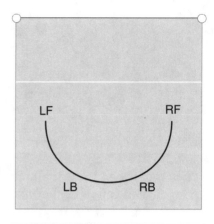

Figure 3.1   Four-player U serve-receive pattern.

each takes position about 8 to 10 feet (2.4-3 meters) from the end line to promote forward movement after the serve is contacted.

As you can see in figure 3.1, several seams are still present in the four-player U formation, just as in the five-player W. The receiving principle that applies to the W also applies to the U—that a serve traveling between the two passers closest to the end line is received by the player in the left-back area because this player is moving toward the intended target (the setter). Further, a serve landing between two passers who are staggered front to back is passed by the deepest passer because it's easier to pass a ball while moving forward than when moving backward. The four-player U can be used effectively as long as all players understand who should take balls that are traveling between players into open areas of the court. With enough practice, players will respond automatically to such serves.

PERSONNEL REQUIREMENTS

Assuming your team is using the same four passers in all six rotations, these passers should pass with greater efficiency than those players who aren't part of the serve-receive pattern. (For a method of assessing passer effectiveness, see page 237.) Specialized passers with responsibility for covering the entire court must have sufficient reading and movement skills, including forward and back as well as lateral movement abilities. Reading skills include watching the server before the toss for clues to help determine where the serve might be going; reading the toss to determine if the server is going to serve short (usually a toss behind the server's head indicates a short serve), crosscourt, or line; and anticipating the flight of the ball once the server has made contact. Average ball control (see chapter 2) is the minimum standard for the four specialized passers in this system.

ADVANTAGES AND DISADVANTAGES

Compared to the five-player W, the four-player U offers some advantages. For one thing, fewer seams are present in a four-player U, making it less likely for miscommunication to occur when a serve is going between players or to an open area of the floor. Having one less player receiving serve compared to the W system tends to make the four passers more aggressive, knowing they must cover more court. In demanding more movement from passers than the five-player W requires, teams using the four-passer system develop players who better understand the overall movement demands of volleyball. Finally, when a team is using all of its players in the four serve-receive positions within this system, all players are developing the skill of receiving serve.

One disadvantage of the four-player U is that when one of a team's four passers has an off night it means that a struggling passer is thus exposed to the opponent to target with their serves. You can't just reassign or drop the struggling passer from their spot in the U because it's difficult for a team to adjust from a four-player serve-receive to a three-player format in the middle of a tournament, match, or game (unless of course, you have prepared them for that adjustment by rehearsing it in practice).

Because a team is more or less specializing with their passers within this system, passers must be positioned in the serve-receive pattern when in the front row. Players struggling with their front-row responsibilities (hitting and blocking) might let their struggles in those areas get the best of them, making their passing also less than perfect.

Finally, with four players identified as passers, lack of ball control becomes a concern when compared to the three-player serve-receive pattern (see chapter 4), since not all four may be highly skilled passers. Despite the possible disadvantages to this system, the benefits gained by passing with four players rather than five generally appear to be worth the risks.

OPTIONS

When a team is developing a four-player U, many options present themselves. Because the four-player reception pattern by and large specializes with the same passers in each rotation, it's possible to design the serve-receive to allow your best passers to receive serves most of the time in the area in which opponents are most likely to serve. Even when specializing with your four best receivers, there will likely be one or two passers who you want to receive more serves than the others. Very rarely do all four passers receive with the same efficiency.

Teams might consider modifying the typical four-player U, for instance by moving passers at the bottom of the U up six or seven feet from the end line as a response to opponents serving shorter zones of the court. The setup of the U can be tinkered with depending on a team's capabilities and the strategy of opposing teams.

As mentioned earlier as a disadvantage to the four-player system, a difficult situation occurs when one of the passers is struggling. In such a case, a couple of options exist. First, the coach might choose to use the same four passers, but encourage the other three passers to step up and cover more court, and limit the struggling passer's area. Second, the struggling passer might be subbed out for a bit, especially if a player on the bench has near equal reception skills. Giving the player a chance to relax might provide the break he or she needs to regain composure and confidence. Good coaches will give some thought to what they will do *when* something happens as opposed to *if* something happens. Acknowledge that passers will struggle and train another option in each rotation so when it does happen your team is still able to perform within a system that they are comfortable and confident with.

An understanding of the overlap rule should guide coaches and players in developing the four-passer system. In general, teams must understand the principle of adjacent players and be able to adjust as necessary. Players must realize they need be concerned only with teammates in adjacent positions. Here are the adjacent positions for each player on the court:

- Left-front player—adjacent players are left back and middle front.
- Middle-front player—adjacent players are left front, right front, and middle back.
- Right-front player—adjacent players are middle front and right back.
- Right-back player—adjacent players are right front and middle back.
- Middle-back player—adjacent players are right back, left back, and middle front.
- Left-back player—adjacent players are middle back and left front.

Official USA Volleyball rules stipulate that the overlap rule is in effect for players who are adjacent to one another, either side to side or front to back. Players must always know who they are adjacent to in each rotation because they must keep the same rotation pattern until the opponents have contacted the serve. For example, before the serve, the left-front player must be closer to the left sideline than the middle-front player is to the left sideline and closer to the center line than the left-back player is.

In another example, before the serve, the player playing middle back must be closer to the end line than the middle-front player is, closer to the right sideline than the left-back player is, and closer to the left sideline than the right-back player is.

Players in serve-receive would be considered overlapped if they're not in their correct rotational order before the opponent contacts the ball on the serve. In the above example just described, if the middle-front player is closer to the left sideline than the left-front player is, an overlap violation will be called, resulting in a point for the opposing team. In a front row–back row adjacent player situation, if the right-back player is closer to the net than is the right-front player, an overlap violation will occur. Of course there's no possibility of an overlap violation unless players are in fact adjacent.

COACHING POINTS

Although the four-player serve-receive effectively eliminates your weakest passers on a consistent basis, you need to be sure these players still have a role in the serve reception. For instance, a coach should teach nonpassers how to read and anticipate the serve that's coming into play. Many servers give accidental hints on where they're going to serve. A toss behind the server's head, for example, indicates the serve is likely going to be short. Also easy to recognize is the traditional jump serve because the toss is high, typically with topspin. In addition, many players have been taught to face the direction in which they're going to serve as a way to line up the serve and potentially intimidate the targeted passer.

Giving nonpassers the duty of communicating what kind of serve might be coming gives them a useful role in the serve reception. Encourage them to call out their best guesses, even if they're wrong sometimes. Young players who lack confidence in their ability to read situations can tend to stay quiet and say nothing at all, which hurts a team's overall communication. Coaches should reinforce players who call out their best guess, even when they're incorrect. The more such players anticipate out loud, the better they'll become at recognizing what the opposing team is doing. Other roles for the nonpasser include helping call the ball in or out or short or long. They might also call the passer's name that should receive the ball.

In other situations, encourage the nonpassers to become cheerleaders during serve reception. They need to stay emotionally involved in the game. The emotional role can be as valuable as a physical role.

Front-row passers should do a lot of drills that combine individual passing and hitting. Although it's simpler to create two separate drills, one for passing and one for hitting, this is not the best way for learning and transfer to occur. Instead, create a gamelike drill that requires a player to pass and then to transition and hit. This might look sloppy, but it will allow players to better transfer what they learn from practice to games. Be willing to endure some error-filled drills while you require passers to receive serve, transition to their hitting location, and terminate a set, knowing you're teaching the game of volleyball exactly as it's played.

Front-row passers must also be trained to pass serves from difficult places on the court and then still transition to become available hitters. For example, imagine a left-front player passing from the left-back position. The server hits a short serve that requires the passer to go to the three-meter line to receive it, and she then finds herself six or seven feet inside the sideline. Assuming the left-front player will be hitting a ball from near the left-side antenna, this player has a long way to go before she's available to hit. This movement might seem difficult, but with training, front-row passers can pass from anywhere on the court and still transition to get available to hit, thus giving your setter more options.

During practice sessions, instruct servers to challenge the passers, forcing them to receive serve in many locations, with many different trajectories and speeds, so they can develop proficiency at transitioning to their next responsibility. Always instruct servers to try to serve aces. It does a team no good when servers ease up to help their teammates succeed, when in a competition their opponents will not be so considerate.

Finally, all players need to learn and fully understand the overlap rule. Clear understanding of this rule allows teams to manipulate their serve-receive patterns and get their best passers passing more often. Quiz players on who they must be concerned with regarding overlap. This rule is often misunderstood, so make sure all players are clear before they take the court.

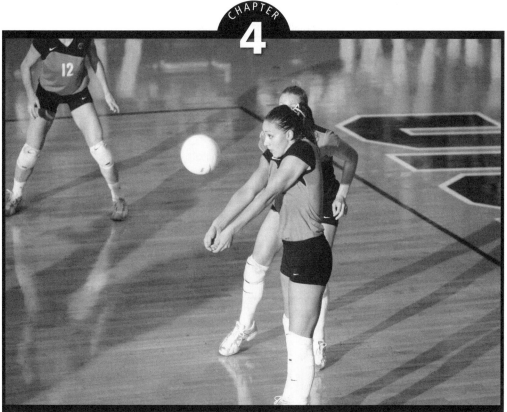

Three-Player Serve-Receive System

EXPLANATION OF TACTIC

As mentioned in chapter 2, many teams like to specialize with primary passers and receive serve with a three-player serve-receive pattern. Although it's quite possible to use the three-player reception system using five players (everyone but the designated setter) who each rotate through the three passing positions on the court in each rotation, we'll focus here on a three-player serve-receive pattern using only the same three primary passers in each rotation. This pattern allows for greater consistency of passing with three strong passers receiving all the serves. Incorporating such a system obviously requires choosing your best three passers, regardless of position (even a setter can be a primary passer if your offensive system uses more than one setter), and having them pass in every rotation. This system is quite popular at all levels of play, from junior high through college, and even beyond.

The three passers align in either a semicircle (figure 4.1) or in more or less a straight line across the court. Where the passers position before the ball is served depends on what the coach wants to accomplish. If coaches want to promote forward movement, the passers should start 23 to 26 feet (7-8 meters) away from the net; this makes it very likely that all their movement will be forward (because a server must have outstanding ball control to serve to the deepest part of the court).

A possible problem with positioning your passers 23 to 26 feet (7-8 meters) back is that this might be too deep to

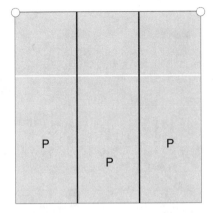

Figure 4.1   Three-player serve-receive pattern and its passing lanes.

allow effective reception of a short serve. Some coaches prefer to start their passers about 20 feet (6 meters) from the net because most serves end up traveling about that far, but of course this positioning allows a good serving team to force passers to move backward to receive, making an accurate pass more difficult (unless you also train your passers to receive high and deep balls with an overhead pass technique rather than with the forearm pass technique).

In general, where passers are initially positioned (this is referred to as the base or home position) should depend on their skills and abilities. For example, a passer with outstanding movement skills should position between the other two passers so that he or she can receive the most serves. Also, it's quite normal for the middle-back passer to be slightly deeper in the base position, giving him or her more responsibility to receive serves traveling to the deep corners of the court. About the only time your best passer shouldn't be receiving in middle back is when you have determined that he or she has a far better passing percentage when passing from either the left-back or right-back position.

The three-passer system allows the use of passing lanes, meaning that the court is basically split into equal thirds with each passer responsible for a particular area. But keep in mind that in a three-player reception pattern one passer (the best passer, usually the middle back) can and should handle more serves in more areas of the court. A common approach is to give the best passer authority over which serves he or she will receive. Another approach is to designate passers according to their strengths, so that if a serve is to the left portion of the court, for instance, the passer best at moving in that direction is positioned in the area most likely to receive that serve.

As explained in chapter 3, the ball traveling between the left-back and middle-back passers should typically be passed by the left-back passer because he or she is typically moving toward the target (the setter) and so can better establish a platform that faces the target. In the same way, if the ball is falling between the middle back and the right back, the middle back should take it. An exception to this principle is when your middle-back passer is so much more skilled than your other two passers that he or she should take *any* serve reasonably within reach.

PERSONNEL REQUIREMENTS

Employing a three-player serve-receive, and designating the same three passers to handle all the passing duties all the time, implies some built-in assumptions regarding what your passers are able to do. Primarily, they must be skilled forearm passers but comfortable passing with the overhead pass technique as well.

Recall the three-point passing rating system from the appendix (0 = service ace; 3 = perfect pass). A serve-receive pattern that's as specialized as the three-passer system should have passers who pass above a 2.0 and preferably higher (depending on the age and level of play of your team). Many teams believe that the left-side attackers should be two of the three primary passers in the three-player reception system, but it makes just as much or more sense simply to designate your three best overall passers regardless of position. Assuming a solid understanding of the overlap rule (see chapter 3), serve-receive formations can be worked out to always position the three best passers to receive serve in all six rotations.

Passing well requires a balance of physical and mental skills. Physically, passers must be able to consistently execute the technical skills of forearm passing (feet balanced and stable; arms out early and away from the body, pointing toward the target). Overall, they should have above average movement skills and be able to move efficiently forward, backward, and sideways. Mentally, passers must understand the opponent's overall serving strategy as well as what the server might try given the circumstances of the point, game, and match. As a match progresses, servers tend to settle into their most comfortable serve and location, but good passers remain alert, ready for the surprise meant to catch them off guard. Savvy and experienced passers have a knack of reading the server and can anticipate what's coming.

Executing a successful serve reception begins when the opposing team's server gets the ball and before the referee blows the whistle to signal the serve into play. Good passers are always thinking ahead. What is the server's favorite serve? What did he or she do last time? It's late in the game, and we have the advantage, so what's the server's safest serve? This far into the match, has the server recognized our weakest receiver? Will the server try to serve to him or her? Good passers also always expect the ball to come to them on every serve.

Once the server serves the ball into play, all three passers read where the serve is going—which depends largely on where the server is facing and where the toss is. Passers who have done their mental work before the served ball approaches the net will have good success in preparing themselves physically and receiving serves efficiently. Those who begin physically preparing to receive the serve only after the ball has reached the net will find themselves late and out of position for many serves.

ADVANTAGES AND DISADVANTAGES

If you compare the diagrams for the five-player W (p. 12), the four-player U (p. 18), and the three-player serve-receive, you'll likely notice a visible advantage to the three-player reception pattern: fewer seams created by the passers. As long as passers and other teammates are communicating well, this pattern should result in more effective service reception.

Further, the three-player reception allows passers and their teammates to get into a game rhythm, knowing their movements and court responsibilities will be similar from rotation to rotation. Once such a groove is established, it's far easier to focus on the tactical elements of the game.

Although the game of volleyball lends itself to specialization in all positions (one or two setters, one or two back-row players, primary passers, etc.), a major disadvantage of specialization is when one of those specialists is unable to perform to his or her usual ability. In such a case, teams must resort to using a lesser-skilled and lesser-practiced player in place of the regular, which can of course disrupt the team's rhythm and flow. When one of the injured, absent, or slumping specialists is one of your key passers, the disadvantage to your team might be too much to overcome.

Specializing with three passers too early can stunt the development of others on the team who might develop and later grow into passers who could be used as primary passers (passing specialists). Coaches should be careful not to overlook players who aren't initially identified as primary passers but who might be well equipped to develop the necessary skills to evolve into excellent receivers later. In other words, teams should avoid becoming so specialized that they become blind to making passing personnel adjustments that might better the team.

OPTIONS

Although three-player serve-receive patterns are common, subtle differences in the system exist among teams. If you took photos of 10 teams using the three-player system, you might see slight variations in each photo regarding where passers are stationed. For instance, one team might place its best passer in the left-back position and another team in the middle-back position. Teams that face opponents who tend to serve primarily to the middle of the court might place their best passers in the middle of the serve-receive pattern. This would be just one example of how to align your serve-receive pattern based on an opponent's serving strategy.

As mentioned earlier, many coaches choose to designate different areas of responsibility to each primary passer. For instance, if a team has two great passers out of three and a third who is at least reliable, they might align their passers in a three-player receive pattern but position the two great passers to receive the large majority of the serves (at about an equal depth from the net with equal space between them and their sideline). Why not use a two-player serve-receive in such a situation, you might ask. Having two great passers know they have a third passer helping them tends to take the pressure off of them to pass every serve. The third passer provides not only competence at passing certain areas of the court but also a lot of emotional support.

Emotional support should be considered when choosing positioning and strategy in your passing game. Even the strongest passers can't be expected to carry a team alone. They need to know they can count on teammates to back them up on occasion. All players are most comfortable in a passing system in which they know they can handle the technical, tactical, and emotional demands required of them.

COACHING POINTS

Once a coach has decided to use a three-player reception system, he or she must commit to spending a lot of time working on individual and team serve reception skills. To work on developing their technical skills, passers must have opportunities to pass in drills in which they are the only passer. Equally important is that players have opportunities to pass alongside the same players they'll be passing next to during competition. As you prepare for upcoming competition, have your passers receive the types of serves that they're likely to face during those matches and problem solve the kinds of scenarios they'll likely see. For instance, if you know from scouting reports that an opponent excels at the jump serve or likes to alternate serving short and then deep, use this knowledge to prepare your passers during practice.

As always, it's critical to practice skills under gamelike conditions. Create serve-receive drills that require passers to receive serve and then to transition to their next responsibility. For some passers, this might be transitioning to become a hitter; for others it might be moving into a coverage position based on where the setter sets the ball. It is important that players practice with the preceding action (in this case the live serve), the main action (the serve-reception pass), and the following action (the transition movement) in a gamelike sequence for best transfer of skills to the actual game.

Remember that a coach's subjective evaluation often doesn't match up with what's really occurring on the court. To avoid making mistakes, consider keeping statistics during practice, especially on your passers' performances. Statistics can confirm that you have identified and are using your best passers, and can also help you in justifying making a change involving a passer who's being moved out of the serve-reception pattern.

Serve-Receive Drills

The drills presented in this chapter are designed to work on serve-receive skills. The chapter is organized with drills working on five-player serve-receive first, followed by drills working on four-player, then on three-player systems.

Five-Player Consecutive Pass, Set, and Hit

Category: Use with chapters 2, 3, and 4.

Objectives: To establish good communication between two passers who make up part of the five-player W serve-receive and generate the ball control that allows them to successfully pass, set, and hit three in a row after two minutes of passing repetitions.

Players Required: 8

Procedure: Server serves down the line to left-front and left-back passers, who must communicate and decide who will receive the serve. The passer passes to the setter, who sets the left front, who then hits against the blocker. The team receiving serve will pass, set, and hit for two minutes before being required to convert three pass-set-hit combinations in a row to end the drill and cue a change of personnel or a rotation. The objective is the same for the right front, right back, and setter on the other half of the court. The setter setting the right-side attacker should set from as close to her normal setting position at the net as possible while also avoiding the other setter setting the left-side attacker from the same side of the net. The servers can help by slightly alternating their serves to the passers.

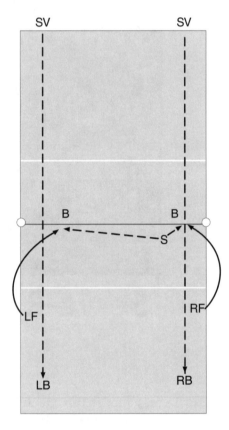

Variations: The two groups (setter, back-row passer, front-row passer) can run this same drill from opposite sides of the net, with both groups passing and hitting from the left side of the court first, followed by both groups switching to pass and hit from the right side. Servers should slightly alternate their serves. Hitters can also be allowed to hit different options out of the serve-receive pattern.

Common Errors and Corrections: Beginning servers might have trouble serving into the specified zones the passers are in. If so, have the servers step into the court to initiate the serve, or have them throw the serve into play.

Five-Player Pass, Set, Hit Middle vs. Middle

Category: Use with chapters 2, 3, and 4.

Objectives: To establish good communication between three passers (left back, right back, and middle front) and generate sufficient ball control to successfully pass, set, and hit while using the middle front as the only attacker.

Players Required: 10 (or 5 if drill is run from only one side)

Procedure: Position one middle front, left back, right back, and setter on each side of the net. Servers on each side alternate putting the ball into play. The server must serve so that the middle front, left back, or right back is required to pass. The setter is required to set only the middle-front player. The middle front tries to reach 10 kills before the opposing middle-front player gets 10 kills. The middle front who's not hitting is allowed to block and receives one point for each successful termination of the ball with a block.

Variation: Add more than one blocker to defend the quick attack.

Common Errors and Corrections: When passers can't pass well enough to allow the setter to set the middle attacker, have the setter set either the left back or right back out of the back row to assure a pass-set-hit repetition.

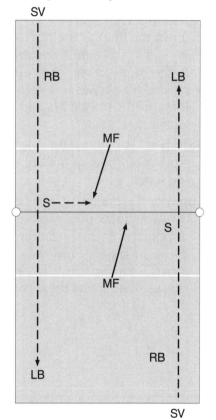

Five-Player Pass, Set, Hit Right Side vs. Right Side

Category: Use with chapters 2, 3, and 4.

Objectives: To establish good decision making and communication between the right front and right back relative to who should pass the ball. Also works on the right-front hitter terminating the ball for points.

Players Required: 10

Procedure: The server serves crosscourt (or down the line) to the receivers, requiring either the right front or right back to receive the serve. The ball is passed, set, and hit. Servers will alternate serves. Right fronts must compete to score 10 kills first.

Variation: Have the right side hit various types of sets both in front of and behind the setter.

Common Errors and Corrections: Passers sometimes don't recognize who's responsible for balls landing between them. In general, the passer who can move forward toward the target to receive should pass the serve.

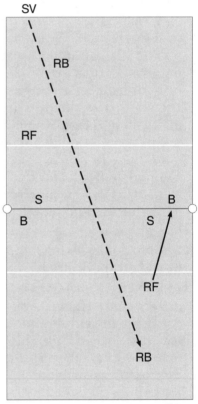

Five-Player 10 Before 4

Category: Use with chapters 2, 3, and 4.

Objective: To establish consistency in the five-player W serve-receive to successfully pass, set, and hit for points.

Players Required: 8

Procedure: Team of six (team A) sets up in a five-player W serve-receive. Server initiates the ball into play, trying to ace the receiving team. Team A tries to pass, set, and kill 10 balls before the servers score 4 aces. In this drill an ace can be defined either as a ball that's overpassed or is untouchable after the pass is made. Team A rotates after one side reaches their goal (4 aces or 10 pass-set-kills.)

Variation: Determine the appropriate ratio of perfect passes to aces. For teams that lack ball control, more aces might be required than perfect passes. Setter can either penetrate from a back-row position on each save or stay at the net in the S target.

Common Errors and Corrections: Teams that struggle with ball control will have trouble completing 10 perfect passes, sets, and hits. If the number of successes for them is reduced, it might still be necessary to help the team that's passing, setting, and hitting by giving half points or full points for a perfect pass even if play doesn't result in a successful attack.

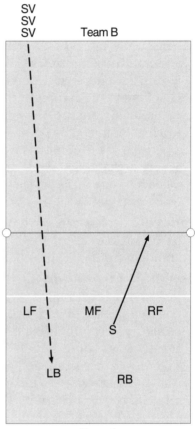

Four-Player Passers vs. Passers

Category: Use with chapters 2, 3, and 4.

Objective: To train consistency of left- and right-back passers (who will probably be required to receive more serves in a four-player U).

Players Required: 8

Procedure: Servers serve simultaneously from each end line to passers anywhere behind the opposite three-meter line. Passers must communicate, decide who is to pass, and receive serve to target (T). Passers on each side try to score 10 points before the opposing passers reach 10 points. One point is given for a perfect pass, 1 point taken away for a service ace, and no points are given or taken for a ball that's passed but doesn't reach its target.

Variation: Servers can serve only to the passers at the top of the U (left front and right front).

Common Errors and Corrections: Because many seams are present between passers in a four-player serve-receive, passers might be unsure who should pass some serves. To correct this problem, encourage passers who can move forward toward the desired target to receive the serve.

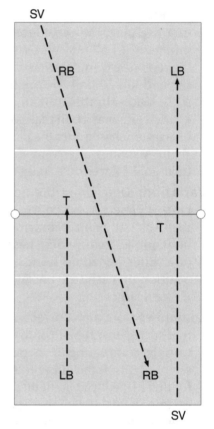

Four-Player Setter Attacks

Category: Use with chapters 2, 3, 4, 15, and 17.

Objective: To pass well enough to enable the front-row setter to attack on second contact.

Players Required: 12

Procedure: Servers alternate serving to four-player U serve-receive pattern. The ball is passed and attacked by the setter if the pass is to target and high enough for the setter to attack. Servers alternate serving for the first three minutes, then change to a single side, continuously serving to give one setter the chance to terminate three balls in a row off the pass. If the setter doesn't successfully terminate on the second contact, the server on the other side initiates serve.

Variation: The setter can also set rather than attack the pass that is to the target and high enough to attack.

Common Errors and Corrections: The setter might attempt to attack the second contact when the pass isn't high enough or close enough to the target to allow success. Work with the setter to know how close the ball needs to be to the target and how high a pass would need to be to warrant attempting attacking the second ball.

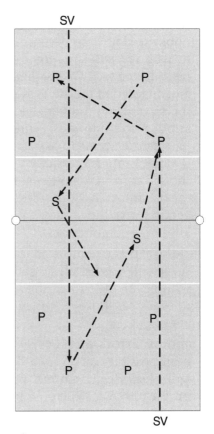

Four vs. Four

Category: Use with chapters 2, 3, 4, 15, 16, and 17.

Objective: To generate consistent serve-receive in the four-player U.

Players Required: 12

Procedure: Server on one side initiates serve to four-player U formation on opposite side. Passers communicate as to who receives the serve. The ball is passed, then set (to a designated player), and attacked. If the attack is successful, the server from the same side initiates another ball into play, with the same passers attempting to pass, set, and kill. If a ball is not successfully terminated, the server from the other side initiates the ball into play. Both sides attempt to get five consecutive successful pass-set-kill (PSK) combinations.

Variation: If you're more concerned with successful passes, allow setters to set whomever they like, allowing them to work on those sets they feel need attention.

Common Errors and Corrections: It's quite possible that one phase of the PSK will break down. Correct by focusing on the phase at which the breakdown occurs.

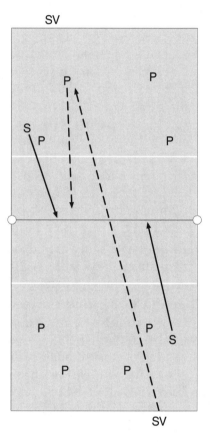

Four-Player Pass, Set, Quick Attack

Category: Use with chapters 2, 3, 4, 15, 16, 17, 20, and 21.

Objective: To generate consistent serve-receive, enabling the setter to run quick attacks with front-row players.

Players Required: 8

Procedure: Servers initiate serve to four-player serve-receive, trying to serve aces. The four passers communicate and pass to target. The middle hitter transitions off the net after the serve is contacted, and is set by the setter.

Initiate serves for four minutes, and then ask middle hitters to hit four kills in a row, requiring perfect passes.

Variation: Less experienced teams might have trouble terminating four balls in a row. If so, reduce the number of consecutive hits required. Blockers may be used.

Common Errors and Corrections: Sometimes the passing doesn't allow the setter to run a quick attack. If the objective is to run a quick attack, have servers step into the court to initiate the serve.

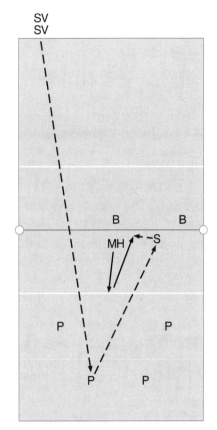

Four-Player 25

Category: Use with chapters 2, 3, and 4.

Objective: To require all primary passers in a four-player U serve-receive to successfully pass 25 serves to a target.

Players Required: 12

Procedure: Servers initiate serves simultaneously on both sides. Passers on both sides pass to target. Servers serve for three minutes, giving players opportunities for repetitions. After three minutes, a coach counts perfect passes until a team (or combined on both sides) reaches 25.

Variations: Place a time limit on reaching 25 perfect passes. Or reduce the number of perfect passes required for teams who struggle with ball control. Or each side attempts to get to total of 25 points first.

Common Errors and Corrections: Because this is a team goal of achieving 25 perfect passes after the three minutes have elapsed, some passers might not focus well enough to contribute to the 25 perfect passes. If this occurs, penalize a team if they allow a certain number of balls to be served that are not passed perfectly. You can also give bonus points for a specified number of consecutive perfect passes.

Three-Player Pass, Set, and Back-Row Attack

Category: Use with chapters 2, 3, 4, 19, 20, 21, and 22.

Objective: To generate consistent serve-receive and effective back-row attack capabilities.

Players Required: 10

Procedure: Servers alternate serving to a three-player serve-receive pattern. Passers pass to the setter, who sets a back-row attack to any one of the three primary passers. Servers alternate serving for three to five minutes; then teams see which side can convert 10 successful PSK combinations first.

Variation: You can use a front-row attacker in addition to the back-row attackers. Or require setters to set only to the back-row player who passed the ball.

Common Errors and Corrections: Back-row attackers, especially if they have received the serve, will often fail to get into position to generate a full and fast approach. If passers must move forward to receive the serve, be sure they are backing up, allowing enough room to generate a full and fast approach.

Three-Player Pass, Set, and Left-Side Attack

Category: Use with chapters 2, 3, 4, 19, 20, 21, and 22.

Objective: To consistently pass from a three-player serve-receive pattern to ensure the setter can effectively set the left-side attack.

Players Required: 8

Procedure: Servers initiate the serve to a three-player serve-receive. Passers receive the serve, and the setter sets the ball to the left-side attacker. (Note that if the left-back passer is a front-row attacker, he or she must be incorporated into the left-side attack.) The left-side attacker attempts to terminate the set. One of the left-side hitters serves as the solo blocker, requiring the hitter to hit around a block. The blocker performs one repetition, and then gets in line to hit. Servers serve for three minutes; the coach can then require 10 successful PSK combinations.

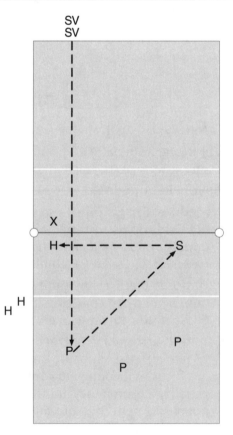

Variation: If you're putting equal value on the pass and the hit, require that a perfect pass be executed. In this case, even if the ball is terminated, the team will not get credit if the pass isn't perfect.

Common Errors and Corrections: If the passer is the left-side attacker, it's common for him or her to pass and then fail to get into position to approach, jump, and swing. If this occurs, make a successful transition from passer to hitter a part of the scoring.

Three-Player Passing Quads

Category: Use with chapters 2, 3, and 4.

Objective: To get repetitions as individual passers while focusing on individual technique.

Players Required: 12

Procedure: For this drill, the group of 12 is divided into 3 groups of 4 each with 1 server, 2 passers, and 1 target/catcher. Each group occupies a long and skinny court within a regular court (each about 10 feet wide on a regular court). All three servers simultaneously serve to the passers on the other side of the net that make up their quad. A passer stands out of bounds to serve as a ball retriever (if necessary) for five serves, then trades places with the passer who is in front of him or her. Servers first serve for three to five minutes; then they serve until passers successfully pass seven perfect passes. Once seven passes are completed, passers trade places with the catcher and server in their group.

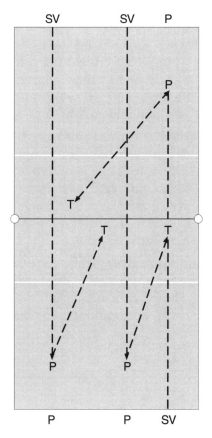

Variations: Turn this into a server versus passer competition (similar to the Five-Player 10 Before 4 drill). Or have both passers in the small group on the court pass the serve, forcing communication and decision making for the passers.

Common Errors and Corrections: When several repetitions are executed within a set time, servers and passers tend to lose concentration. If this happens regularly, either reduce the number of timed reps or eliminate them altogether.

Three-Player Serve Plus Conditioning

Category: Use with chapters 2, 3, and 4.

Objective: To practice successful passes and serves while increasing conditioning.

Players Required: 8

Procedure: Servers on both sides initiate serves over the net. The ball is passed, and everyone rotates to the next position, following the path of the ball through the drill. For example, after a player has served as a target, he or she sprints over to the other side of the net to become a server. After serving, the server sprints over to the other side to prepare to pass. Continue the drill until a conditioning benefit has been gained.

Variation: Because this is a conditioning drill, add push-ups, sprints, tuck jumps, and so on to provide variety of movement, especially if a player is wating in line to play the next ball.

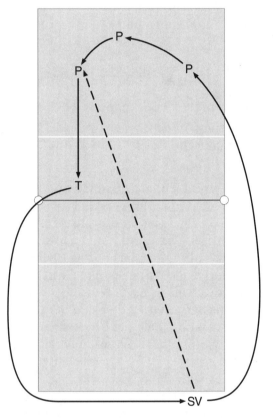

Common Errors and Corrections: Passers and servers are at some point asked to perform while fatigued, so execution suffers. Focus on players whose performance suffers dramatically by helping them regain attention and concentration, even while fatigued.

Three-Player Receivers vs. Servers

Category: Use with chapters 2, 3, and 4.

Objective: To practice successful passes and serves while increasing conditioning.

Players Required: 9

Procedure: In this serve-receive drill, servers score "small" points for aces or when they force bad passes. Receivers score "small" points for passes that make it to the setter inside the 10-foot, or 3-meter line. Four "small" points for either side equals one "big" point. The first side to reach three "big" points wins. Three to four receivers rotate after five serves. Four players alternate serving, using a variety of serves. If a player serves an ace, he or she continues serving.

Variation: If run on one side only, the servers serve only from one end of the court to the passers opposite, who pass to the target. If you have more players, run this same drill on both sides of the net, with three servers at each end line, three passers in each back court, and coaches or extra players or setters in the setter targets.

Defensive Systems

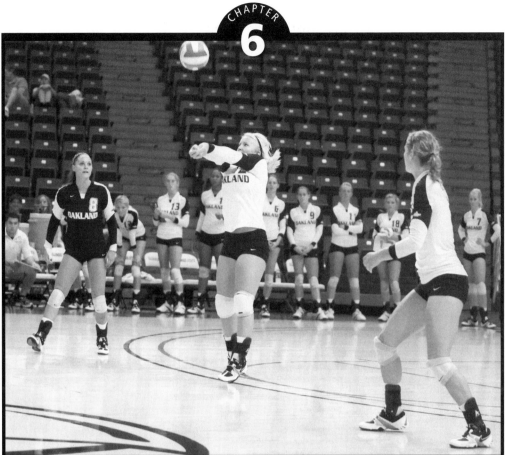

© Alan Look/Icon SMI

Player-Back System

EXPLANATION OF TACTIC

The traditional player-back defensive system (also called the perimeter or white defense) is one in which back-row defenders position around the edges of the court, close to the sidelines and endline. Left-back diggers hug the left sideline; right-back diggers hug the right sideline. The middle back hovers near the end line about equal distance from the left and right sidelines. This positioning tends to promote forward movement among players at left back, right back, and middle back, which is what you want for your diggers, who are much more efficient and effective when moving forward rather than sideways or backward.

Assuming a team is incorporating a two-blocker system against an opponent's outside hitters, one front-row player (called the off-blocker) pulls off the net to the three-meter line and sideline corner and has digging responsibility; primarily this player is responsible for sharp-angled hits, tips, or off-speed shots that fall inside the three-meter line between his or her base position and the blockers. It requires extraordinary strength and jumping ability for a hitter to hit a hard-driven ball inside the three-meter line, so the majority of balls hit to this area will not be hard driven. Although we'll operate in this chapter on the assumption that two blockers are being used, the player-back system can be used with a one-blocker system (or even a zero-blocker system), as we'll discuss in chapter 9.

Figures 6.1a-c show the basic positions of the players against the opponent's left-side, right-side, and middle attacks. As you look at the basic blueprint of the player-back defense, notice that regardless of where the opponents are attacking from, your team maintains balanced defensive positioning. This balance is achieved by a back-row player who can dig an opponent's line attack or crosscourt attack and a middle-back player who can dig an attack to either of the deep corners.

Notice also what is sometimes perceived as a vulnerability of open space in the middle of the court in this system. Of course all defenses leave areas of the court relatively uncovered, and in the player-back defense it's the middle that's left most open. A basic assumption of the player-back defense is that it's easier for back-row players to come forward to cover the middle than for players stationed up in the court to back up to cover an open area in the back. Also, any ball targeted to the middle of the court will ideally be blocked by the two blockers (or force the hitter to hit higher and slower shots over them), or at least

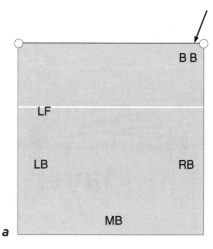

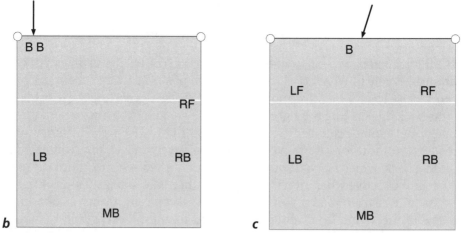

Figure 6.1 Basic player-back positioning for a *(a)* left-side, *(b)* right-side, and *(c)* middle attack.

slowed down by the block enough to allow remaining defenders time to dig the ball and mount an offensive attack. If all goes as planned, and assuming the block is well formed, balls hit to the middle of the court will rarely be terminated against this defense.

Now let's look at specific digger responsibilities when opponents are attacking from each of the front-row positions (left front, middle front, and right front).

1. Opponent's left-side attack: At most levels of the game, most teams attack more often from the left than from the middle or right. In figures 6.2*a* and *b* notice that once the ball has been set to the attacker, the left-back and middle-back diggers move to station themselves in the crosscourt zones of the court. The left back should be about 1 to 3 feet (.3-.9 meter) inside the sideline and about 18 to 20 feet (5.4-6 meters) away from the net. From this position the left back can dig the hard-driven ball that isn't blocked or deflected by the blockers while still adhering to the principle of forward movement. The middle-back digger remains deep—25 to 30 feet (7.6-9 meters) from the net. Because left-side attackers, especially younger ones, prefer hitting crosscourt, the middle back will shift to a position about 2 to 3 feet (.6-.9 meter) to the left of center court. This allows two diggers to dig in the strong crosscourt zone. The line digger (right back) remains tight to the sideline (with the right foot actually touching the right sideline), anywhere from 15 to 20 feet (4.5-6 meters) from the net, when the outside blocker is blocking crosscourt (figure 6.2*a*). If the outside blocker is taking away the line, the digger should be deeper (20 feet, or 6 meters) and possibly even a bit inside the sideline, because any ball hit down the line must go either over the block and deeper or be slowed down enough that the digger can pursue the ball (figure 6.2*b*). Conversely, if the blocker is taking away the crosscourt shot, the line digger moves slightly forward (up to

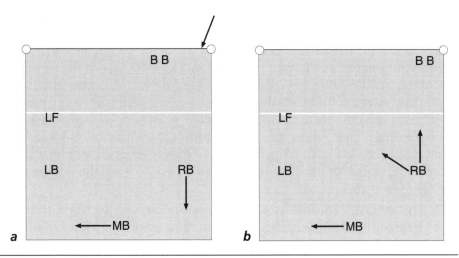

Figure 6.2 Positioning for a left-side attack with the right-side blocker *(a)* blocking crosscourt and *(b)* blocking the line.

15 feet, or 4.5 meters, from the net) because the hitter doesn't have to worry about a blocker blocking the line shot and so may hit hard down the line. The off-blocker (left front), who has no blocking responsibilities, pulls off the net anywhere from 5 to 10 feet (1.5-3 meters) from the net and as far in as 15 feet (4.5 meters) from the left sideline, depending on whether or not the player has tip coverage responsibilities. This puts him or her in position to dig balls that are tipped inside the three-meter line behind and inside the blockers. This positioning assumes that the opponent's left-side attacker lacks the ability to attack a sharply angled, hard-driven ball to the left-front position. This is a difficult shot that requires strong upper body strength and an ability to hit high above the net. If you face hitters who can hit this shot consistently hard, the left-front digger would stay much closer to the left sideline (1 to 3 feet, or .3-.9 meter) and come off a little deeper from the net (8 to 10 feet, or 2.4-3 meters). Of course, you'll want to adjust the diagrammed player positions and distances from the sidelines, end line, and center line to best suit your team's abilities and what your opponents attacking tendencies are.

2. Opponent's right-side attack: Teams that attack from the right side require similar placement as just described, but now that the right-side attacker is hitting, the right-back and middle-back diggers become the crosscourt defenders. The right-back defender positions 1 to 3 feet (.3-.9 meter) from the right sideline and about 18 to 20 feet (5.4-6 meters) from the net. Just as the middle-back digger positioned slightly to his or her left during the opponent's left-side attack, he or she will also shift slightly to the right during the opponent's right-side attack, once again providing two diggers defending the strong crosscourt attack. If you know that a particular right- or left-side hitter can effectively hit the line, the middle-back digger can stay in more of a neutral position (2 to 3 feet, or .6-.9 meters) inside the end line and more in the middle of the backcourt, to be in better position to help the line digger with hard-driven shots down the line. The left-back digger mimics what the right-side digger does when the attack is coming from the left side. If blockers are taking away the line, the left-back digger stations 18 to 20 feet (5.4-6 meters) from the net and touches the sideline with the left foot (figure 6.3a). If this digger reads that the hitter has no chance of driving a hard-driven ball down the line, he or she may release a bit inside the line (figure 6.3b). If the line is open and no block takes away this shot, the left-back digger must step forward, anticipating the hard-driven attack down the line. In turn, the right-front off-blocker also mimics what the left-front off-blocker did in the earlier example, either staying more to the middle of the three-meter line for tips or toward the sideline to dig the hard sharp angle shots.

3. Opponent's middle attack: If opponents are hitting a quick set (see chapter 20), defenders will stay in base position to defend that attack (figure 6.4). Here we'll assume that the quick attack is a higher tempo ball, at least 2 feet (.6 meter) above the top of the net, which is a common tactic. Thought must be given regarding how many blockers will be used to defend

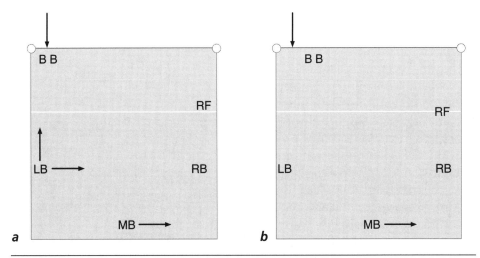

Figure 6.3 Opponent hitting to the right-side and the left-side blocker *(a)* blocking the line and *(b)* blocking crosscourt.

the attack. A hitter must be able to dominate as a middle attacker to warrant two blockers. If you do go with two blockers, a decision must be made on who will assist the middle blocker on the block—which boils down to three major questions. One, do the middle hitters like to hit crosscourt (to left back or middle back) or cut back and hit to the right-back position? If they hit crosscourt (the way they face on their approach) predominately, having your left-side blocker assist on the block makes most sense. Second, what kind of blockers do you have on the left and right side? If the hitter likes to hit crosscourt, but your right-side blocker is bigger and better than your left-side blocker, you now have a tacti-

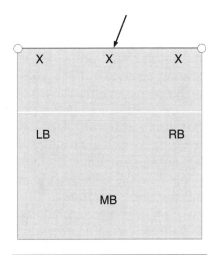

Figure 6.4 Base position for opponents hitting a quick set.

cal dilemma. Third, who would you rather have the middle hitter hit to—your left-back and middle-back diggers or your right-back digger? Your answers to these questions should help you determine which tactical decision to make.

Let's assume your team is blocking with your left-front and middle-front blockers. The left-back digger, who has now made a move from base position, will dig about 18 to 20 feet (5.4-6 meters) from the net and 2 to 3 feet inside the court (figure 6.5). Because the right-front player (off-blocker) has primary duty to get tips right behind the block and any junk that rolls off the blockers' hands inside the three-meter line, the left back can release from base position deeper into the court without having to be concerned with covering the tip behind the block. The middle back will typically shift slightly to the left side of the court to provide another crosscourt digger. However, because we're working on the assumption that the left-side blocker is helping block the middle attack, it's then also possible to think that the middle-back digger might actually need to shift slightly to her right because some balls hit crosscourt will ideally be blocked or slowed down, or toward her left if the hitter tries to cut the ball toward the right-back area of the court. The right-back digger, responsible for the cut-back shot, is once again 18 to 20 feet (5.4-6 meters) from the net and 2 to 3 feet (.6-.9 meter) inside the court. (Again, recall that these numbers are guides, not exact positioning requirements.) If you decide to use your right-front blocker to assist your middle blocker, the roles are basically reversed from the above example.

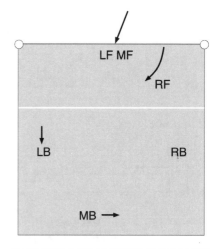

Figure 6.5 Player-back defense with opponent hitting high-ball middle attack with left and right fronts blocking.

Once your team has a basic concept of how the player-back system works, you need to understand how to deal with an opponent's attack that's traveling between two diggers. Most common are the attacks that go between the middle back and left back and the middle back and right back. The ball traveling between middle back and left back should be taken by the left-back digger as long as he or she is moving forward and to the right toward the target and can contact the ball within a comfortable range of motion (i.e., from below the waist to slightly below the shoulders). If the ball is passing the left-back digger higher and deeper than

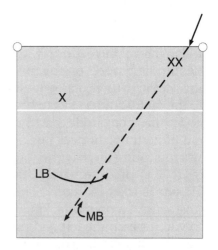

Figure 6.6 Player-back defense with ball traveling between diggers.

this, then the middle-back defender, who's moving sideways and behind the left-back digger (who's moving forward) should take the ball (figure 6.6). The same principle is at play when solving the situation of the ball going between the middle-back and right-back diggers. This is referred to as seam coverage. In general, the player nearer the net should move across in front of the deeper player, who moves behind and across to attempt to cover the seam in the defense.

PERSONNEL REQUIREMENTS

We would all like to have tall, athletic players with great overhead passing skills and outstanding movement skills, but unfortunately we can't always get what we want. Critical to overcoming a disadvantage in height and athleticism is training players to anticipate, read, and adjust consistently well. All players on the court should know, or quickly recognize, the following details regarding their opponent:

- which hitter or type of set the setter most likely to set;
- their hitters' best shots; and
- the shot their hitters can't hit, either because of their limitations or because the block is taking it away. Reading such situational details makes it possible for diggers to be outstanding on defense—because much of their work as diggers can be done before the ball is even attacked.

Once players have developed the tactical skills of reading, anticipating, judging, and timing, the physical requirements of diggers in the player-back system include strong individual digging technique (feet balanced and stable), arriving early with arms together and in front of the body, and an ability to direct the ball to the desired target.

Having players who assume that every ball is playable and reachable goes a long way toward making any system work. Players with the attitude of *I can get to any ball*, coupled with the ability to anticipate and accurately read opposing hitters, makes the player-back system extremely effective.

ADVANTAGES AND DISADVANTAGES

The player-back system promotes forward movement because diggers have the entire court in front of them. The distance any digger must move is not terribly far. This is not to say that good movement skills are not important in this system, but they might not be as critical as they are in other systems.

The player-back defense is widely popular and promotes confidence since the diggers can see and play all balls in front of them. Coaches should not underestimate the degree to which player confidence in a defense can serve as an advantage.

The primary disadvantage to the player-back defense is that it exposes the middle of the court, which becomes a potentially vulnerable spot if blockers are doing a poor job of anticipating, reading, judging, and timing the opponent's attack. Even when blockers are doing their jobs, some opponents might be able to hide or disguise their attack well enough to exploit the exposed middle and counter this defense with success.

OPTIONS

One of the beauties of volleyball is that any system can be modified to meet the demands a particular opponent creates—as long as time is taken to train the modifications you have in mind. What happens, for example, when an opposing team's left-side hitter's favorite shot is to hit deep between the middle-back and right-back diggers? We mentioned earlier that the middle-back digger would shade in one direction to help dig the crosscourt attack, but now it makes sense to shift him or her slightly in the other direction, because the attacker is more confident in hitting in that direction. Such modifications to defensive positioning can occur with every blocker and digger on the floor based on what's happening in a given game, as long as players have worked on the modification in practice.

Another option that needs to be explored more is the court position from which diggers play defense. Many times it's court position by default—for example, if you're a left-back digger, you'll dig in the left-back position whenever you are in the back row. This is how many teams determine backcourt positioning. An alternative is to put your best defender in the position in which most balls will be hit, typically the middle-back or left-back areas. If you know that most balls are attacked to the middle-back digger, it only makes sense to station your best digger in that position. This is usually referred to as switching into your backcourt defensive specialty after the ball crosses over the net to your opponent's side the first time during any rally.

COACHING POINTS

First, coaches need to be aware of three situations that must be defended that require players (primarily back-row players) to position differently from what's done in a typical player-back defense. These positions are commonly called base positions and allow a team to defend against the first of three situations that might develop following a serve or attack: the overpass. If the overpass doesn't develop, watch for a second possibility: the setter attack. If the setter attack doesn't develop, beware of a third option: a quick attack. Note that the figure shows that the left- and right-back defenders are about 4 to 5 feet (1.2-1.5 meters) inside their respective sidelines and about 12 feet (3.6 meters) from the net or 2 feet (.6 meter) behind the three-meter line. Unless the setter is extremely skilled and strong enough to attack the ball to deep parts of the court, the majority of overpasses and setter attacks will be handled by the left- and right-back defenders, if positioned as shown. If you watch the teams that you play and chart where overpasses and setter attacks travel to, you'll find most go to the middle of the court anywhere from 10 to 15 feet (3-4.5 meters) from the net. Positioning your left- and right-back defenders as shown allows for coverage of these attacks without defenders being forced to move large distances to keep the ball in play.

If opponents run a quick attack (the most common is a front 1 to the middle attacker, though more-skilled teams also run a back 1 to the middle attacker, and 31s with either the middle- or left-side attacker), balls are often hit about where you have already placed your defenders in this base defensive position. Players will stay in their base positions until all three of the possibilities (overpass, setter attack, and quick attack) can be eliminated. When the ball isn't overpassed, attacked by the setter on the second contact, or set to a quick attacker, defenders then transition to the areas as shown in figures 6.2-6.6 in order to read the developing attack. As you train these various defensive systems, keep in mind that training players to move into and out of base positions is critical regardless of what defensive system you use.

Develop drills that force your players to do many repetitions in which they must read what attackers are doing, anticipate where attackers are hitting, and judge where the ball will end up (assuming it isn't blocked). To help your diggers become adept in reading, anticipating, and judging, use this ball-setter–ball-hitter checklist:

1. Ball: Once the ball is on the opponent's side of the net, defenders should watch the ball, tracking it to whoever is making the first contact and judging its quality. Any information the players gain should be communicated verbally to teammates, helping them to be successful as well. This gives the defense information regarding what the setter might be able to do, or more important, not do (e.g., set a quick attack because of a less-than-perfect pass). Obviously, when defenses eliminate opponent's options by reading the pass quality, defending is made much easier.

2. Setter: Once the first contact has been made and the defenders know where the ball is going, they quickly turn their attention to the setter, who might give some clues as to where she will set. If the setter arches his or her back, this signals a likely backset. The setter might also signal by looking at whom the set is going to. Defenders should avoid watching the ball from first contact all the way to the setter because the flight is predictable; more knowledge can be gained by transferring focus to the setter instead.

3. Ball: Defenders at this point have gathered information from the setter regarding what he or she might do. They now turn their attention to the ball again (briefly) as the setter is setting it and until just after it's released. Helpful information defenders can gather by watching the ball come out of the setter's hands includes direction of release; whether the ball is traveling to its intended target or falling short; how tight the set is to the net (is a tip likely?); and how high (slow) or low (fast) the set is. Such information helps defenders know what shots are available to the hitter. Of course, these details must be read extremely quickly, in terms of milliseconds rather than seconds.

4. Hitter: The ball is now out of the setter's hands and on its way to the attacker. Because the laws of gravity are constant, it does little good to watch the ball travel through the air all the way from the setter to the hitter. Rather, as soon as the ball has left the setter's hands, defenders should turn their focus to the anticipated hitter, who might inadvertently signal the intended shot in a variety of ways. First, watch the hitter's approach angle. If he or she is facing the line, that's where the ball will probably go. Also watch the hitter's eyes—some hitters actually glance to the area they intend to attack. Consider also the speed of the attacker's approach. A slower approach signals a possible tip or off-speed shot, as does an early extended arm/hand position.

Training players to read, anticipate, and judge is best done in game situations. Attackers should be hitting live sets whenever possible rather than have coaches standing up on a box and hitting balls to diggers (or, worse yet, standing on the same side of the net as the diggers). Players should work on the ball-setter–ball-hitter sequence until it becomes automatic. Requiring diggers to verbalize this sequence as they move through it helps them become confident and adept at the process, while also allowing the coach to be aware of what the defenders are seeing, and when.

In chapter 24 we'll cover the concept of making positive rather than negative errors; this concept should be emphasized in all defensive systems. Keeping the ball on your side of the net and too high rather than too low gives your team greater chances to transition and get an aggressive swing back to the opposition.

© MUSTAFA OZER/AFP/Getty Images

Player-Up System

EXPLANATION OF TACTIC

You might already be aware of the several varieties of the player-up defensive system, which is commonly referred to as the red defense. Whichever form a team chooses, the system is generally designed for use against opponents that tip often, particularly to areas right behind the block. In this chapter we'll look at three common forms of the player-up system: the off-blocker player-up, the setter-up, and the middle-back player-up.

1. Off-blocker player-up defense: As you can see in figures 7.1*a-c*, positioning in this defense looks similar to the player-back defense discussed in chapter 6. You may sometimes see this version referred to as a "blue" or "box" defense. The primary difference is when and where the off-blocker positions behind the block. For example, when the opposing team is hitting from their right side, the right-front player (off-blocker) pulls off the net to just inside the three-meter line. Generally, this position is somewhere between 5 and 7 feet (1.5-2.1 meters) from the net and either right behind the block or lined up on the inside shoulder of the middle blocker. The positioning of the player-up defender is determined largely by the tendencies of the opponent. Opposing teams that generally tip right behind the block call for the off-blocker positioning right behind the block (splitting the block or in the seam). As to when to make their move, off-blockers should position as soon as the setter sets the ball to the hitter away from their blocking side. This "up" player is not trying to read what shot the hitter might attempt; rather, he or she is moving into position first, and *then* reacting to a ball that's tipped behind the block. It's important to understand that this digger is responsible not only for the tip but also for any ball that falls behind the block and, in most cases, all balls that fall inside the three-meter line. So beside an attacker's tip, the off-blocker (now the player-up digger) is responsible for balls that might be overset on the second contact as well as attacked balls deflected by the block or that fall behind the block and inside the three-meter line. As you see by the positioning of the remaining diggers, the principles of base defense (see chapter 6, p. 49) and

overall positioning stay basically the same as in the player-back system. When using the off-blocker player-up defense against teams that traditionally attempt to score by tipping, especially right behind the block, you force them to devise other ways to score, which tips the scale in your favor, defensively speaking. An important consideration when deciding what version of the player-up defense to implement is how you will transition your hitters from this player-up position. Each version has advantages and disadvantages in this area.

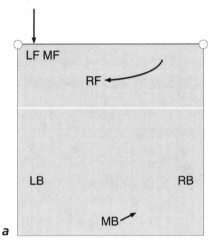

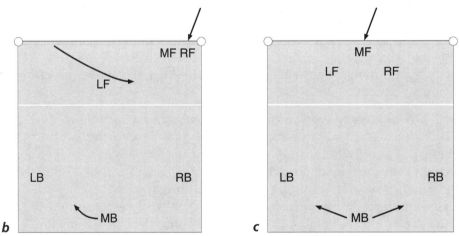

Figure 7.1 Off-blocker player-up defense with opponents hitting from their *(a)* right side, *(b)* left side, and *(c)* middle.

2. Setter-up defense: In this variation of the player-up defense, the setter (when the offensive system used is a 5-1 or a 6-2) or the off-setter (the setter who plays in the backcourt in a 4-2 offensive system) is the one chiefly responsible for tip coverage behind the block. The base position for this digger when in the back row is about on the three-meter line halfway between the side lines. From this base position the player-up digger can handle the majority of overpasses or move to a position behind the block no matter where the opposing team's setter sets the ball. This up-digger must also be aware of the opponent's quick attack options to avoid being caught by surprise. The blockers are ultimately responsible for protecting this digger from line-drive attacks to the head or body. Assuming that the opponent overpass, setter-attack, and quick-attack options have been eliminated, the up-digger moves from base position to behind the block, as described in the off-blocker player-up position. Once again, this digger is responsible for tips behind the block, deflections off the block, and any other ball that lands around the block or inside the three-meter line. Because the up-digger is standing on or near the three-meter line when the opposing team is making their first contact of the ball and getting ready to mount their attack, the positioning of the remaining back-row diggers is somewhat different than in the player-back positions. The basic principle of base position for the remaining back-row diggers involves balancing the court. These diggers are

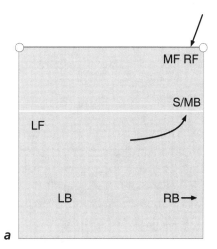

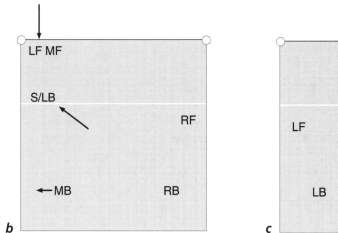

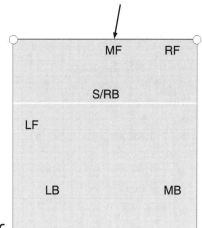

Figure 7.2 Setter-up defense with opponent hitting a *(a)* left-side, *(b)* right-side, and *(c)* high-middle attack.

positioned deep in the court with equal distance between them and their respective sidelines, which allows them to handle deep overpasses, deep setter attacks, and deep quick attacks. Once the opponent's setter puts up a higher set to any hitter, the remaining back-row diggers move to their digging positions, as illustrated in figures 7.2a-c. Another key to this system is the role of the off-blocker. Pay attention to the off-blocker's position relative to the three-meter line. In some cases (especially when the opposing team can't hit a hard sharp-angle attack from the left side or right side), the off-blocker digger might position on or even behind the three-meter line, essentially providing a third back-row digger because one of the true back-row diggers (the setter) has left the backcourt to handle tips and other balls from behind the block.

3. Middle-back player-up defense: Though we specify the center-back as the player-up in this version, in reality any of the back-row players could be designated as the "player-up" in this defense. The other two back-row players then balance the backcourt and the off-blocker drops off the net to play more of a crosscourt digging position as well. If using a nonsetter back-row player as the player-up, after the serve has been contacted (or after the ball travels across to your opponent's side of the court the first time) the designated back-row player will switch into the player-up position near the middle of the three-meter line, while the other two backcourt players balance the court. The player-up digger will then shift toward the block after reading the direction of the opponent's set, and dig any tip or roll shot over or around the block that falls into their area of responsibility. So, if the player in right back is the better digger at this up position, coaches could have him or her switch into this up-digger position, or if it is the left-back player that is better at running down and controlling tips, you could choose to switch this player into the up position. In the back-row player-up options the problem of the left-front or right-front players moving widely out of position to dig tip, then having to cover great distances to transition outside again for an attack has been eliminated.

In each of the three variations of the player-up system, bear in mind the primary reason to use this system is to defend against teams that tip often, or that pick on the short zones of the court with higher, slower roll shots. If you're facing teams whose mantra on offense is to swing away each and every time they get a set (and such teams are out there), this defense is not the one to choose because you're wasting a digger to cover tips that are seldom if ever hit. On the other hand, if you have a weak defender, and your opponent does *not* tip that often, you can "hide" that weaker defender and give them less responsibility by having them switch into that up behind the block digging position. Your opponents may not realize the player covering tips is a weaker defender, perhaps instead thinking, "we'd better not tip, they have it covered."

PERSONNEL REQUIREMENTS

As you can see in the figures, in the off-blocker player-up system the movement demands for the off-blocker to get into defensive position are minimal. But notice, for example, in figure 7.1, where the right-front player is positioned for tip coverage. Assuming your team controls the dig, the right-front digger, who is pulled way into the court and basically on the opposite side of where she'll attack from, has a long transition to make herself available to hit. The same is true when the opponent's left-side attacker is hitting, as shown in figure 7.2, when the left-front digger must move way right to cover behind the block. So for this defense to work and still allow an effective transition back to offense, the off-blockers (whoever is playing left side and right side) must have above-average speed in order to transition back to their offensive position and become available hitters.

This is also a major concern for the front-row setter who is the right-front player (when the attack is coming from the opponent's right side), or for the back-row setter who must transition to the setter's target at the net to set. The setter who moves to the left side of the court to position behind the block must have adequate foot speed, efficiency of movement and the technical training to get back to target to initiate the offense after the ball is dug.

Another personnel requirement is having disciplined blockers who know that a digger is being committed to covering the tip, eliminating the need for blockers to reach back or make a sudden "heart attack" type play on a ball falling right behind them. (Younger blockers especially tend to panic when a tip is moving slowly over their outstretched arms; sometimes they make a last-minute dig to keep the ball in play, forgetting that a digger is already in position to cover them.)

The personnel requirements for the setter-up defense are somewhat different. Because you're now moving a back-row digger up in front of the three-meter line, it's critical for the remaining two back-row diggers to have above average to excellent ball control, especially when it comes to handling overpasses, setter attacks, and quick attacks, because they are essentially the only diggers left in the backcourt. Also, because you're asking the off-blocker to move deeper into the court and basically to become a back-row digger, their movement skills off the net need to be quick, efficient, athletic, and strong. A lesser athlete playing right front when the opposing team sets to the right side, and who must make the move from the net back to the three-meter line and sometimes deeper, will have trouble because of the distance involved. The same is true when the opposing team sets their left-side attacker, forcing the left-front digger to make a long move off the net. You can't teach athleticism, but coaches can and should spend time making sure their players know the principles and skills of moving efficiently. Efficient movement in diggers, no matter how far they're asked to move, makes this defense effective, ending with a terminal dig, set, and hit sequence.

Requirements for the back-row player-up version are the same as for the setter-up option, however with the added concern about transition for a back-row setter if not in the player-up role, but is left as one of the two diggers splitting the backcourt. This setter must be a strong digger with quick transition skills to get back to the net to set the second ball if he or she does not dig the first ball. Choosing to use the back-row player-up defense with this option may require the coach to also train someone other than the primary setter to set the second contact if the setter digs the first contact.

ADVANTAGES AND DISADVANTAGES

Off-Blocker Player-Up Defense

In the off-blocker player-up defense, as is true for all "up" defenses, your team is committing someone to covering the tip, which you hope neutralizes your opponent's success in scoring points via tips or short soft shots. The movement demands for the off-blocker are not that significant relative to getting into digging position. For those players whose anticipation skills are still developing, the player-up defense minimizes the need for anticipation because the defender moves into coverage before the ball is actually attacked. The defender is stationed at the net, waiting to block, and when the ball is set to the opposite side of the net (i.e., to the opponent's right-side attacker if you're the right-side blocker for your team), it's a relatively easy move to go from the net to behind the block. Any time you can minimize movement demands in going from one position to the other, you've gained a technical and physical advantage because your players will tire less easily making these moves.

As for disadvantages to the off-blocker player-up defense, there are a few. First, once a ball is dug, the off-blocker has quite a distance to move to transition into position to be set for an attack. The physical advantage gained relative to the defensive movement demands might be handed right back to the opponent during a transition attack. This is especially true with your left-front player moving all the way right to position behind the block formed on the opposing left-front attacker, since the transition move is now back to their left to get outside the sideline to attack. This is often a difficult move for right-handed hitters, and may result in them not getting fully outside to take a strong approach and producing a weak attack, if they are in position to take a swing at all. This may be a slightly easier transition for your right-front digger in the player-up position behind the block facing the opposing right-front attacker, since for a right-handed player the move back out to the right sideline is easier and more comfortable to perform. Plus if this player is taught a one-foot slide approach, they can still be a very effective transition attacker from their player-up position behind the block.

In any form of "up" defense, you're using one of your diggers solely for tip coverage. This player is in no position to dig any ball except for the short ball. If your team's overall ball control depends on the defender you've assigned to dig only tips, you might be better off playing perimeter defense, which allows this skilled defender to dig both tips and hard-driven balls, possibly resulting in keeping more balls in play.

Setter-Up Defense

A team using a setter-up defense enjoys one key advantage over a perimeter or player-back defense. If the setter (in a 5-1 or 6-2 offensive system; see chapters 15 and 16) doesn't have to take the first ball, he or she can actually begin moving back to the net into the target area where diggers are instructed to dig the ball. Ideally, they'll be at least halfway back to the desired target before the ball has been dug because they have read the attack direction and anticipated another player will have responsibility for the dig. Getting this kind of head start is not as possible when the setter is in the back row and engaged in a player-back or perimeter defense. Depending on whom you play against, it's quite possible your setter won't have to dig the first ball, allowing him or her to make the second contact and enabling your team to run a more efficient offense. The transition from digger to attacker is also easier for the left- and right-front off-blocker defenders.

As for disadvantages to the setter-up system, note that the setter's base position is in the middle of the court and near the three-meter line. This creates a significant disadvantage if the blockers responsible for blocking balls fail to protect this vulnerable digger stationed directly in the middle of the court. If one or both blockers get faked out or otherwise don't close the block, the setter-up defense exposes this digger to high-speed attacks. If playing a 5-1 offense and utilizing the setter as the player-up, when the setter is a front-row player and is involved in the block, one of the back-row players or the off-blocker must now be trained as the player-up behind the block.

The movement demands for the off-blocker, who might travel well behind the three-meter line, are also significant. Teams able to attack aggressively crosscourt require the off-blocker to make a move from the net to at least the three-meter line, if not further. Any hesitation by the off-blocker in making this move will result in being inadequately stopped, balanced, and positioned to dig the opponent's attack.

Back-Row Player-Up Defense

In this player-up version, an advantage may be that this allows a setter to be utilized as a strong digger if she is one of the better defenders on the team, but a disadvantage may be if the back-row setter is not the player up behind the block, then she is exposed to taking more first contacts or faces a greater transition distance to the target to set the second contact.

OPTIONS

Those who diagram the perfect defensive system on paper may run the risk of establishing a too rigid set of expectations relative to player positioning. As you review the three types of player-up defenses discussed in this chapter, various distances from the net and spacing relative to the end lines, sidelines, and other teammates have been suggested for you to consider. Please keep in mind, though, that the diagrams presented here are merely blueprints ready to be modified as necessary for your team's personnel, as well as for your needs against the specific opponents you will play. For instance, look at figure 7.2 *a-c* that propose that the setter in the back row starts on the three-meter line in the setter-up defense. If opposing teams tend to place overpasses, setter attacks, and quick attacks deeper than 15 feet (4.5 meters), it would make sense to adjust your setter's base position to be in front of the three-meter line, because all three tasks they had responsibility for will now become the responsibility of the remaining back-row diggers. Also, it's quite possible to modify the position of the setter relative to where he or she is stationed behind the block. If teams tend to tip around the block on either side (outside the outside blocker and inside the middle blocker), it might make sense for the setter to position in the seam between the blockers, enabling him or her to get either one of the tips described.

In the off-blocker player-up defensive system, consider a couple of options that might help your team. If during a match you notice your opponents successfully hitting a hard sharp-angle ball, keep your off-blocker closer to the side line rather than bringing him or her in close to the block. This adjustment counters the opponent's tactic. Further, just because you bring in your off-blocker for tips on one side of the court or against one hitter, this doesn't commit you to bringing him or her in on the other side. In other words, if your opponent, when attacking from the right side, doesn't have the ability to hit the hard sharp-angle shot, it makes sense to bring in your right-front player to cover tips. But if the opponent does in fact have a hitter who can hit the hard sharp-angle shot from the left side, you can pull your left-front digger off the net 8 to 10 feet (2.4-3 meters) and 1 to 3 feet (.3-.9 meter) from the sideline to have more opportunities to dig the sort of ball just described. Training your left-front digger in this case to hit something other than the traditional high outside set may also be important in running a still effective transition offense or counter attack off the dig.

COACHING POINTS

Again, the three forms of player-up defenses create movement demands for each of the diggers. Continue to train the movements of each of the players who have digging responsibility, which is in effect everyone on the floor. Many times, coaches work on the skill of digging without requiring the player to demonstrate the movement that's necessary before the actual dig occurs. A player might be a great digger when he or she isn't forced to produce any movement before the dig, but very rarely does a digger get to dig in a game without having to generate some sort of movement first.

Although we're covering a different defensive system than discussed in chapter 6 (player-back), the coaching points in that chapter generally also apply here. Giving diggers in the player-up defensive systems movement training while also having the chance to dig a live ball that's coming from the opposing team's side goes a long way toward developing proficient diggers. The ball-setter–ball-hitter approach (p. 53) to training defenders in what to watch works here as well, giving the defenders opportunities to develop their skills of reading, anticipating, judging, and timing. Finally, be sure your players are being exposed to digging opportunities in this system at gamelike speeds.

Two-Blocker System

EXPLANATION OF TACTIC

In a two-blocker system the primary objective is to get two blockers up at the point of attack against the opponent regardless of where the attack is coming from. This is accomplished by the middle blocker taking part in every block, whether the block is formed on the right, middle, or left side of the court. Who the second blocker will be is determined by where the ball is set: Left-side blockers will team with the middle blocker when the opposing team has set their right-side attacker, whereas the right-side blocker will team with the middle blocker when the opposing team has set their left-side attacker. Who helps the middle blocker when the opposing team sets their middle hitter? Either the left-side or right-side blocker, depending on who is more skilled at blocking and also on the tendencies of the opposing team's middle hitters. Clearly, if one of your outside blockers has a decided blocking skill advantage, that player should be the blocker to help the middle blocker in slowing down the middle attack. But a tactical dilemma occurs when an opposing team's middle hitter prefers to hit to crosscourt (toward your left back and middle back), but your best outside blocker is your right-side blocker. In such a case teams must sort through what gives them the best opportunity to win the rally. The earlier such decisions are made and trained, the better.

It's important to consider the hitting ability of your opponents when deciding whether to commit two blockers to defend their attack. Many teams, at all levels, commit one third of their team (two blockers) to blocking attackers who don't really have the ability to put the ball away. Teams whose hitters have slow approaches and slow arm swings will have minimal success with putting the ball down to the floor for a point. In general, hitters must be good enough to deserve two blockers. But also consider the ability of your team's diggers to control a particular attacker's shot. If blocking with one or zero blockers gives your team little chance to dig and transition to offense, then using two blockers makes sense. Teams with good ball control and proficient diggers might be better off digging a lot of balls from the attackers rather than trying to block them. So coaches must teach defenders when to *not* block as well as when to block.

We have discussed the principle of base positions for back-row players in earlier chapters. Blockers also have base positions at the net that need to be discussed. Most typically expect outside blockers to block the hitters directly across the net in front of them (left-side blockers block right-side hitters; right-side blockers block left-side hitters), so a common practice is to start the outside blockers near the opponent's anticipated point of attack. Many right- and left-side hitters hit the traditional higher outside set (and typically in a crosscourt direction), which is near the antenna on their respective side. Positioning your blockers at or near this position puts them already in a place where minimal movement will be necessary to block the respective hitter. For the middle blocker, base position will be about the middle of the net. This puts him or her in position to get to the point of attack regardless of where the ball is set.

PERSONNEL REQUIREMENTS

Blocking is the one skill in which the opponent's ability to attack determines your personnel requirements. The stronger the opponent's ability to aggressively attack the ball from all positions, the greater the need to have blockers who can defend against those types of hitters. Assuming opposing attackers have the ability to consistently terminate the attack, several personnel requirements exist.

First, blockers must possess the ability to get hands over the net to intercept the ball that has been attacked. Recognizing that once the hitter has made contact with the ball, it's perfectly legal to reach over the net to block it, blockers must have the physical characteristics to jump and reach high enough to do this. A common misunderstanding is that blockers must get considerably above and over the top of the net (elbows above and across the net) to be effective. At most levels, once attackers contact the ball, the ball will cross the net just slightly above the top of the net. So although it's helpful to get across the net as high as possible (which takes away more area and angles, and might intimidate the attacker), it's critical to get just over the top of the net (hands and wrists are over) to intercept the ball that crosses this close.

Blocking with success requires above average upper body strength. A blocker who can get over the top of the net but who lacks upper body strength can't accomplish much because attacked balls will deflect off a weak block, leaving diggers behind the block small chance of retrieving the ball. Upper body strength, particularly in the shoulders and chest, allows blockers to keep their arms and hands firm and to block balls back into the opponent's court or deflect them in such a way that diggers can retrieve the ball and transition to offense.

Ideally, blockers will also possess the lateral movement skills required to effectively get in front of the hitter's approach angle and the likely zone on the net at which the ball will cross. Good outside blockers possess the reading skills to be able to set the block at the correct point on the net in front of the hitter, which allows the middle blocker (in a two-blocker system) to move to close a solid block. Good middle blockers also possess good reading skills allowing them to watch the pass and setter for clues that will help them anticipate the direction of the set to release and close quickly with the outside blocker.

Quick, efficient lateral movement skills are very important for blockers, especially middle blockers. There are several different footwork patterns that blockers need to rehearse and become proficient at in order to set the block quick enough, and if a middle, close with their feet to the point of attack. Some patterns work better for shorter distances and some better for longer distances, but basically the blocker needs to keep the upper body parallel to the net with hands high as they either side shuffle, or for longer distances, turn their feet and hips to run to the point of contact. Whichever footwork is used, once there it is important for blockers to turn feet, hips, and shoulders back parallel to the net (square up) and prepare to jump to block.

Another personnel requirement is effective timing by the blocker. Blockers who have the ability to get over the net do themselves and their teams little good if they can't successfully time when they should jump. A common error blockers make is to jump at the same time as the attacker. Because the attacker has more to do while in the air (cock the arm back and finish a complete arm swing), the blocker should wait to jump until after the hitter has left his or her feet. How soon the blocker jumps after the hitter is best determined by the height of the set, the attacker's height and jumping ability, the speed of the attacker's approach and arm swing, and how close the set is to the net. In general, the faster the set and the faster the hitter's approach and arm swing, the sooner the blocker will jump after the attacker has done the same. Of course the key is to be at maximum height on the block jump when the attacker begins the arm swing toward the ball.

Finally, effective blockers must have the mental skills to recognize what's required of them in all situations and to quickly adjust as necessary. Hitters tend to do what they feel most comfortable doing. This is especially true in close matches when hitters are under stress. In particularly meaningful matches (championship matches, tournament matches, matches against ranked opponents) and in those matches in which every point seems crucial, hitters are likely to resort to what they feel most confident doing. This might be attacking crosscourt, for example, or hitting some kind of off-speed shot. Whatever a hitter's tendencies are, blockers must be able to read them and try to take them away. Clearly, if you can force hitters to go away from or change their most comfortable shots, your team gains an advantage.

ADVANTAGES AND DISADVANTAGES

When a team commits two players to defend one attacker, they do so believing they can positively influence what occurs when that attacker hits. If a team has the required personnel, a two-blocker system can help swing the momentum of a game and match very quickly. Though it can be difficult for blockers to maintain persistence, because they don't see results in every effort, those who stay with it and come up with a great block late in a game feel amply rewarded.

As mentioned earlier, when you block with two blockers it's much easier to take away an opposing hitter's bread-and-butter shot. Many teams have hitters who have only one attacking option they can execute with high levels of success. Taking that option away forces their team to make big adjustments on the fly. Even when a team has a star hitter capable of attacking in many ways, making that hitter do something just a little different from what he or she excels at doing will frustrate the hitter and generally disrupt the opponent's game plan.

Another advantage of a two-blocker system is that it better allows a team to hide its blockers' deficiencies. Say your team's outside blocker is having trouble slowing down an opponent's aggressive swing. This blocker might try positioning slightly outside the attacker's favorite shot, perhaps giving a taller or more accomplished middle blocker the opportunity to block the shot. Such adjustments can be easily made in a two-blocker format as long as both blockers recognize and respect the skills of the other.

A final advantage to using two blockers is the greater impact this defense can have against opposing teams with seasoned and aggressive hitters. As you likely know, when all else is equal, teams with excellent attackers usually win the battle over teams with excellent diggers. A two-player blocking scheme can often reduce the tactical and technical advantages that great hitters have over great diggers.

The most obvious disadvantage of the two-player blocking system is that you commit two of your players to defending one of your opponent's. Built into the system is the concession that one of your blockers can't do the job alone. If the attacker can get the ball past the block, your team has only four players to play the ball. In choosing this system, you are gambling that your two blockers will be able to block (or touch and slow down) enough balls to win the match, but of course it doesn't always turn out that way. If it did, all teams would use the two-blocker system.

Another disadvantage arises when your two blockers don't block side by side; if this happens, all benefit of the system is lost. A common example of this occurs when a middle blocker fails to get all the way out to the outside blocker when the opponent has set to the right- or left-side attacker. A middle blocker who is feet or even inches away from the outside blocker has a far tougher ball to block and gives diggers a far more difficult challenge to contend with since there has been a seam created between the blockers.

Also common is poor timing by the two blockers. If either or both blockers jumps too early or too late, the attacker gains options not present had the block been properly timed. Clearly, when a team commits to a two-blocker system it also commits to practicing it until blockers can communicate and read each other perfectly, and can be totally synchronized on their block jump.

OPTIONS

Volleyball teams at all levels need to understand how to implement the various blocking options available within the two-blocker system. Teams often become locked into where they place their blockers. The front players are usually referred to as left-side hitters, middle hitters, and right-side hitters. Forgotten in this terminology is that these players also have significant blocking responsibilities. In addition, some coaches tend to think too far ahead, asking, "What can our hitters do from their hitting positions after the opponents have hit and we're now digging and transitioning into offense?" while forgetting that they may have to block first.

One option is for coaches to determine the opponent's likely point of attack and have the best front-row blocker move to defend that attack. If you're in a tight match and your team has a one-point lead late in a game, the opposing setter is likely going to set the ball to the attacker believed to have the best chance of ending the point. Assume this is their left-side hitter and that your best blocker in this rotation is your left-side blocker. In such a case, your team might quickly switch the left-side blocker with the right-side blocker so that your best blocker defends your opponent's best attacker. This can be accomplished by altering the base position of your blockers right before the ball is served (figure 8.1). Bunching your three blockers into the middle of the net before the serve gives all three time

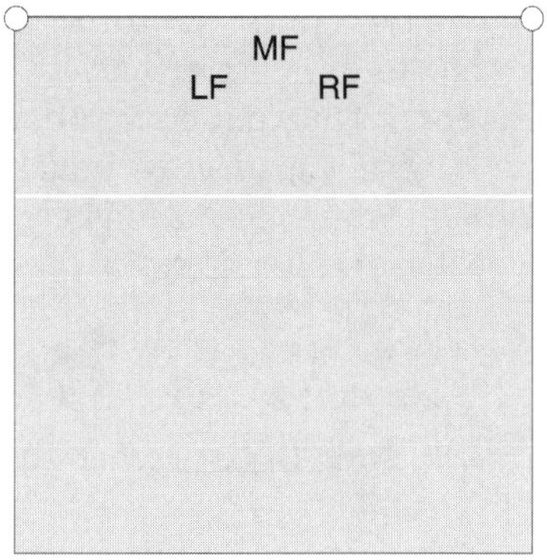

Figure 8.1 Blockers' base positions when switching after a serve.

to get to their blocking position. More highly skilled teams, if trained to do so, can assume this bunch position after their team has attacked and the opposing team has successfully dug the ball in transition and is now moving to offense. By bunching your blockers' base positions you give your team the opportunity to deploy its best blocker against the most likely point of attack. In any case, the blocking team has gained a tactical edge.

Another option within the two-blocker system is the soft block. Every team will experience a situation in which their blocker is physically shorter than the attacker, or can't get as high on the block as the hitter can on the attack. Sometimes blockers can rise to the challenge, but many times they simply can't win such a point. Attempting a soft block, in which blockers point their palms up toward the ceiling, won't result in a stuff-block on the opponent's side but might allow the ball to be hit off the palms and rebound high enough to give the defense behind the block time to pursue the ball.

Many teams are predictable in terms of where they like to set the ball in certain situations or rotations. If you know a team's offensive tendencies, take advantage by shifting your blockers' base positions toward the likely point of attack. For example, if the likely point of attack is the opponent's left-side hitter, it makes sense to shift your middle blocker's base position slightly to the right. Similarly, once you have determined which outside blocker will usually assist the middle blocker with the middle attack, you can shift that blocker along the net more into the middle of the court.

Typically, when blockers have less distance to travel along the net to thwart an attack, the more success they'll have. So it's often a good idea to alter all your blockers' base positions based on most likely point of attacks and on the opposing hitters' favorite shots. Of course, the better you know your opponents, the easier it is to implement such a plan.

COACHING POINTS

Players who understand the technical demands of blocking go a long way toward forming an effective blocking team. In general, once your blockers understand the technique and movements required of them, they should practice blocking against live attackers who are attempting to terminate the ball. Initially, your blockers might have minimal success, but through such practice they'll gain valuable experience in several skills, including the following:

- Reading (e.g., does the setter have fewer options because of the quality of the pass or dig?)
- Judging (e.g., to what direction and location will the setter deliver the ball?)
- Anticipating (e.g., what is the hitter most likely to do in this situation?)
- Timing (e.g., when do I jump to most effectively neutralize the attacker?)

Generally speaking, middle blockers must also have efficient lateral movement skills—because you're expecting them to block no matter where the ball gets set. In drills, incorporate lateral movement while giving your middle blockers chances to read, judge, anticipate, and time the block. Such drills promote optimal learning.

In practices and games blockers may correctly form blocks, jump, and never get a block touch or kill. So when training your blockers against live attackers, be sure to reinforce them, especially when they may not realize they've done something well. A common example is when your blockers force a hitter to hit the ball out of bounds because of what the well positioned block took away. Although your blockers didn't touch the ball, they forced the hitter error and should be recognized for a job well done.

Also look for occasions when your blockers can't have a positive impact through no fault of their own. For instance, when an attacker is not aggressive, it might be difficult for your blockers to influence the game—simply because they don't have to. The hitter isn't being aggressive enough to merit aggressive blocking. Such situations might not call for two blockers to jump, but if they do, reinforce them for being in good position for a well-formed and timed block, even if the hitter's lack of aggressiveness isn't allowing them to positively influence that point. Be sure players understand that a good block is not just a stuff or kill block and reinforce blockers who touch or slow down attacks that can be controlled by teammates as well.

Whatever blocking strategies are decided upon before or during a match, focus on individual blocking in practices. Individual blocking training coupled with knowledge of what opposing hitters like to do will give your team a leg up in the tactical battle of winning rallies.

Along with practicing technical skills, middle blockers need to be trained to emotionally deal with the demands of the position. It's not uncommon for great blockers to score fewer than two points from blocks in a game. Because ideally the middle blocker is involved in every play that involves an attack, this low rate of return can be emotionally unnerving. Remind your blockers that two blocks for points per game might be the difference between winning and losing, especially when your team and the opponent are about evenly skilled. When not properly trained emotionally, blockers tend to get down on themselves when not touching balls or scoring points and become discouraged. Keep them at the top of their game by consistently applauding their efforts, whether they result in direct points or not.

Finally, coaches must decide how much practice time to devote to blocking. It's widely agreed that the skills of serving and passing should be practiced during every session, but views differ when it comes to blocking. In general, the younger or less experienced your players, the less likely it is that blocking will influence a game. So, while coaches have the responsibility of introducing all aspects of the game to all skill levels, those with young teams might be better off introducing individual blocking skills and concepts and working on them periodically but focusing most practice time on those skills that can determine outcomes of games. That said, of course, teams that face opponents whose attacking skills are above average to excellent must devote ample practice time to effectively defend against quality attackers. Opponents who consistently attack with velocity will require regular training of your blockers in the skills necessary to neutralize the attacker's strengths.

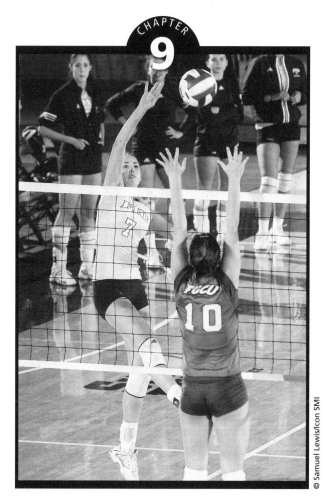

© Samuel Lewis/Icon SMI

One-Blocker System

EXPLANATION OF TACTIC

The one-blocker system is employed when a team has only one or two efficient blockers in the line up or when a nonaggressive opponent doesn't warrant using two blockers to defend their attacking game. The one-blocker system is commonly used to defend the middle attack of the opposing team.

Here we'll discuss using one blocker when your team has two blockers with the ability to affect the outcome of games in positive ways. In this example imagine that your team's remaining players either lack the physical size to get their hands and wrists at least over the net or else lack experience in blocking to the extent that it's unwise to use them as blockers when they're in the front row.

If your team has two able blockers, place them in opposite positions within the starting rotation. The opposite positions of volleyball are right back and left front, middle back and middle front, and right front and left back. Placing your two blockers opposite each other ensures that you'll have one of the blockers on the front row at all times, allowing you to use the one-blocker system effectively.

Conventionally, the two blockers would play the middle-blocker position, allowing them to start their base position in an area that lets them cover the entire net, or position their base in front of the opponent's primary attacker, ,and ideally get stuff-blocks and "slow downs" on opponent attacks. Recall from the explanation of tactics for the two-blocker system (chapter 8) that the middle blocker adjusts his base position slightly to the side on which he expects the ball to be set. This principle remains valid in the one-blocker system as well. The blocker must not cheat over so far, however, that he won't be able to defend any unexpected maneuver by the opponent's setter.

Your blocker in this system should focus on taking away the opposing hitter's favorite and most effective attack. Because there's only one blocker and one hitter, a sort of cat and mouse game might develop between the two. In any case, the single blocker (like the double blockers) should always have these primary objectives (in order of preference): stuff-block the ball for a point; force the hitter into an unforced error; slow down the attack, making it easy for remaining defenders to dig; or channel a ball (even if it's hard driven) to one of the diggers. If the blocker does one of these four things, he or she has done the job.

What do the other two front-row players do since they're not involved in the block? Figure 9.1*a-c* shows one possibility. Because the players at the right-front and left-front positions know ahead of time they won't be involved in blocking, their base position is about 5 feet (1.5 meters) from the net and anywhere from 5 feet (1.5 meters) inside their respective sideline to as far in as 10 feet (3 meters) inside their sideline. When the opponent is attacking from their left side (figure 9.1*a*), your right-side player is behind the blocker, out of harm's way. More important, he or she is in position to cover tips that are inside the three-meter line and as far into the court as 15 feet, or 4.5 meters (halfway between the sidelines). The left-front digger is closer to the three-meter line and sideline (the "short corner" of the court) to dig any ball the left-side hitter hits at a sharp angle. The left-front digger also retains tip responsibility for balls inside the three-meter line that are 15 feet (4.5 meters) or closer to the left sideline. The same alignment occurs (flip-flopped) when the opposing team is hitting from the right side (figure 9.1*b*), with the left-front player now positioning behind the blocker. The left-front digger is again out of harm's way yet in position to dig the same tips inside the three-meter line that are 15 feet (4.5 meters) or closer to the left sideline.

Keep in mind that if the opponent (from the right side, left side, or both) lacks ability to hit a sharp-angle shot, the sharp-angle digger (either the left-front or right-front player) will move in closer to the net and probably further into the court. Remember the principle of placing diggers in areas in which the opponents are most likely to attack; don't waste your diggers by stationing them in areas that opponents are too weak to attack.

When the opponent is attacking from the middle, the left- and right-side players' positions are somewhat determined by the kind of set the middle runs. If it's a quick attack (a ball that's set 1 foot [.3 meter] above the top of the net), the left-front and right-front players will simply stay in their base positions to read and react to what the hitter does (figure 9.1c). If the middle hitter is hitting a slower tempo set (at least 2 feet [.6 meter] above the top of the net), the left- and right-front players will have time to move, although probably still inside the three-meter line, to get in position for likely shots from the middle attacker. If you have a general sense of what your opponents will do from the middle, your left- and right-front players should position accordingly.

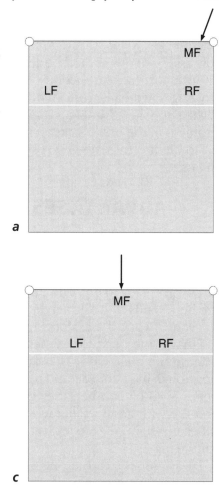

Figure 9.1 The off-blocker's role in a one-person block when the opponent is *(a)* attacking from the left, *(b)* attacking from the right, and *(c)* hitting a quick middle attack.

PERSONNEL REQUIREMENTS

In this system the two single blockers must possess the same qualities as those mentioned for blockers in the two-blocker system (chapter 8, p. 66), and in some ways must possess even more mobility since you are relying on only one of them to patrol and block the entire net. For the most part a team needs two solid blockers with great game awareness (ability to read, anticipate, judge) who can move efficiently, especially laterally, score points through stuff-blocks, and touch or slow down attacks to give teammates opportunities to dig and transition. These blockers must be resilient; capable of handling many repetitions of blocks but aware that great blockers often get fewer than two blocks for points per game.

The remaining players require strong digging and ball-control skills. In a one-blocker system this requirement is magnified. Diggers in both the front row and back row should be able to dig the ball high enough and accurately enough for the setter to move into position to set. A blocker effective in slowing down balls from an opponent's attack must be able to count on the diggers to take advantage. Diggers who can't control their digs are a major problem in the one-blocker system. Blockers skilled enough to force attackers to hit directly at diggers require teammates with the skills to dig that ball to target.

ADVANTAGES AND DISADVANTAGES

Because many opponents won't have outstanding attackers, committing only a single player to blocking them often makes sense. Only the most dominant hitters can terminate balls against a one-blocker system because five diggers are always ready to dig. The single blocker in this system, knowing all blocks are hers, tends to be hungry and aggressive. She knows she can't point her finger at anyone if the blocking game isn't working.

Finally, the one-blocker defense obviously presents fewer seams to the offense and makes for easier digging around the block. Ask any good digger how tough it is to dig behind two blockers who are only inches or centimeters apart. Such balls, when they get past the blockers, are hard to prepare for and dig with accuracy because diggers can't see them coming. In the one-blocker system, diggers expect to stay busy, so they remain focused, ready for the dig.

Disadvantages to the one-blocker system begin with the blocker. If the blocker is having a rough day, every teammate is going to know it. Opponents too will recognize a struggling blocker and will of course key on the blocker. A blocker who's not blocking for points, forcing hitters to make unforced errors, or deflecting balls will cause severe problems for the diggers behind her and fewer points will be scored out of defensive transition. The one-blocker defense is physically taxing for the blocker, so fatigue might be a factor late in a game or match, especially if opponents run a fast-tempo offense or a spread offense along the whole width of the net.

This system requires players to have specialized skills. Both blockers and diggers must be strong in their areas. A blocker with only adequate skills in reading, judging, anticipating, and timing will have difficulty if an opponent's offense requires him or her to move a lot. Diggers in this system who lack ball-control skills will be exploited by strong hitters.

Finally, a one-blocker defense isn't usually able to neutralize a hot-hitting attacker. Great offense tends to beat great defense, so a hitter on a hot streak is going to get her points, no matter how good the blocker is. There's often nothing a defense can do to stop a hitter with an extremely hot hand, but the one-blocker defense will be particularly susceptible to losing points to such a player.

OPTIONS

Speaking of hot-hitting opponents, one option when you run into one is to mix things up on defense over the course of a match in an effort to cool their hitters off. For instance, you might alternate using one and two blockers to show the offense something different and disrupt their flow.

Usually teams want their single blocker in a base position that will allow him or her to move to block the opponent's best attacker. Occasionally, however, a team might move the blocker into the zone of the most likely attack, which invites the opponent's setter to set someone other than that hitter. This maneuver probably works best early in a match, assuming that later in the match their best hitter is going to get set most often, no matter what. Inviting the opponent's setter (by where you start your blocker) to set a lesser-skilled attacker can create a tactical advantage for your team.

Similarly, when an opponent has two strong attackers (assuming they're in opposite positions and never in the front row at the same time), you might consider devoting all your single blocker's energy to defending the dominant attacker in the front row, treating any other hitter who gets set as a down-ball attack (which doesn't require the blocker to jump and block).

COACHING POINTS

For the one-blocker system to work, the blocker must be trained physically (anaerobically more than aerobically), technically, tactically, and emotionally. Training the blocker anaerobically means requiring many short bursts of movement at optimal speeds under gamelike intensity. Such movements don't require using oxygen as fuel, so the blocker's anaerobic system is developed. Many resources are available that address how to train athletes using the energy systems most prevalent in the game of volleyball.

A blocker who can get to the point of the opponent's attack efficiently is only as good as the tactical application a coach allows him or her to develop in training. Such training involves moving to front the hitter's point of attack with arms in a comfortable position above the waist and in front of the body, getting feet balanced and stable before jumping, and pressing over the net, leaving no space between the arms and the net (called sealing or penetrating the net). To be able to do all of this consistently requires much specific training under gamelike conditions.

Train your blockers to continually ask two questions:

- Who's most likely to be set in this situation?
- What shots does this hitter most like to hit?

Based on the answer to these questions, the blocker must then determine where to position to have the best chance of blocking the ball. Usually, being able to correctly answer these questions indicates that your blocker has good game sense and an ability to read opponents well. A coach who provides gamelike drills so the blocker can learn to answer these questions quickly and correctly will be training a blocker who can positively affect the outcome of many plays.

As for the emotional element in the one-blocker system, above all, coaches should train resiliency in their blocker. The single blocker will have times of frustration when the opposing team has scored several points in a row and he or she has been able to do nothing about it. A coach needs to help the blocker stay focused and emotionally strong. One way of doing this is to provide encouragement after every point, even when the blocker has not touched the ball.

In practice, run gamelike drills that pit your hitters against your blockers, and keep score. Create opportunities for your blockers to win points (by giving them the goal of a specific number of blocks or playable deflections to score before the hitter gets a set number of kills), allowing them to train physically, technically, tactically, and emotionally.

Of course your remaining players, the diggers, should be working just as hard on digger alignment. A one-blocker system allows more opportunities for diggers to affect the outcome of matches. Once you have chosen this system, be sure that diggers also get plenty of practice so that the system rewards them rather than penalizes them.

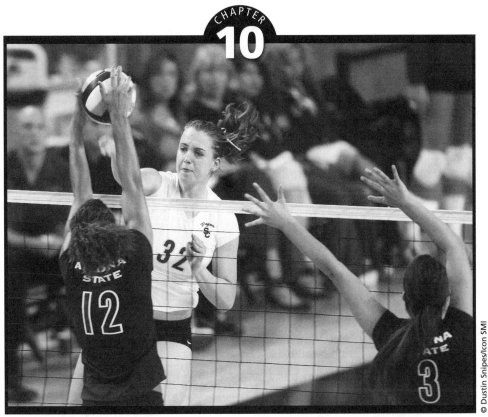

CHAPTER

10

© Dustin Snipes/Icon SMI

Defensive System Drills

The drills presented in this chapter are designed to work on the defensive systems presented in Part II. Many, however, are designed to develop skills across other systems and strategies as well. The "category" section of each drill will help you determine all of the skills each drill can be used to develop.

Digging the Left-Side Crosscourt Attack

Category: Use with chapters 6, 7, 8, 11, 12, and 13.

Objective: To effectively dig hard-driven crosscourt shots with only one blocker blocking.

Players Required: 9

Procedure: The tosser on side B initiates a ball over the net to the passer on side A, who passes to the setter, who sets the left-side attacker. The 5 defenders on side B start in base position, and then move to player-back defensive positions after the ball is set. The team B defense digs, sets (either to their left-side attacker or back-row hitter), and hits. The tosser initiates balls to the other side for three minutes; the defense successfully converts three consecutive dig-set-kills (DSK) to complete the drill. The defense then becomes the attackers, and the drill repeats.

Variations: A team with solid ball control can have the tosser initiate an aggressive down ball (a standing self toss and overhand attack) versus the toss. A team must win on both defending and attacking sides to win the drill.

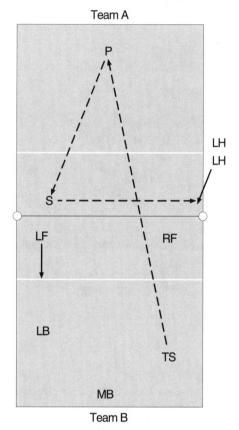

Common Errors and Corrections: Because this drill focuses on the outcome of the defensive contacts, players might take less seriously the actual movement before the ball is dug. Watch for efficiency in the defense's movements that puts them in position to dig, possibly awarding points only if the movement is executed correctly and results in a dig-set-kill sequence.

Plus 10

Category: Use with chapters 6, 7, 8, 11, 12, and 13.

Objective: To successfully score 10 points on defense using a player-back system.

Players Required: 10

Procedure: The tosser initiates a free ball or down ball to the side of four (team A), who dig, set, and hit to the side of six (team B) across the net, trying to terminate the ball. Team B attempts to block the opponent's attack or successfully dig the hitter and run a transition attack. Teams stay in a rotation until plus 10 points are scored (by either team). Scoring is as follows:

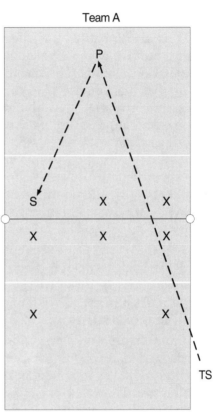

Team A

Team B

- + 2 points for a successful terminal block or successful DSK sequence.

- + 1 point for successful (i.e., up and playable) dig, regardless of outcome of play.

- –1 point for digging ball over the net or an unforced error (net violation, hitter hitting ball into net).

- –2 points if the ball is merely touched or no effort is made to dig the attack.

- The drill continues until the defensive team (team B) rotates through all rotations.

Variation: There are many ways to develop scoring systems for this drill. Coaches may choose to award more than 2 points for a successful block, dig, set, or kill.

Common Errors and Corrections: Less experienced teams will struggle with digging balls on their side of the net. If players are having difficulty, reward them for the times when the dig is kept on the same side of the net or when blockers touch or slow down the attack.

Dig Plus 1

Category: Use with chapters 6, 7, 8, 9, 11, 12, and 13.

Objective: To train successful digs, sets, and kills off of defensive transition attacks.

Players Required: 12

Procedure: The tosser initiates a free ball or down ball to the side of five (team B), who digs, sets, and hits. Team A must win the rally by either blocking for a point or successfully digging, transitioning, and terminating the set. If team A wins the first rally, the tosser on the other side initiates a free ball to them. Team A must win both rallies to score the point. Team A stays in the same rotation until they score 5 points. Continue until team A has rotated through all six rotations.

Variation: This drill can be turned into a dig plus 2 drill, assuming ball control is effective.

Common Errors and Corrections: If the side of five is struggling with getting a dig, set, and hit after the ball is tossed, create a way to solve this. Maybe substitute a better player to the team of five. Or initiate the toss to the setter rather than to the digger, especially if the drill is breaking down with the dig.

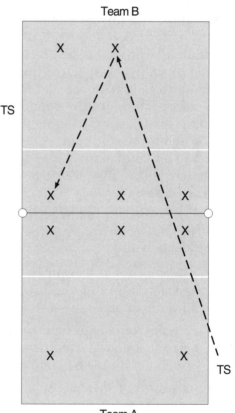

Serve Plus 1

Category: Use with chapters 2, 3, 4, and 6.

Objective: To work on player-back defense efficiency against a team of six (team B).

Players Required: 12

Procedure: Team A serves to team B, who pass, set, and hit to team A. Team A plays player-back defense and tries to win the rally. Once the ball is terminated by either team, the tosser on team B's side initiates a free ball to team A, who once again tries to win the rally. A point is scored for team A if they win both rallies in succession. Team A must score three points in order to rotate. Team A must rotate through all six rotations to win the drill.

Variations: Require team A to score more than three points. Require a team to win more than two balls in succession. Coaches could arrange their top six players so that three play front row on team A and three on the front row of team B, or arrange them as team A back row and team B back-row players, or even three as front row on team A with the other three as the back row on team B, depending on which skills they wish to stress.

Common Errors and Corrections: In this format, it's not uncommon for one team to dominate a game. Consider balancing the teams (putting top players on both teams) to ensure good competition.

Digging the Right-Side Crosscourt Attack

Category: Use with chapters 6 and 9.

Objective: To effectively dig hard-driven crosscourt attacks from the right side using one blocker.

Players Required: 10

Procedure: Tosser initiates a free ball over the net to a digger on team A. The setter back-sets to the right-side attacker. Team B (on defense) digs, sets, and hits, trying to win the rally. The tosser initiates free balls to team A for three minutes; then team B (on defense) must dig, set, and hit three balls in a row to score a point. Team A needs to score three points to rotate.

Variations: If a team has good ball control, the tosser can initiate a down ball instead of a free ball. Consider awarding extra points for correct movement by diggers.

Common Errors and Corrections: Pay attention to the movement of the defensive team prior to the dig. Efficient movement by the diggers allows for successful digs, sets, and hits.

Off-Blocker Hitting Transition (Left Side)

Category: Use with chapters 6, 7, 8, 11, and 12.

Objective: To give the left-front off-blocker experience in transitioning from player-up digger to hitter when opponents are hitting from the left side.

Players Required: 8

Procedure: The tosser on team B's side initiates a free ball across the net to a digger, who digs to the setter. The team A left-side hitter tips or hits an off-speed shot to team B's left front, who has moved into position as the player-up digger behind the block. Team B's left front digs to the front-row setter who has just landed from participating in the block, then transitions out to left front and gets available to hit. The setter sets team B's left-side attacker, who attempts to terminate the play. Two other left-front players are waiting off court and will alternate with the left front on each side after each set. The tosser initiates free balls for three minutes; then the team B left-front players must successfully dig, transition, and terminate three balls in a row to end the drill.

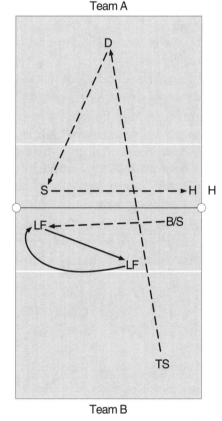

Team A

Team B

Variations: The left-side attacker who's tipping or hitting an off-speed shot can alter where he or she puts the ball (as long as it's in the area that the off-blocker is responsible for defending). The drill could also be run as a competitive game with team A's left-front off-blocker dig and hit vs. team B's left-front off-blocker dig and hit for points or time.

Common Errors and Corrections: The off-blocker might be in a hurry to dig the ball so he or she can begin the transition as a hitter. In this case, emphasize defense first. The off-blocker (who has ultimate control in this situation) might dig the ball so low that he or she has no time to transition to their attack position and hit. If so, tell the off-blocker to dig higher to give him/her more time for this transition move.

Off-Blocker Hitting Transition (Right Side)

Category: Use with chapters 6, 7, 8, 11, and 12.

Objective: To give the right-front off-blocker experience in transitioning from player-up digger to hitter when opponents are hitting from the right side.

Players Required: 8

Procedure: The tosser on team B's side initiates a free ball over the net to team A's digger, who digs to the setter. The team A right-side hitter tips or hits an off-speed shot to team B's right front, who's positioned as the player-up digger. Team B's right front digs, then transitions out to right front to get available to hit. The setter sets team B's right-side attacker, who attempts to terminate the play. Two other right-front players are off court and will alternate with the right front on each side after each set. The tosser initiates free balls for three minutes; then the team B right-front players must successfully dig, transition, and terminate three balls in a row to end the drill.

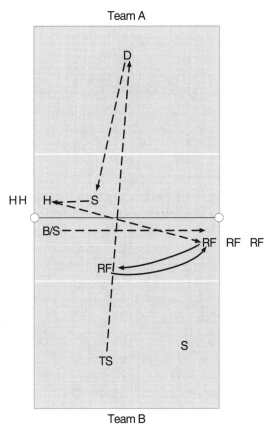

Team A

Team B

Variations: The right-side attacker who's tipping or hitting an off-speed shot can alter where he or she puts the ball (as long as it's in the area that the off-blocker is responsible for defending). Could be played as a competition between team A and team B's right-side players as in Digging the Left-Side Crosscourt Attack. It is also easy to train the right-side players to approach and hit from a one-foot slide approach in this transition drill.

Common Errors and Corrections: Watch for the breakdown of movement from digger to hitter (in this case the right-side player). Assuming that the right-side hitter is right-handed, his or her transition will be an inside-out approach, giving them less distance to travel to establish an approach angle (as compared to the left-side attacker in Off-Blocker Hitting Transition [Left Side]). Ensure that the right side digs high enough to allow for this approach angle to be established.

Setter Digging First Ball

Category: Use with chapters 7, 8, and 9.

Objective: To develop the skill of terminating balls after the setter-in–setter-up defense must dig the first ball.

Players Required: 7

Procedure: The tosser initiates a ball to the team A digger. The team A setter sets the left-side attackers, who alternate after each hitting attempt. The left side either tips or hits an off-speed shot behind the team B block, requiring the setter, who is up behind the block, to dig the first ball. The setter digs the ball to the team B right-front player (who has just landed from participating in the block), who then sets either the middle hitter or the left-side hitter on team B. The tosser initiates free balls to the same side for three minutes; then the blocking team must convert three balls in a row to end the drill.

Variation: If the right-side player, who's now the front-row setter after the back-row setter dug the first ball, is tall or athletic, he or she may choose to attack the second contact if it is high and close to the net.

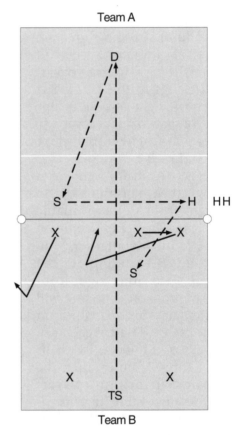

Team A

Team B

Common Errors and Corrections: Any time a nonsetter must set from right side to left side, there's a possibility of the set not getting all the way outside to the left-side attacker. Work with this player on setting a hittable ball that's high enough and far enough outside for the left-side attacker to hit, or run a medium- to high-tempo set to the middle-front attacker.

Serve-Receive to Quick-Attack Defense

Category: Use with chapters 2, 3, 4, 6, 7, 8, and 9.

Objective: To work on making an effective transition from serve-receive offense to defending the opponent's quick attack.

Players Required: 11

Procedure: The server serves to the side of six (team B), who runs their serve-receive offense and a transition to defensive position. After the ball is terminated, the tosser tosses a ball to the setter on side A, who sets a quick attack (can be in any of the three positions if quick attack is run with multiple hitters). The team on defense (team B) digs, sets, and terminates after successfully defending team A's quick attack. Team B stays in position in the same rotation until five successful defensive transitions occur, or four minutes pass, whichever occurs first. Teams then rotate once and begin again.

Variations: The team on defense can defend against the quick attack with various options, including using one, two, or three blockers. The team on defense can play a player-up or player-back defensive system.

Common Errors and Corrections: Middle hitters typically have a favorite shot. Be alert to the middle attacker who's getting successful swings (kills) to the same zone each time. Instruct the defense (specifically the blockers) to play a cat-and-mouse game with the middle attacker by taking away different zones periodically.

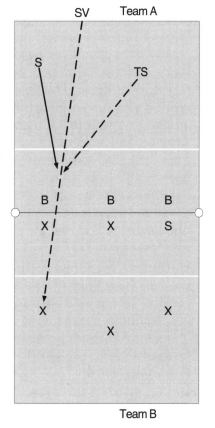

Player-Up Dig to Quick-Attack Transition

Category: Use with chapters 7, 8, 9, 11, 12, and 13.

Objective: To gain efficiency in running the middle attack after the player-up digger digs the ball.

Players Required: 8

Procedure: The tosser tosses to the setter on side A, who sets the left-side attacker. The left-side attacker tips or hits an off-speed shot to the player-up digger on team B, who's behind the block. The team B middle front (quick attacker) transitions off the net to get available and hits a quick set (either in front of or behind the setter). Alternate the middle-front players after each repetition. The tosser tosses for two minutes; then the quick attackers terminate five balls to end the drill (need not be consecutive).

Variations: Depending on the offense the team is running, the quick attacker can hit various sets both in front of and behind the setter. Can start with a toss across the net to the team A left front who must then pass to the setter to start the series.

Common Errors and Corrections: Any time the opposing team tips right behind the block, the middle attacker has very little time to block and transition off the net to get available to hit a quick attack. In this case, the digger must dig the ball high enough to ensure the quick attacker has adequate time to block, transition, and approach. This drill is good for training the middle hitter to figure out a quicker two-step attack approach when unable to get off far enough to take a full approach.

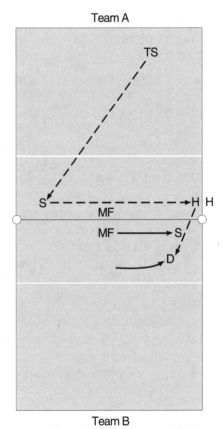

Team A

Team B

Front Row vs. Front Row (With Front-Row Setter)

Category: Use with chapters 6, 7, 8, 9, 11, 12, and 13.

Objective: To give middle blockers experience in reading to see where the set will go (to one of two front-row hitters) so a two-player block can be formed.

Players Required: 10

Procedure: The tosser on team B tosses to the digger on the other side. Team A digs, sets (to either front-row attacker), and hits, while team B blockers defend the attack. Once the ball is terminated, the tosser from the other side tosses across the net to a digger, and the drill repeats. Play a rally score game to 15 points.

Variation: Allow teams to score only on defense, by blocking for points or to get block touches or slow downs. Alternate with additional middle hitters.

Common Errors and Corrections: This drill will fatigue the middle attackers/blockers because they're required to move a moderate to long distance every single play. Train the middles to have the attitude of relentless pursuit and persistence.

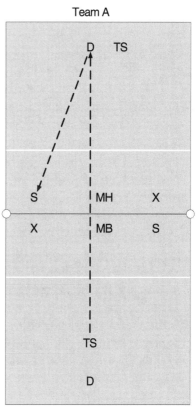

Team A

Team B

Front Row vs. Front Row (With Back-Row Setter)

Category: Use with chapters 6, 7, 8, 9, 11, 12, and 13.

Objective: To give middle blockers experience in reading where the set will go (to one of three front-row hitters) so a two-player block can be formed.

Players Required: 11-12

Procedure: The tosser on team B tosses to the digger on team A. Team A digs, sets (to any one of the three front-row positions), and hits, while team B blockers defend the attack. Once the ball is terminated, the tosser from the other side tosses to a digger, and the drill repeats. Play a rally score game to 15 points.

Variations: Instruct the setter to set balls that require the middle blocker to travel the greatest distance; this also gives the setter some eye training. This drill can also be played to fewer than 15 points, but start the score so the game will finish on the normal end point (for example, start at 15-15 and play first team to reach 25).

Common Errors and Corrections: Because the middle blocker is being physically taxed, ensure that efficient movement skills are maintained.

Middle Blocker to Quick-Attack Transition (Opponent's Right-Side Attack)

Category: Use with chapters 6, 7, 8, 9, 11, 12, and 13.

Objective: To give middle blockers experience in forming a two-player block against the right-side attacker and transitioning off the net for a quick attack.

Players Required: 7

Procedure: The tosser initiates the toss over the net to a digger on team A. Team A's setter sets the right-side attacker as team B's left front and middle front (quick-attacker) form a two-player block. When the ball is hit, if terminated or gets by the block, team B's quick-attacker transitions off the net as the tosser tosses a ball to team B's setter. Team B's middle front hits a quick attack. Continue for two minutes; then require the quick-attacker to successfully terminate three balls in a row to end the drill.

Variation: After the attacked ball from team A is terminated, the tosser can toss various types of tosses to the setter on team B, including higher than normal, faster than normal, off the net, left of center, and so on to simulate what a dig would look like in a game, forcing the middle hitter to adjust.

Common Errors and Corrections: One of the more difficult things for a middle blocker to do is transition off the net and prepare to hit a quick attack. Middle blockers must land, open up quickly, and work at keeping desirable spacing between themselves and the setter based on where the toss (dig) is.

Middle Blocker to Quick-Attack Transition (Opponent's Left-Side Attack)

Category: Use with chapters 6, 7, 8, 9, 11, 12, and 13.

Objective: To give middle blockers experience in forming a two-player block against the opposing left-side attacker and transitioning off the net for a quick attack.

Players Required: 7

Procedure: The tosser initiates a toss over the net to a team A digger. The setter on team A sets the left-side attacker as the right front (setter) and middle front (quick-attacker) on team B form a two-player block. When the ball is hit, if terminated or gets by the block, team B's quick-attacker transitions off the net as the tosser tosses a ball to team B's setter. Team B's middle front hits the quick attack. Continue for two minutes; then require the quick-attacker to successfully terminate three balls in row to end the drill.

Variation: Allow or require the middle blocker to hit various types of sets both in front of and behind the setter.

Common Errors and Corrections: The key to making this drill gamelike is the pace at which the ball is tossed after the first attack is completed. The tosser should immediately toss the ball to the setter (simulating the dig), forcing the middle attacker to quickly transition off the net.

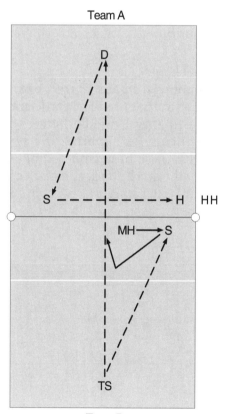

Team A

Team B

Middle Blocker vs. Middle Blocker

Category: Use with chapters 6, 7, 8, 9, 11, 12, and 13.

Objective: To train middle blockers to successfully block from the middle-front position.

Players Required: 8

Procedure: The team B tosser tosses to the setter on the same side of the net. The setter sets the middle front (quick-attacker) a quick attack (can be in front of or behind the setter) while at least two blockers on the team A side defend the attack. After the ball is terminated, the tosser on the team A side repeats the process. Play a rally scoring game to 10.

Variation: The tosser can challenge the setter and the hitter by not tossing perfect tosses.

Common Errors and Corrections: Because this drill has two blockers defending the quick attack, middle hitters will have difficulty terminating the set. Work with these hitters on getting up early for the quick attack and hit deep corner shots, negating the two blockers and one attacker.

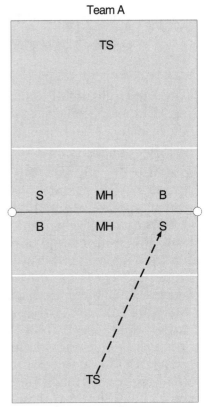

Team A

Team B

Middle Blocker Transition

Category: Use with chapters 8, 9, 11, 12, and 13.

Objective: To give the middle blocker repetitions to develop movement skills and conditioning to block the opponent's left-side attacker.

Players Required: 8

Procedure: The tosser on team B tosses to the setter on the same side of the net, who then sets the left-side attacker. Team B's middle front (single blocker) makes the move to defend this attack as a single blocker, while team B's setter backs off to cover tips. After the ball is terminated, the tosser on team A repeats the process, tossing to the team A setter, and team B blocks and digs. Play until one team scores 15 points via kills or stuff-blocks.

Variation: Tell the setter to occasionally stay up to help block the attack so the left-side attacker must pay attention to how he or she is being defended.

Common Errors and Corrections: The middle blocker will have some difficulty consistently getting outside to block the opponent's left-side attack. Watch for proper footwork. Because the setter only has one attack option (left-side attacker) the middle-front blocker will sometimes cheat over before the set is released. Have the blockers focus on reading the setter and set, then releasing to go block.

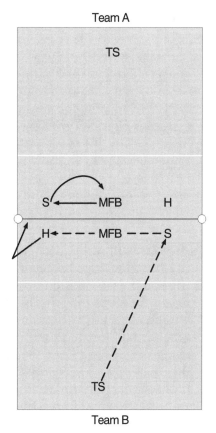

Middle Blocker Conditioning

Category: Use with chapter 9.

Objective: To give the blocker in a one-blocker system enough conditioning work to develop the stamina to block across the entire net.

Players Required: 6

Procedure: Team B's tosser tosses a ball over the net to the digger on team A. Team A's setter then sets the left-side attacker, while team B's blocker makes the move over to block. Immediately after the ball hits the floor, the tosser tosses another ball over the net to the digger, while team A's setter sets the right-side attacker, requiring team B's blocker to make the opposite move over to block the opponent's right-side attack. Continue for three minutes, and then put in a new blocker.

Variations: If the middle blocker is having trouble blocking the second attempt (opponent's right-side attacker), the right-side hitter can hit sets inside the antenna, giving the middle blocker a better chance to defend the attack. Count a set number of repetitions for the single blocker, or count the number of block touches or block kills.

Common Errors and Corrections: Because this drill requires the middle blocker to make the longest move possible as a blocker, focus on this player's movement skills. Many times a blocker who has just made a block attempt of the opponent's left-side attack and is now attempting to cover ground to block the opponent's right-side attack will focus too much on footwork. Remind them to move as fast as they can by turning and running, then getting squared up to the net as they reach their blocking position.

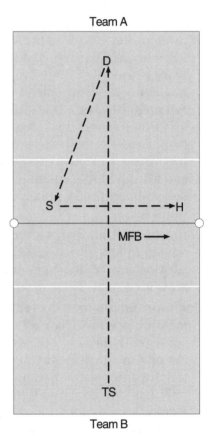

Team A
Team B

Four vs. Six Plus 10

Category: Use with chapters 6, 7, 8, 9, 11, 12, and 13.

Objective: To successfully dig, set, and terminate a rally, against one blocker.

Players Required: 10

Procedure: Team B's tosser initiates the ball over the net to team A's back-row player in middle back. Team A (team of four) runs an offensive attack against team B (team of six). Team B's middle front (single blocker) blocks regardless of where the ball is set. Team B attempts to reach +10, scored the following way:

- + 2 for a stuff-block by the single blocker
- + 1 for a ball that isn't blocked but is dug and converted into a point (or + 1 for any block touch)
- –1 for blocker who commits unforced error as a blocker (net error)

Variation: Many different scoring systems can be used. For example, a younger team might be given points for effort alone. Or points may be increased for positive actions.

Common Errors and Corrections: Any time a drill uses a one-blocker system, it's likely the blocker will get fatigued and frustrated. Watch the blocker and help him or her stay focused and controlled.

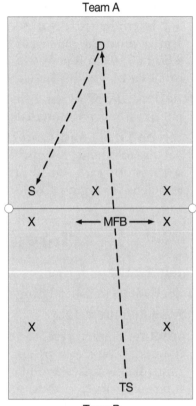

Team A

Team B

Serve Plus Three Digs

Category: Use with chapters 2, 3, 4, 6, 7, 8, 9, 11, 12, and 13.

Objective: To successfully convert balls into points from defense—one after a served ball and three after free balls to the opponent.

Players Required: 12

Procedure: Team A serves a ball to team B. The ball is played out. After the ball is terminated, the tosser on team A initiates three free balls to team B. Team A must play defense and win three out of four defensive rallies to score a point. If team B wins two or more rallies, no points are scored. Team A rotates until arriving back at their starting positions.

Variation: Any of the three free balls can be put in as down balls and can be put to various positions, both front row and back row.

Common Errors and Corrections: Watch for proper transitioning from defense to offense. Require defenders to go back to their home base defensive position each time to read the opponent's pass and set, and *then* move to defensive digging positions based on the set and attack.

Serve Plus Two Digs

Category: Use with chapters 2, 3, 4, 6, 7, 8, 9, 11, 12, and 13.

Objective: To transition from defense to offense to score points.

Players Required: 12

Procedure: Team A serves to team B. Regardless of which team wins the rally, the tosser initiates a free ball to team B and when that rally terminates, immediately tosses another free ball to the same side. Team A must win three rallies in a row to score a point. If team B wins either the first, second, or third rally, they rotate and become the serving team. Play until one team scores eight points.

Variations: Down balls can be introduced instead of free balls. Coaches can modify how the receiving team earns the right to serve.

Common Errors and Corrections: The serving team often has difficulty winning the last rally after having won the first two. This usually occurs as a result of individual skill breakdown. Be aware of what skill tends to break down and what player (if there are one or two people causing the breakdown) is responsible. Correct the skill as necessary.

PART

III

Defensive Strategies

© Stan Liu/Icon SMI

Block the Line and Dig Inside Strategy

EXPLANATION OF TACTIC

Assuming that most of your team's opponents will prefer to hit crosscourt, the strategy to block the line and dig inside is a good choice for a team who has better diggers than blockers. Lining up the block to take away the line shot, which at most levels is not hit as often as crosscourt anyway, still provides an opportunity for the blocker to protect the shot from being hit for a kill. In essence, this strategy invites your opponent to continue hitting their favorite shot because your team knows its diggers can dig the best shot their hitters have to offer. If effective, this strategy can have a demoralizing impact on hitters, as time and time again their best shots are dug. This can also allow your line diggers to come off the line and angle slightly crosscourt as well, providing an additional digger in the area more likely to be attacked, or allow her to release forward for a possible tip or short roll shot over the block.

Teams that incorporate this strategy will have their outside blockers set the block with their outside arm just inside the antenna, giving the attacker limited opportunities to attack the line. The outside blocker should be lined up close enough to the antenna that there's not enough room between the blocker's outside hand and the antenna for the ball to fit through.

The backcourt, again working on the assumption that hitters hit crosscourt more than down the line, should "flood the zone," which means placing more than one digger in the crosscourt position (figure 11.1a-c). Notice in the figures that the left-back and middle-back diggers are in position to dig any type of crosscourt shot the hitter attempts, including the sharp shot hit from 20 to 25 feet (6-7.6 meters) deep and shots hit to the deepest part of the court.

From the middle-hitting perspective, even though middle hitters might be more confident hitting back to the defender's right-back position than outside hitters are in hitting the line shot, the middle-back and left-back diggers are still placed in the crosscourt zone. If the middle hitter begins to hit more balls to the right-back area between the right-back digger and middle digger, the flooding-the-zone tactic can still be implemented simply by moving the middle-back digger toward the right-back position rather than the left-back position. Be sure that one digger remains committed to handling any ball an attacker might hit down the line.

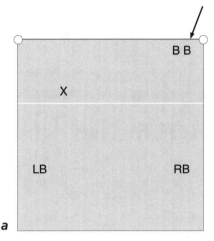

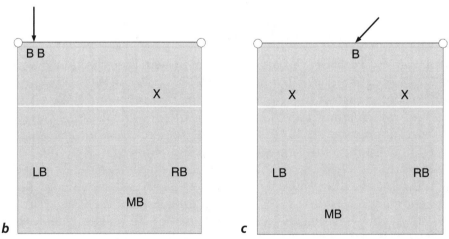

Figure 11.1   Flooding the zone during a *(a)* left-side, *(b)* right-side, and *(c)* middle attack.

It's easier to use the block-the-line-and-dig-inside strategy in a two-blocker system, but it can also be used with one blocker, especially if a team's digging skills far exceed their ability to stop the opponent's attacks at the net.

PERSONNEL REQUIREMENTS

Diggers must have the skills to consistently dig the ball to target. They must be able to dig high enough to allow the setter to run any offensive option desired. If your diggers can't dig hard-driven balls, this strategy is not for your team. Diggers flooding the zone must have good reading and anticipation skills to determine what kind of crosscourt shot is going to be hit. Within any defensive system, diggers (as long as they're good readers) should have the freedom to alter their positions to get directly behind the path of the ball, making it easier to dig. Diggers who react to the ball after it has been hit will have less success than those who watch approach angles, speed of the approach, and what the hitter's eyes are telling them about where the ball is likely going.

As the speed of the game continues to increase, diggers who have good ball control and who can cover large sections of court will make this strategy an attractive option for their team.

ADVANTAGES AND DISADVANTAGES

Diggers should have greater success than usual in digging balls because they know beforehand where the block is going to be formed to defend the attack. Thus, diggers can focus fully on the attacker.

Again working on the premise that outside hitters prefer hitting crosscourt rather than down the line, and that your diggers will flood the zone, you gain the advantage of giving hitters little to choose from. Their main choices are to try to beat the block down the line or else hit directly to a well-prepared digger. Neither choice is all that attractive.

The main disadvantage to blocking the line and digging inside arises when your team faces a dominant and powerful attacker. Even with two diggers taking responsibility in the crosscourt zone, a skilled attacker will be able to score. Remember that great hitting beats great digging in most cases. Predetermining where your block is going to be opens up opportunities for powerful attackers to hit crosscourt winners.

This strategy of play works well for teams with great diggers but might not be advantageous for teams with super blockers. In a sense, you're wasting your skilled blocker on the line in this system because he or she won't get many opportunities to win points via the block. To make things worse, your blocker might feel demoralized because he or she feels his or her skills aren't being used wisely and he or she can't contribute to determining the outcome of the match.

Finally, the strategy of blocking a certain shot regardless of what the hitter can do has potential pitfalls if used against teams you don't know well. A team might have hitters who can hit a wide variety of shots and cause problems for your diggers. For example, committing to blocking the line no matter what invites a smart attacker to tip or roll short shots over the block. So, knowing this, train your line digger to read, recognize, and release forward off the deep line for tip coverage.

OPTIONS

When using a predetermined strategy, your team can choose from among many options that can unbalance and confuse your opponents (if the options have been trained in practice). One option is to give your blockers the freedom to block the opponent's attack for a point. This is especially useful if a team's hitter has had success hitting one shot repeatedly. Allowing your blocker the freedom to block that shot (as opposed to always lining up to take away the line) forces the hitter to consider what the blocker is going to do from one play to the next. Of course in this situation you will have trained your back-row diggers to adapt to the freedom you have given your blocker. Diggers continue to play within the system, reading and anticipating how points will unfold and making the necessary adjustments behind the blockers.

Another option is to position your best diggers in the crosscourt angles. Based on scouting information, if you learn that an opponent has a particular crosscourt shot they hit repeatedly, you might place a digger right in that spot to force hitters to hit elsewhere. Moving a digger to a nontraditional position to defend an expected attack makes the opponent adjust to your strategy rather than the other way around.

Because many teams don't have the ability to hit into the deepest parts of the court or straight down the sidelines, a third option is to move your diggers—both crosscourt and on the line—further forward into the court. This allows them to defend the part of the court most likely to be attacked, while still adhering to the principle of forward movement. Of course before choosing this tactic, you must know the abilities and tendencies of your opponent's hitters.

COACHING POINTS

Your team has scouted your opponent, and your opponent has scouted your team, so they know that blocking the line and digging inside is a strategy they might see from you. Does this give them an advantage? Perhaps under one of two conditions: if your team has not sufficiently trained the strategy in practice, or if you lock stubbornly into the strategy and allow no flexibility for your blockers. For instance, if as a game progresses you recognize that the opponent's hitters are having too much success against your diggers, set your blocker free occasionally to contest the crosscourt attack. Sometimes a strategy works best with some flexibility.

When training the strategy to block the line and dig inside, make sure your diggers are facing the center of the court so that hard-driven balls can be dug up into the middle of the court, allowing for an offensive transition. Because you'll probably flood the zone in conjunction with this strategy, train your diggers in movement skills that allow two or more diggers to cover areas not covered by others. An example is the movement of the middle-back and left-back digger when the opposing team is hitting from the left side. The middle-back digger, who's flooding the zone, should be trained to move mostly laterally, whereas the left-back digger's movement should be forward and into the court. A left-back digger who moves backward more than a couple of steps is in essence shoulder to shoulder with the middle-back digger and is to be avoided because of possible miscommunication and confusion about who should dig the ball.

A key principle of individual digging technique is being in a stopped and balanced position an instant before the hitter strikes the ball. Diggers will read, anticipate, judge, and time the hitter, but they should progress through these stages *before* the hitter makes contact with the ball. Diggers who are still moving on the hitter's contact will disadvantage themselves severely if they are going one way and the hitter hits it the other way. Emphasize that all diggers must be stopped and balanced in a low neutral position just before contact. This puts them in position to move forward, left, or right (or even backward), if necessary.

The block-the-line strategy is generally preferred by teams with strong diggers, and highly skilled diggers welcome the challenge the system brings. Blockers, however, delegated to blocking the lines, might feel less useful in this system and simply go through the motions of blocking. Blockers who do this might fail to attend to the technical execution of their blocks, giving hitters a decided advantage. Be sure to train your blockers to block with the purpose and intent of taking away that zone of the court, so when hitters challenge them, they will be ready to do battle.

Finally, consider how you might manipulate your off-blocker in this defensive scheme. Because you're likely flooding the zone with two diggers in the crosscourt area, adding a third digger into the crosscourt zone puts three players relatively close to one another. Consider if the opposing hitter has the ability to hit a hard-driven ball to the sharp angle (defined as a ball that's hit hard and will land inside the three-meter line). If the hitter doesn't have this ability, move your off-blocker inside the court to take more responsibility for off-speed and tip shots. If, on the other hand, the opponent's hitter is able to hit hard-driven balls sharply crosscourt, align your off-blocker to dig this type of attack.

© Stan Liu/Icon SMI

Block Inside and Dig the Line Strategy

EXPLANATION OF TACTIC

This defensive strategy is used against teams that hit primarily crosscourt, which is the majority of teams. Choose this strategy when your team has a size advantage over your opponent and blockers skillful enough to generate stuff-blocks and slow down a hard-driven attack. This defense cuts off your opponent's most common hitting angles. The defense is also commonly used to invite opponents to try to hit down the line from the outside hitting positions, forcing them to hit shots they are likely less comfortable with (because they haven't trained it in practice and also because there's less space to hit the ball into) and which ideally result in unforced errors. This defensive strategy also makes it easier for diggers to dig because balls hit down the line generally aren't as powerful as crosscourt shots.

Although this strategy is designed for defending an opponent's outside attack, it can also be used in defending a middle attack. In this case, the middle blocker would take away the ball that the opposing middle hitter would hit to the left or middle back, coaxing the hitter to turn and hit to your right-back digger, which is a cut-back ball that's more difficult to hit with accuracy. Middle hitters generally are used to hitting to the left- and middle-back areas because that is where they face on their approach, so this strategy takes them out of their comfort zone.

Contrary to blocking the line and digging inside (chapter 11), which requires strong diggers, this defense requires strong blockers. Within this defensive strategy your blockers have greater flexibility in positioning for the inside (or crosscourt) block inside the antenna. For instance, giving your blockers the latitude to move their feet significantly inside the antenna (by as much as 4 feet, or 1.2 meters) should pay off in terms of the number of stuff-blocks they can collect.

In executing the inside block for the crosscourt shot, some outside blockers choose to set the block with their inside arm at the point where the ball will cross over the net and the other arm outside (figure 12.1a) to still have a chance for a stuff-block while protecting some line as well. This also is an alignment that allows the middle blocker to close to that position with her outside hand and take away more of the crosscourt angle. At other times, the outside blocker will place the outside hand where the ball will cross the net, effectively sealing off any opportunity for the hitter to hit strong crosscourt with success especially if joined by the middle blocker, but completely giving up the line or cut-back shot (figure 12.1b). Still other times the outside blocker will choose to split the difference, basically lining up

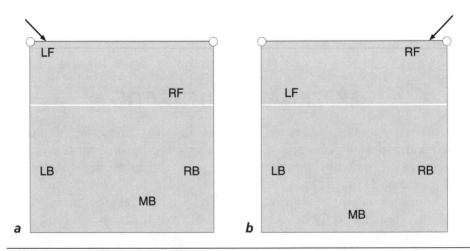

Figure 12.1 Outside-blocker alignment when blocking inside with *(a)* inside hand on the ball and *(b)* outside hand on the ball.

with his or her head on the point of contact so one hand is inside and the other outside that point, protecting against both shots equally. If unsure of hitter tendencies or if blocking one on one, sometimes this is the smart alignment to start with.

The first alignment discussed is used when the outside blocker is a single blocker, and the second is used more if the single blocker is your middle blocker since this alignment requires less movement. If forming a double block the outside blocker would assume the first position to set the block and the middle blocker moves to the second position.

The positioning of your crosscourt diggers in the defense will depend on where and how your blockers set up. For instance, if the outside blocker chooses to block with arms splitting the difference (as shown in figure 12.1), crosscourt diggers will flood the zone to defend balls that get past the block. If blockers block with their outside hand on the ball, which moves them inside the court even more, this will cover significantly more of the zone area, so diggers likely won't need to flood the zone. In this case, the crosscourt digger reads, anticipates, and digs balls that come crosscourt, whereas the middle-back digger reads and anticipates as well but tends to stay closer to the middle-back position, allowing the backcourt diggers to be equally balanced.

PERSONNEL REQUIREMENTS

As mentioned, the primary personnel requirement for this defense is strong blockers—at least two of them. If your team has stronger diggers than blockers, you'll want to choose another defense, such as the block-the-line-and-dig-inside defense discussed in chapter 11, which has the blocker channeling the ball to strong diggers.

If you have two strong blockers and then a significant drop-off in skilled blockers after that, try to put your two strong blockers in opposite positions within the rotation. The benefits of doing so are obvious (you'll always have a strong blocker in the front row), but sometimes it's not feasible. In general, you'll always want to have your two best hitters playing in opposite positions, and if one of those is also one of your best blockers, sometimes this means your two best blockers can't be opposite of each other.

If your two best blockers aren't opposite, you need a third blocker who can play within the defense (i.e., he or she must be able to block hard-driven crosscourt swings). If your team doesn't have such a player, he or she will need to be developed through training.

In earlier chapters we've discussed the impact that effective reading, anticipating, judging, and timing can have for your team. Good skills in these areas are always useful, but they are crucial for a team using a strategy geared toward blocking an aggressive crosscourt attack, even more so if choosing to block with only one blocker. A player who struggles in only one of these perceptual skills will have trouble being an effective blocker.

In general in this system, diggers need competent but not excellent skills. But because outside blockers will sometimes move the block 4 to 5 feet (1.2-1.5 meters) inside the antenna to take away the crosscourt attack, a sizable opening is often left for hitters to attack the line. The line digger must be able to retract quickly from base position and get back to a court position deep enough to dig the hard-driven attack while maintaining a body position that allows for forward movement. The line digger must also have quick reactions, ready to stand in the line of fire when the block adjusts and an outside hitter spots the opening between the blocker and the antenna. This ball will probably not be blocked or slowed down by the blocker, giving the digger full responsibility to keep the ball in play. And if it is touched by the blocker, it may deflect out of bounds, which then requires the digger to be fleet enough of foot to react and run it down.

ADVANTAGES AND DISADVANTAGES

As mentioned earlier, the primary advantage of this defensive strategy is that it takes hitters out of their comfort zones. Their favorite shot is either taken away or must be adjusted to challenge the block. A particularly strong attacker will be able to excel even against this defense, because they'll beat the block more often than not, but such attackers are rare.

As you recall, generally speaking, the less blockers and diggers must alter their position in order to make a play, the more success they'll have. In this defense, because they know they'll be blocking some portion of the crosscourt, blockers can establish an initial base position closer to that possible shot so that movement demands are minimal, allowing them to focus more fully on the hitter.

The main disadvantage of this defense is revealed against teams with dominant attackers who can hit down the line effectively (exclusively one line or the other, or angle or line at will). Teams who choose to block inside against such teams do so because they haven't scouted their opponent well enough, or because they believe their diggers will be up to the task of digging many hard-driven balls down the line. Such teams might be fooling themselves, however, because even the best diggers will have trouble digging these shots consistently.

Another disadvantage of this system is the amount of time a line digger has to respond to the ball. Because the line ball travels less distance, a hard-driven ball gets to the line digger faster than a hard-driven ball hit crosscourt. You hear players and coaches speak of the benefits of "slowing the game down." Well, that doesn't happen here. The hard-driven ball can come like a rocket at the line digger, and only the best diggers can handle such a ball.

One last thing to consider: If you play a defensive system in which your setter plays defense in the right-back position, blocking crosscourt leaves the setter exposed to taking the first contact more often, resulting in the setter being unable to run the transition offense to his or her hitters.

OPTIONS

Options in this defense depend largely on the blockers because diggers will react to what the blockers choose to do. When a blocker sets the block farther into the court, the farther up the line the digger should move, while continuing to hug the line. Because the block in this situation is set up to defend the crosscourt attack, any shot down the line will clear the net and tend to travel in a downward trajectory. Conversely, the farther outside the block is set (i.e., the closer the outside blocker's outside hand gets to the antenna), the deeper the line digger stays, recognizing that balls hit down the line will either be blocked, will deflect off the block, or be hit high over the block sending the ball deeper into the court. An exception to this rule is when the digger is confident the hitter won't try to hit down the line at all because the blocker is completely taking away that shot; in this situation, the line digger will read, anticipate, release, and move forward to defend a tip that goes down the line.

Similarly, crosscourt diggers will also be heavily influenced by blockers in this defense, often sacrificing a clear vision of the ball to allow themselves room enough to play the ball. In general, left- and right-back diggers should line up shoulder to shoulder with the inside blocker's inside shoulder, in such a position that if the digger ran forward toward the blocker, she would in effect line up as the third blocker. Diggers who need to constantly reposition to fully see the ball might put themselves out of position to play the ball well. Crosscourt diggers must remain alert and focused, but also ready for balls to come at them seemingly out of nowhere if the blocker has blocked their view.

COACHING POINTS

Coaches choose this defense when they know their blockers are capable of defending shots hit by talented crosscourt attackers. We've discussed earlier the skills associated with effective blocking (reading, anticipating, judging, and timing). In drills, ask your blockers how they determined where they ended up jumping from based on what they were watching. Many times your blockers won't know what led them to jump from a particular spot, which tells you they weren't doing much thinking or observing what the hitter was doing. If a player says, "I don't know," ask him or her to perform a few more reps, and then ask the question again. Be assured that during follow-up repetitions, your blockers will pay greater attention to the hitter's approach angle, speed, hips, eyes, and shoulders, allowing them to be more efficient blockers by becoming better observers.

If you have utmost trust in the blocker setting the block (typically the outside blocker in the two-blocker system), give this player leeway to establish the position from which the block will jump. Players see many different things on the court that are harder to see as a coach on the sideline. (This is a good reason that when coaching blockers, coaches should be on the court either behind the blockers or across the net in front of them to see what they are seeing and help give them the proper cues about what to look for.) If a player communicates to you that he or she feels a ball is going to be set to the left-side hitter and that the hitter is going to try to attack the line, this might be a time to trust your blocker and allow him or her to block the line, although the strategy by and large is to block inside. Trust your players—until they give you reason not to.

Coaching points for the back-row diggers involve the same principle as just described for blockers—give your diggers opportunities to observe gamelike hitters, and train them to move to areas without infringing on someone else's territory in order to dig a ball. There will be times when diggers move to a position you instructed them to move to, only to see the ball hit elsewhere. Sometimes a digger will not possess the sense of responsibility needed in order to chase down this ball. You and your team work hard at teaching efficient movements and reading to your diggers, but ultimately, if the ball is hit somewhere else, the digger is still responsible for doing what it takes to keep the ball in play. Instill in your diggers the attitude of relentless pursuit of every ball. Don't allow them to decide whether or not a ball can be dug. *Every* ball should automatically be pursued until it hits the floor.

© Dustin Snipes/Icon SMI

Middle-Block Strategies

In this chapter we'll look at three of the primary strategies for blocking in the middle: read blocking, release blocking, and commit blocking. These strategies can be implemented into most defensive systems and are each most effective in specific situations, which we will discuss in this chapter.

◀ READ BLOCKING ▶

EXPLANATION OF TACTIC

Let's start with read blocking, a common strategy that can be implemented within most defensive systems (e.g., block the line and dig inside, one-blocker system, two-blocker system, etc.). In read blocking, the middle blocker invests time in assessing (reading) what's happening on the other side of the net before committing to a particular mode of defending. Read blockers ask, What options does the setter have? Who is the player most likely to get set? What type of set and location is likely? They answer these questions for themselves and then shift position accordingly.

Most teams use this strategy with the assumption that the middle blocker will have time to move to the point of attack after the setter has released the ball, implying that the opposing team does not run a fast-tempo offense. However, some defenses opt to read block against faster-paced offenses, as long as their blockers have time to react to the read. If blockers use the proper technique of keeping hands high enough (above the shoulders) and legs slightly bent while sliding along the net to front the hitter, they might be able to read block with success against even fast-tempo sets. But, usually, unless a team has supersmart and superfast blockers, it's wiser to commit block with your middle blocker (discussed later in chapter) than to have him or her read block against any offense that runs a highly effective fast-tempo attack.

PERSONNEL REQUIREMENTS

For success with read blocking, your team needs an intelligent blocker who can

- judge the quality of the opposing team's pass or dig and determine what offensive options it has,
- read the setter to gain information about where the setter will set the ball, and
- move efficiently to the area from which the ball will be attacked.

Note that these personnel requirements all deal with tasks that occur *before* the attacker hits the ball, so to read block effectively, your blockers must have a high level of game intelligence. Once blockers have made the move to the point of attack, they must of course be able to close the two-player block and seal the net.

ADVANTAGES AND DISADVANTAGES

Read blocking allows a blocker to read the opponent's pass or dig and recognize what options the setter has and doesn't have. This allows the blocker to eliminate wasted movement and move directly toward the attacker most likely to be set. However, read blocking should also permit the blocker enough time to recover and adjust in the event of a misread. Compared to commit blockers (discussed later), read blockers get significant opportunities to read and anticipate what the opponent is going to do.

Read blocking trains smart volleyball players. If you have the luxury of a long preseason and many hours of practice time, begin your young players read blocking early to help teach them the nuances involved in reading opponents.

The main disadvantage to this blocking strategy is that it's far from fool proof. No matter how adept your blockers are at reading, the opponent's setter might be even more adept at disguising his or her sets (or reading the blockers' cues). The more deceptive the setter, the less effective the read blocker. Also, as mentioned, read blocking is not usually effective against a fast-paced offense.

OPTIONS

Many of the options within this blocking strategy are based on the blockers' ability to recognize setters' tendencies—as well as their tendencies to stray from their tendencies. One option that makes for a cat-and-mouse game between setter and blocker is to have your middle blocker shift far enough over to the most likely point of attack that he or she invites the setter to do something else. Will the setter fall for the ploy? Or will he or she recognize it and exploit it? If the latter, will the blocker be able to read the setter's recognition and intent? If so, the blocker gains the advantage. Coaches can set up and train these types of setter-blocker cat-and-mouse scenarios in practice.

Once your blockers have grasped the strategy of commit blocking, discussed later in the chapter, you can choose to commit your outside blocker to the opponent's quick attack (if no offensive options are available behind the setter and therefore no blocking responsibility there), allowing your middle blocker to read and get outside to the most likely remaining point of attack (in all probability the left-side attacker), knowing the quick attack is being defended by the left-outside blocker. This is also especially useful if the opposing setter is in the front row. Let your left-front blocker step inside to start on the front-row setter (to take her attack away) and help the middle blocker on the front quick. This enables the middle to shift as well and get outside quicker to join the right-front blocker in a two-player block against a strong left-side attacker.

COACHING POINTS

Healthy debate continues regarding which position in volleyball requires the most movement—a setter who's running a 5-1 system (setting in all six positions) or a middle blocker who's part of a two-blocker system and thus required to attempt to block every legitimate attack attempt. If this same middle blocker is also a primary quick-attacker, forcing him or her to get off the net to get available to hit, the movement demands are of course even greater. In any case, playing middle blocker is going to be physically taxing, requiring many quick, explosive, short movement patterns, so these players must be extremely well conditioned.

Assuming the physical elements have been trained, middle blockers who are part of the read system must execute several technical tasks before the ball is set to best prepare for the block. If the opponent passes or digs a perfect ball to target, for example, the middle blocker must get hands above the head to defend the quick attack. The better the pass or dig, the higher the hands in the block read position.

Along with high hands, the middle blocker should have slightly bent knees, allowing for a first move up (rather than down into a knee-bend), backward, or sideways, depending on his or her read of the setter's intentions. What a blocker does before the set is as important as what he or she does after the set. Look for ways to reinforce proper preparation during practice sessions.

Finally, although read blocking might suggest the blocker doesn't move much until the ball is set, any movement that a blocker can make before the ball is set is helpful in getting to the point of attack sooner, providing more time to watch the attacker. The important skills of reading and anticipating on defense should be developed through gamelike drills with live hitters during practice. Standing on a box and hitting balls to blockers and diggers does not require the same reading, anticipation, judgment, and timing skills as with a live attacker.

◀ R E L E A S E   B L O C K I N G ▶

EXPLANATION OF TACTIC

The release block strategy is one in which the middle blocker moves relatively early to a specific area in order to focus on a particular hitter (or sometimes on a particular attack that has been repeatedly successful) to ensure that a block is made for the hitter to contend with. The strategy allows the middle blocker to ignore other attacking options so that he or she can block the attacker most likely to be set or the hitter who requires considerable skill to block or slow down (i.e., the opponent's "go to hitter"). Basically, the release block is like a chess move: If the blocker reads the play correctly, he or she is there to defend it—but if the blocker misreads the setter, he or she risks being rendered useless on the play. However, even that might give the defense an advantage, since the presence of the blockers may force the setter to set away from her go-to hitter to a less effective attacker. In this strategy, the middle blocker releases to the most likely point of attack based on several avenues of information, which include the following:

▶ Scouting report. Observing an opponent's tendencies and practices (either live or via videotape) informs a team from where the opponent will most likely attack.

▶ Statistics. In the absence of a scouting report or video, information on which hitters get the most sets, who has the highest hitting percentage on the squad, and who has the highest kill percentage can help a team develop its defensive strategy, as does any information on who *doesn't* get set much in each rotation.

▶ Situation. This one is related to statistics. In a situation in which an opponent has had several points in a row scored on them, the setter will usually become very predictable and set to her best hitter, thereby making the release block more likely to be effective.

▶ Gut instinct. In the absence of other information, players or coaches must sometimes resort to trusting their intuition. Of course the reliability of a hunch tends to relate directly to the player's or coach's experience level.

PERSONNEL REQUIREMENTS

Smart blockers who remember the scouting report, the prepared game plan, and an opponent's statistics and tendencies even in the midst of a tight and prolonged match come in very handy for teams wishing to use the release block with success. Yes, the coach is there to relay information about the opponent, but there will be many times during a long rally when the coach can't clearly communicate with the middle blocker.

Other than the kind of smarts and instincts that come with years of experience, the chief requirement for this strategy is effective blocking abilities. It does no good to consistently read an opponent with accuracy if you don't have the skills to get above the net and stop the attack you see coming.

ADVANTAGES AND DISADVANTAGES

As you might guess, the major advantage of the release block rests in the ability of the middle blocker to get a head start in arriving at the point of attack. Being able to do so with consistency will challenge an opponent's best hitters and prevent kills during crucial points of a match.

What happens, though, when the middle blocker releases to a likely point of attack only to see the setter deliver the ball elsewhere? The likelihood of this occurring is the first disadvantage of the release system. An opponent who expects your team to use the release strategy will counter by instructing their setter to be unpredictable, causing problems for the middle blocker. Countermoves to the release block can be fatiguing for the middle blocker, especially if she has released to the opponent's left-side attacker, only to see the setter deliver the ball to the right-side attacker, because now she must reverse her path to traverse back across the whole width of the net in order to participate in the block. The best scouting and statistical information won't save the middle blocker from experiencing this scenario at times. This disadvantage is compounded when the hitter that you didn't anticipate getting a lot of sets is getting more than you expected and proving to be productive, with lots of kills and a high hitting percentage.

OPTIONS

First, remember that flexibility is the basis of many teams' success. You always have the option to change what you're doing. Let's say that you go into a game having instructed your middle blockers to release to a given area in certain situations in order to block the attacks of certain hitters. The game progresses, and things unfold differently from what you expected. You tell your middle blockers to quit releasing and revert back to the read strategy (or fake the release and stay with the read). This produces more effective plays from your middle blockers because they can now watch a play unfold and react to what they see. The change of strategy also forces your opponent's hand. They must adjust to your adjustment. But because they were having success with their original strategy, they are slow to let go of it, giving your team a tactical advantage. You enjoy this advantage because you were more flexible than your opponent in adjusting to what was happening on the court.

Of course if you're having success with the release strategy, you should stay with it as long as you can. Typically, success using this strategy depends on your other blockers knowing the intent of your middle blocker on as many plays as possible (with the understanding that in many cases such knowledge is not possible because the middle blocker can't communicate it). The middle blocker's communication will tell the other players what their responsibilities are so they can respond accordingly. As an example, before your team serves, your middle blocker tells your left-side blocker that he's going to release to the opponent's left-side attacker, leaving your left-side blocker responsible for covering any attack the opponent might make to their right side. Taking this information into account, the left-side blocker alters his base position by moving slightly farther inside (because most right-side attacks are crosscourt). Such scenarios have of course been practiced endlessly during practice sessions.

Another tactic to stop a strong crosscourt hitter who has now switched to an effective line shot, is to release your stronger middle blocker to the left-side attacker, but all the way to the sideline and have your right-side blocker step off the net and around the middle to take the inside (middle) blocker spot. This can be an effective change if your right-front blocker is a shorter or weaker blocker and the opposing left-front attacker is picking on the line shot over her, negating your middle blocker's influence on the play. If this switch is quickly accomplished as the hitter is in the air, the hitter may never realize it until she is swinging away down the line right into a suddenly bigger blocker.

COACHING POINTS

Because a major reason for using the release system is to give your middle blockers more time to get to the likely point of attack, your middle blockers should always know the opponent's tendencies and who their best hitter is. Get in the habit of quizzing your middle blockers on what's most likely to happen in given situations. During matches, they should always be asking themselves questions such as these:

- Where does the setter like to set when the pass or dig is 10 to 12 feet (3-3.6 meters) from the net?
- How does the setter deal with the tight pass?

- What are the tendencies of the setter when his or her team is behind and trying to stage a comeback?
- What does the setter do to try to end a long rally?
- What hitter becomes less aggressive as the game wears on and the score is tight?
- Which attackers don't warrant a middle-blocker release?
- What is the right-side hitter's favorite shot?
- Where does the left-side hitter tend to hit when hitting a certain kind of set?
- What does the hitter do after being blocked several times?

Having ready answers to questions such as these gives your blockers opportunities to use the release strategy to your team's advantage.

◀COMMIT BLOCKING▶

EXPLANATION OF TACTIC

The strategy to commit block is implemented when an opponent has one or more dominant quick-attackers who can be blocked or neutralized only by committing a blocker to them. In a commit block, the blocker jumps (and thereby commits) just before the quick set is released by the setter, ensuring that the block is above and over the net when the setter sets the ball. The commit blocker often has no idea if the setter will set the quick-attacker or not. Theoretically, if the setter sets the ball to the quick-attacker, and the blocker has committed, the result should be a stuff-block or at least a slow-down.

The commit blocker can be any one of the front-row blockers, or sometimes all three of them. The following situations might require all three blockers to commit:

▶ Left-side blocker commit blocking. Assume that an opponent runs a quick attack right in front of the setter and a traditional outside set to their left-side attacker. The setter is in the front row, so there's no right-front attacker. Your middle blocker who intends to release out to the opponent's left-side attack can do this with confidence, knowing that your left-side blocker is going to commit-block against the front quick set. This enables your defense to have one blocker on the quick-attacker and two blockers on the outside blocker—both situations you can feel good about.

▶ Right-side blocker commit blocking. More and more teams are running their offense behind the setter, using either the right-side or middle attackers or both. Teams that do this are trying to create one-on-one situations between their hitters and the opposing team's blockers. If a team has a quick-attack option taking place in front of the back-row setter (such as a 31), it makes sense to bring the right-side blocker in to commit-block on this quick attack, allowing the middle blocker to release behind the setter, where the two remaining hitters are potentially going to attack the ball. If the middle blocker tries to determine if the setter is setting the front quick attack, and if she has responsibility for defending it, she likely won't have time to move left to get into position behind the opposing team's setter to defend against those hitters. Commit blocking with the right-side blocker solves this problem. Coaches can also commit the right-side blocker to go one on one with a weaker left-side attacker and allow the middle blocker to stay with the greater threat of the middle attacker or help defend the opponent's right-side quick-attacker.

▶ Middle blocker commit blocking. On more and more teams the best hitter is a middle hitter who hits lots of quick attacks. There's no doubt that the setter wants to set that hitter a lot. Especially in a tightly contested game that's nearing its end, this hitter is very likely to get the set. Working on this assumption, the middle blocker commits to the quick middle attacker, leaving the outside blockers to fend for themselves one on one in blocking or slowing down the outside hitter's attack. You wouldn't want to take a risk like this regularly, but when it's pretty clear the quick-attacker is going to get the set, it's an appropriate and effective strategy to employ.

PERSONNEL REQUIREMENTS

We have discussed in several previous chapters the importance of reading, anticipating, judging, and timing in volleyball. When it comes to commit blocking, these skills are much easier to execute. Relative to reading, remember that the commit blocker is not waiting for the quick-attacker to get the set, so the ability to read if the setter is indeed setting the quick-attacker is irrelevant. When it comes to anticipating and timing, these are easier to perform because the commit blocker can be in the air on the jump a little earlier than desired and still accomplish the task. This can also force a setter to *not* set her middle hitter in this case. As for judging, it's important to know where to jump relative to where the quick-attacker is hitting. If the quick-attacker likes to hit to the left back, the commit blocker must judge this well enough to take away that favorite shot. All in all, as long as they can get above the net to block and intercept the quick attack (long arms and good jumping ability are helpful tools), many players should be able to execute commit blocking effectively.

ADVANTAGES AND DISADVANTAGES

The clearest advantage to the commit block is the ability to take away a potentially powerful and terminal quick attack. Quick-attackers who know an opponent is using this strategy will have to make adjustments and work harder to get their kills, which might influence the opposing setter to attempt them less frequently.

This strategy is a good match for the inexperienced blocker who has the physical abilities but not the tactical tools to be effective. Tactical tools take lots of experience to obtain, so strategies depending heavily on tactics, such as the read strategy, are extra challenging for young players. Commit blocking requires no reading. Commit blockers on quick hitters must jump before the setter sets the ball or the hitter jumps, so as long as they can get the height they need and use proper technique, they won't need experience to execute effectively.

When a team chooses not to use the commit block because the opponent lacks a dominant attacker, this is a sound decision. But many teams choose not to commit block because they don't want to risk using their blockers on a play that doesn't involve the quick-attacker after all. This possibility of sacrifice with no reward is a potential disadvantage of the commit strategy. However, when a commit blocker goes up with the quick-attacker and forces the setter to adjust and resort to plan B, the defense has won a tactical battle. So an apparent disadvantage can be turned into an advantage under certain circumstances.

OPTIONS

Once a team decides to commit block, regardless of who does the committing, they are showing their cards to their opponents. Assuming a team does have skills in reading the opponents, veering away from commit blocking for a stretch of plays can be advantageous because this catches the opponent off guard. Very few teams have trouble switching from commit blocking to read blocking (if both have been trained in practice), but it might take a play or two for the opposing offense to adjust to the switch.

Commit blockers also have the option of committing to take away a different shot from the attacker than what the attacker expects. Although commit blocking is fairly obvious to the opposition, exactly where the commit blocker will line up and what he or she will try to take away isn't quite as apparent. Quick-attackers who can hit all areas of the court will have their effectiveness minimized if commit blockers play cat and mouse with them, taking away one area on one attempt and another area on another attempt.

COACHING POINTS

Because all blockers (not just the middle blockers) might be asked to commit block against a quick attack, coaches should be sure their left- and right-side blockers get plenty of opportunities to work on this skill. In fact, taking time to work with outside blockers in all phases of blocking is a worthwhile use of time.

All members of a team should understand when commit blocking will be used. There's no need to commit block on both quick-attackers (assuming there is more than one) if only one of them has the potential to dominate the game. If you have the luxury of knowing your opponent's tendencies regarding the quick attack, you'll be able to read when it's coming. Some teams like to "force the middle," meaning a setter who's several feet off the net will try to run the quick attack, believing there won't be any block up because the blocker has read the quality of the pass as too poor to run a quick set from. Such a time might be an appropriate time to commit block.

Other helpful information you might gain by knowing your opponent is how they establish their offensive schemes. For example, teams commonly want to establish their middle quick attack early in a game or match. If you observe this in an opponent, alert your team that you'll want to commit block earlier in the game or match rather than later.

Also note if an opponent likes to run the quick attack after successfully digging a hard-driven spike. Teams do this to force the tempo of the play, hoping to catch the opposing defenders off guard. This is another tendency that, when read accurately, can be addressed via a commit block, forcing your opponent's setter to think twice about running the quick attack in such a situation.

© Alan Look/Icon SMI

Defensive Strategy Drills

The drills presented in this chapter are designed to develop the skills needed to use the strategies contained in Part III. To be most effective, however, drills should work many skills simultaneously. Therefore, these drills also work on skills needed for many of the other systems and strategies contained in this book.

Flood the Zone

Category: Use with chapter 11.

Objective: To work on converting hard-driven attacks from the opponent's right- and left-side hitters, incorporating the principle of flooding the zone with the backcourt diggers.

Players Required: 9

Procedure: Team A's tosser initiates the ball to the setter, who sets either the right- or left-front hitter. Team B's outside blocker blocks the line (regardless of what they see the hitter do). Team B's back-row players start in base position, and once the ball is set to one side, the middle-back digger shifts to the crosscourt-shot side by making a lateral move, providing two backcourt players to dig the most likely shot. Continue until 10 settable digs are executed.

Variation: Have the setter on team A attack the second ball to keep defensive players in their base, ready to defend against that possibility, or release if the set goes to a hitter.

Common Errors and Corrections: Watch the line digger in this drill to ensure he or she makes the appropriate move to a back-row position. Many times the line digger gets caught in no man's land, getting too far back to cover any tip but not far enough back to dig the hard-driven attack. Emphasize taking a floor position to dig, but in a body position ready to run down a tip.

Team A

TS

S

H ← — — — — — → H

X   X

LB   RB

MB

Team B

Dig the Deflected Ball (Left-Side Attack)

Category: Use with chapter 11.

Objective: To give the right-back line digger (in a block line/dig inside strategy) opportunities to dig balls deflected off the block.

Players Required: 10

Procedure: Team B's tosser initiates the ball over the net to team A's digger, who digs to the setter. The setter sets the left-front attacker. Team B's outside blocker takes away the line shot, while team A's left-side hitter purposefully hits line, causing deflections off the blocker's hands. Team B's right-back digger digs the ball to the target. Continue for three minutes, and then have teams successfully dig five balls to target (they don't have to be consecutive) to trigger a rotation or personnel change.

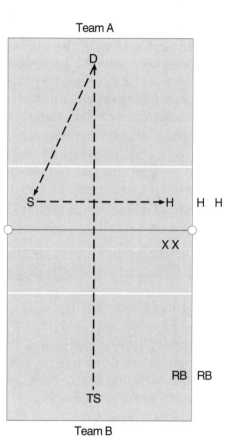

Team A

Team B

Variations: Add a middle blocker to allow more repetitions for diggers. Ask the left-forward attacker to tip over the block so the line digger must read and release for the tip.

Common Errors and Corrections: Hitting the ball off the blocker's hands is a difficult skill. In most cases, hitters hit the ball too low into the blocker's hands, causing a stuff-block. Work with hitters on hitting higher off the blockers' hands than they think they need to, which allows for more deflections. If a hitter is having trouble hitting the ball off the blocker's hands, ask him or her to hit a high toss or set from a hitting platform to simulate deflected balls. However, understand that this removes some necessity for reading and timing for blockers and defenders.

Dig the Deflected Ball (Right-Side Attack)

Category: Use with chapter 11.

Objective: To give the left-back line digger (in a block line/dig inside strategy) opportunities to dig balls deflected off the block.

Players Required: 10

Procedure: Team A's tosser initiates the ball over the net to team B's digger, who digs to the setter. The setter sets the right-front attacker. Team A's outside blocker takes away the line shot while team B's right-side hitter purposefully hits line, causing deflections off the blocker's hands. Team A's left-back digger digs the ball to target. Continue for three minutes, and then have teams successfully dig five balls to target (they don't have to be consecutive).

Variations: Add a middle blocker to allow more repetitions for diggers. Can have the right-front attackers also tip over the block so the left-back digger must read and run down tips. Can also add the left-back digger transitioning to hit a back-row attack after digging.

Common Errors and Corrections: Same as Dig the Deflected Ball (Left-Side Attack).

Close the Block

Category: Use with chapters 8, 11, 12, and 13.

Objective: To give the middle blocker experience in defending a quick attack while still being able to close the block when the setter sets outside.

Players Required: 8

Procedure: Team B's tosser initiates the ball over the net to team A's digger, who digs to the setter. The setter can set either the quick-attacker (middle hitter) or the left-front hitter. Team B's middle blocker defends both sets but must be sure to close the block if the set goes outside. The tosser initiates tosses for two minutes; then the blocker must get three consecutive stuff-blocks or slow-downs to end the drill. Can have the middle blocker and the middle hitter switch after specified repetitions.

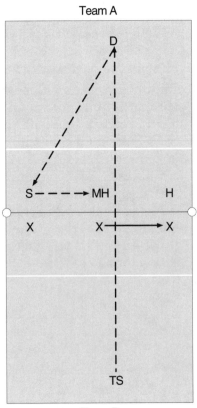

Team A

Team B

Variations: If stressing the middle blocker is desirable, have the outside blockers take away the line, causing the middle blocker to have to travel farther to close the block. Can be done using a read strategy or a commit block strategy.

Common Errors and Corrections: Watch the middle blocker's movement for efficiency in closing the block, especially if the blocker is fatigued. Work with the blocker to maintain disciplined eye focus and efficient movement to the outside and to square up to the net to seal the net.

Dig the Heat (Left-Side Attack)

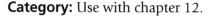

Category: Use with chapter 12.

Objective: To give line diggers opportunities to dig hard-driven balls down the line without a block to stop or slow down the shot. Use this drill when a defensive system requires back-row diggers to dig hard shots down the line (common in player-back systems).

Players Required: 8

Procedure: Tosser on team A tosses to the setter, who sets the left-front hitter. The two team B blockers will block inside, leaving 2 to 3 feet (.6-.9 meters) for the hitter to attack down the line. Team B's right-back digger starts in base defensive position and releases to a deeper digging position (home) after the ball is set to read and react to the ball when attacked. The attacker hits hard down the line. Diggers dig 10 to score 10 points. Score 1 point for balls dug up and playable, 0 points for an overpass, and 1 point if no effort is made to dig the ball.

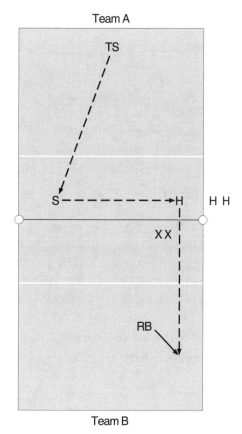

Variation: Have the right-side blocker seal the line, giving the line digger a chance to dig balls that deflect off the block.

Common Errors and Corrections: In a player-back defense, the line digger has prime responsibility to dig most balls attacked down the line. One common error that prevents them from doing so is their defensive positioning. Line diggers often fail to get back deep enough to dig the hard-driven ball. Work with diggers to ensure they're far enough back to successfully dig this attack.

Dig the Heat (Right-Side Attack)

Category: Use with chapter 12.

Objective: To give line diggers opportunities to dig hard-driven balls down the line without a block to stop or slow down the shot. Use this drill when a defensive system requires back-row diggers to dig hard shots down the line (common in player-back systems).

Players Required: 8

Procedure: Team A's tosser initiates the ball to the setter, who sets the right-front hitter. The two blockers on team B block inside, leaving 2 to 3 feet (.6-.9 meter) for the hitter to attack down the line. Team B's left-back digger starts in base defense position and releases to a deeper dig position (home) after the ball is set to read and react to the ball when hit. The attacker hits hard down the line. Diggers dig 10 for 10 points. Score 1 point for balls dug up and playable, 0 points for an overpass, and 1 point if no effort is made to dig the ball.

Variation: Have the left-side blocker seal the line, giving the line digger a chance to dig balls that deflect off the block.

Common Errors and Corrections: Same as Dig the Heat (Left-Side Attack).

Serve-Receive to Defense

Category: Use with chapters 2, 3, 4, 6, 7, 8, 9, and 12.

Objective: To win two rallies in a row, with the last rally ending on a defensive dig and transition attack for a kill.

Players Required: 11

Procedure: The server on team A (side of four) serves the ball to team B (side of six). The ball is played out. Once the rally ends, a free ball is introduced by the tosser to team A. Team B must win both rallies to score the point. If team A wins one point it is then a wash and the series of 2 balls begins again with a served ball. Team B has five minutes to win four points before they rotate.

Variation: Coaches can decide on reasonable goals for each side. For instance, team B might be required to win only one rally to score the point, or a shorter time limit could be imposed.

Common Errors and Corrections: Depending on who's on team A, this team might have substantial success in winning the second rally, making it difficult for team B to win four points in five minutes. At the outset of the drill, try to balance teams as necessary to provide opportunities for both sides to have success.

Three Before 10

Category: Use with chapters 6, 7, 8, 9, and 12.

Objective: To score points by transitioning from team defense when blocking inside and giving line.

Players Required: 12

Procedure: Team B's tosser initiates the ball over the net to team A's digger (team of 5) in middle back, who digs to the setter. The setter may set any of the three hitters in the front row. Team B (team of six) starts in base defense position, working to read what the opposing hitter might do. After the setter sets, the front-row blockers move from base position to block inside, giving up the line to the outside hitters. In each rotation the defense is trying to score three times (on the dig-set-kill transition play) before the offensive team kills 10 balls.

Variation: The first ball over the net could be a served ball or a down ball, allowing team B to run a play out of serve-receive, which still requires team A to work on defense first.

Common Errors and Corrections: Watch for breakdowns in movement, particularly when players are moving from base position to their final digging position on defense.

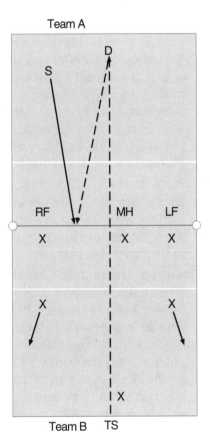

Front and Back Hitting With Blockers Inside

Category: Use with chapters 8, 9, 12, and 13.

Objective: To give blockers repetitions in blocking inside against attackers, even when blockers are showing they're hitting down the line.

Players Required: 12

Procedure: Two tossers toss simultaneously to two setters on the same side of the net. Setters set the left-side and right-side attackers. Two middle blockers on the opposite side of the net move to block the left- or right-side hitter, leaving 2 to 3 feet (.6-.9 meter) of line open. Players toss for three minutes.

Variation: Position blockers in different areas along the net to create gamelike movement demands and alternate middle blockers moving to the hitter that gets set.

Common Errors and Corrections: The middle blockers might move faster than the outside blockers, who are responsible for setting the block. If this happens, work with the outside blockers to move faster to set the block. Also reinforce middle blockers to continue moving as fast as they have in previous reps.

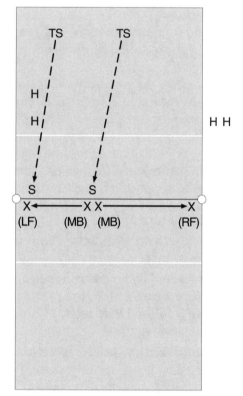

Read and Go

Category: Use with chapters 8, 9, 11, 12, and 13.

Objective: To give the middle blockers experience in reading the dig and the setter and in determining where the ball will be set. Run this drill when your team uses the read strategy for middle blockers.

Players Required: 8

Procedure: Team B's tosser initiates a ball to team A's digger, who digs to the setter. Team A's setter sets the right-, middle, or left-side attacker. Team B's middle blocker watches for the quality of the dig and movement of the setter, and then shifts to where he or she thinks the ball will be set. Once the set is made, the middle blocker moves to attempt to block the hitter. Two middle blockers alternate each play for two minutes, and then they must get two stuff-blocks or slow-downs before team B's offense gets 10 kills.

Variations: To further stress the middle blocker, have the hitters on team A hit a variety of sets. Can be used with a two-blocker or a one-blocker system.

Common Errors and Corrections: The middle blocker will occasionally misread the setter and move in the wrong direction. Remind your blocker that misreads are to be expected but to continue moving to the point of attack, even if it means changing direction.

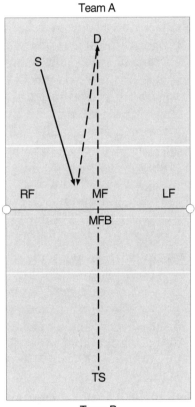

Read, Release, and Go

Category: Use with chapters 8, 9, 11, 12, and 13.

Objective: To give middle blockers experience in reading the dig of a hard-driven ball, determining what options the setter has, and moving in the direction they think the ball will be set before the ball reaches the setter.

Players Required: 8

Procedure: Team B's tosser hits a hard-driven down ball across the net to team A's digger, causing (more often than not) a less-than-perfect dig. Team B's middle blocker reads the quality of the dig and releases to the point he or she thinks the ball will be set. The setter can set anywhere. Two middle-front blockers alternate each rally and must score 10 points to end the drill. Blockers earn 1 point for an accurate read and moving to the correct spot before the ball is set; they earn an additional point if they block or slow down the attacker.

Variations: There are many ways to score this drill. For instance, don't give points for an accurate read, or only award points for desirable outcomes. Can be used with single-blocker system as described or with double-block system by adding a left and right blocker to team B.

Common Errors and Corrections: Because there's only one blocker, it's imperative that the blocker gets squared to the net after making the move to the point of attack. Emphasize efficient movement, but equally important is the blocker getting squared to the net so he or she can seal and penetrate the net.

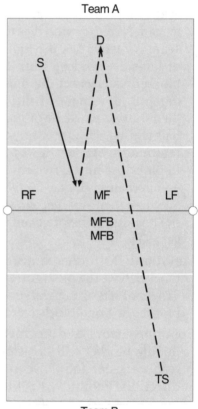

Team A

Team B

Commit to the Quick

Category: Use with chapter 8, 9, 11, 12, and 13.

Objective: To give middle-front blockers experience in timing their jumps when committing to block the quick attack.

Players Required: 5

Procedure: Team B's tosser initiates an easy free ball to team A's digger (ensuring that the quick attack can be executed). Team A's digger digs to the setter, who sets a quick attack. Team B's middle-front blocker jumps into the air before the ball is set to defend the quick attack. Continue for three minutes, and then team B must get three to five consecutive stuff-blocks to end the drill. The group of three middle-front blockers alternate with each repetition.

Variations: To give the middle blocker practice at timing the jump to defend the quick attack, have the setter alternate with sets from the ground and jump sets. Could alter scoring to any three to five stuff-blocks or block touches.

Common Errors and Corrections: Because commit blocking requires blockers to jump and block either before the setter has the ball or as he or she is setting it, a common error is for blockers to jump too late. Spend time working with blockers on the timing of their jumps.

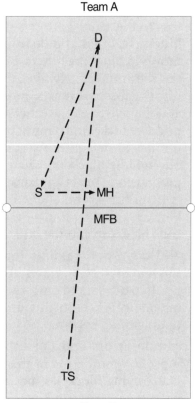

Team A

Team B

Block and Go Plus Conditioning

Category: Use with chapters 8, 9, 11, 12, and 13.

Objective: To give middle blockers conditioning work by moving them from one side of the net to the other to block opposing attackers.

Players Required: 8

Procedure: Team A's tosser initiates a toss to the setter, who sets one of the hitters. Team B's middle-front blocker moves to block the hitter who received the set. Immediately after this ball is hit, the tosser initiates another toss, and the setter sets the other hitter. The middle blocker must move back along the net to defend the second attack. The middle blockers switch after this progression. Tosser initiates tosses for two minutes, and then the middle blockers must get four slow-downs or stuff-blocks to end the drill.

Variations: Award points for efficient movements even when they don't result in the desired outcome. Can add outside blockers in this drill for the double-block system.

Common Errors and Corrections: The most common error in this drill is a late-arriving blocker, especially when defending the second attack. Remind your blockers that it's okay not to get all the way out to block the attack; they should still stop on the attacker's swing and jump there to try to take away what they can, giving the backcourt defense less area to cover.

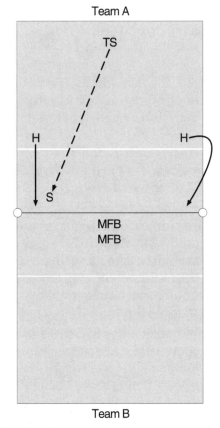

Team A

Team B

Middle vs. Middle

Category: Use with chapters 7 and 13.

Objective: To give blockers practice in stuff-blocks and slow-downs.

Players Required: 6

Procedure: Team A's tosser initiates a toss to the setter on the same side, who sets a quick attack. The ball is played out, with team A's middle attacker trying to terminate the set and team B's middle blocker trying to stuff-block or slow down the attacker. After the first ball is dead, the tosser from team B tosses to the setter on the same side, and the sequence repeats. The middle hitter and blocker compete in a rally score game to 10 to 15 points.

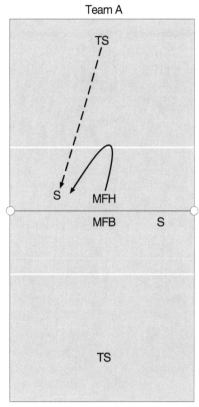

Team A

Team B

Variations: To make the drill even more gamelike, ask setters to mix sets on the ground with jump sets. Setter can set front or back quicks or inside shots (31's) teaching middle blockers to transition from other areas of the court.

Common Errors and Corrections: It's possible that one of the middles will go on a run and score several points in a row, frustrating the other middle. If this occurs, allow each side one 15-second time-out. This allows the team on the wrong side of the scoring run to discuss what needs to be done. Meanwhile, the team on the scoring run can be reinforced for what they're doing right.

Offensive Systems

© Alan Look/Icon SMI

5-1 System

EXPLANATION OF TACTIC

In the 5-1 system for organizing an offense, one player is designated as the setter and is responsible for setting in all six rotations on the court. The remaining five players have no setting responsibilities except in situations in which the setter digs the first ball or is unable to set because of a poor pass or dig. These five players are all hitters and may attack from either the front row or back row. Traditionally, the 5-1 system has two left-side attackers, two middle attackers, and one right-side attacker (often also referred to as the "opposite"). The setter typically sets from the right side of the court, basically from the right-front position, regardless of whether he or she must run in from the back row or is already positioned there. When the setter is in the front row, the two front-row hitters generally start positioned in front of the setter, although we'll look at some variations later in the Options section of the chapter.

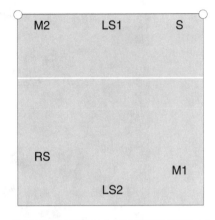

Figure 15.1 illustrates a traditional and suggested rotation for this system. Note that a team's best left-side hitter (LS1) and best middle hitter (M1) are placed directly behind and in front of the setter in the rotation. Putting a high premium on the LS1's and M1's hitting abilities is essential because in a 5-1 system there are three rotations in which the setter is in the front row, leaving only two front-row attackers. Placing the LS1 and M1 around the setter

Figure 15.1 Alignment of players in the 5-1 system.

ensures that the best left-side hitter and best middle hitter will be on the front row with the setter in two out of three rotations, allowing greater opportunities to score points out of serve-receive. Keep in mind that as long as players are placed in the same relative position, you can start the team in any rotation you choose, instead of being locked into the traditional setter in right front or right back in rotation 1. The 5-1 is used at many levels of competition and generally chosen for one or more of these reasons:

- A team has one outstanding setter, able to give hitters opportunities to attack a high percentage of the time.
- No other players on the team have good setting skills.
- It's a highly specialized system in which all players get to do what they are best at all of the time.
- It's a familiar system that many coaches understand better than others.
- It's a system many teams use, so many players are well trained in using it.

In most cases, a team chooses the 5-1 primarily for the first, second, and third reasons, which is the way it should be. Deciding on the 5-1 because it's what other teams run doesn't take into consideration your team's personnel, which should be the basis for most decisions regarding which system you choose.

PERSONNEL REQUIREMENTS

When considering whether to use the 5-1 system to organize your offense, the characteristics of your setter should guide your decision. Teams have different values in a setter who will run the 5-1, but in general you want this player to be athletic, intelligent, competitive, and mentally tough, adept at ball control, a decent blocker, and, ideally, left-handed.

▶ Athletic. Because the setter sets for the entire match, with significant movement demands, you need a player who is quick and efficient in movement skills and above average to excellent in overall athleticism. The setter should be able to move quickly and fluidly in all directions and have good jumping ability. This will allow him or her to get to more balls and thus set more sets.

▶ Intelligent. The setter must be smart enough to understand and run the offense and execute the game plan. If your plan is to run a lot of quick attacks with your middle hitters because your opponent has inexperienced middle blockers or because you have dominant middle hitters, it's up to the setter to manipulate situations as much as possible to effectively set the middles. He or she must understand how to make the most of team strengths while downplaying team weaknesses. The intelligent setter can also recognize when a particular game plan is not working and adjust as necessary.

▶ Competitive and mentally tough. A competitive setter can make an entire team more competitive. Hitters get caught up in their setter's effort level and try to imitate it so they don't let the setter down. He or she understands how to deal with teammates, such as helping a struggling hitter break out of a slump, or keeping pressure off her hitters, keeping hitter confidence levels up. He or she must also be willing to set who is being effective, not just spread sets around to make teammates happy.

▶ Adept at ball control. A setter with good ball-control skills can take any ball, regardless of how poorly passed or dug it is, and provide a hitter with an opportunity to take a swing. If setters can get their hitters good swings, create one-on-ones against blockers, and produce situations in which their best hitter is hitting against the opponent's poorest blocker, they have done their job.

▶ Decent blocker. The setter in a 5-1 must play in the front row for three rotations and must be able to hold her own as a blocker.

▶ Left-handed. Because the setter in a 5-1 system is in the front row for three rotations, he or she might have hitting opportunities as well. Being left-handed allows a setter more opportunities to take a swing on the second contact (after the pass or dig) with effectiveness equal to any other hitter's swing. Left-handed setters have the advantage of having their hitting arms away from the net, allowing them to jump, rotate shoulders into the attack, and produce more powerful swings. Although right-handed setters can also be trained to take an effective left-handed swing, which may catch defenders off guard.

When the setter is in the back row, good ball control among teammates reduces the movement demands of the setter, if she has not had to dig, is already transitioning from the back row into the target area at the net. When the setter is in the front row, good ball control among diggers and hitters means passes and digs will be to target, so the setter need not chase the ball as far. Teams that can pass and dig to target at a high percentage allow the team and setter to be "in system," meaning the setter has all offensive options available to set. The further off the net you have established your setter's target to be, the more often your passers and diggers will be able to pass in system as well.

ADVANTAGES AND DISADVANTAGES

The primary advantage to running the 5-1 is that teams have only one setter for hitters to learn how to adjust to. Other popular systems use two setters, meaning hitters must adjust to different tendencies, timing, heights of sets, and so on. Teams spend a lot of time working with their setters in developing a game plan to be used against an opponent. Developing this plan with only one setter makes this task more efficient and effective.

Another advantage of this system is the option to run a creative offense, assuming a certain level of ball control. Examples include having your middle hitter (especially when the setter is in the front row) hit sets that are behind the setter and incorporating back-row attacks that can cause stress and indecision in the opponent.

A disadvantage of this system is that relying on one setter can be dangerous, especially if teams fail to adequately train a second setter as a back-up (in case of illness or injury or an off night). Even when a second setter has been trained, he or she probably won't be as effective as the regular setter (similar to a back-up quarterback in football). So teams face a dilemma when the starting setter goes down with an injury, or when he or she is having an off night. Do they stick with the 5-1 or try something else?

OPTIONS

Many options are available to the setter running the 5-1 system. As mentioned earlier, hitters can hit sets from positions other than their named position. A team's best middle hitter, for example, who will be in the front row two out of three rotations when the setter is in the front row, can do much of his or her hitting behind the setter, from fast-tempo quick attacks to higher tempo sets. It's fairly common when the setter is in the back row for the right-side hitter to do some hitting in front of the setter because many teams have sufficient ball control to allow the right-side attacker to hit from different locations.

When considering options to run within the 5-1, remember the old coaching axiom, "Only attempt tactically what you can execute technically." So, for example, though running your middle hitter behind the setter for a quick attack can be fun and exciting, it can only be done if the pass and dig are delivered perfectly to target. If you don't have passers or diggers who can get the ball to target, you shouldn't be running quicks as a major part of your offense.

COACHING POINTS

The 5-1 system, perhaps the most widely used organizational system of offense in the country, is often chosen because of its perceived advantages. These advantages, however, are minimized if the coach doesn't address some issues. First and foremost, your setter must be trained with the team in regular team practices but also separately, outside the team's normal practice schedule. Basically, you want your setter to be at least twice as good in setting the ball as your other players must be relative to their responsibilities, so extra practice time is needed. In many cases, 30 minutes before or after regular practice will be enough. In 30 minutes of training the setter alone, you can provide him or her with hundreds of repetitions and a chance to increase their confidence in their ability to get to any ball or set any set.

The setter also needs tactical and technical training, which entails that the coach establish a working relationship with the setter so that questions about decision making and technique can be discussed. Such questions might include the following:

Tactical

- What made you decide to set this player?
- What did you see from the opponent that made you think this set would work?
- What play do you intend to run here? (Ask this question during a time-out.)
- What hitters are hot right now? Which are not?
- Who do you feel confident in right now?

Technical

- Did you notice where your hands were when you set the quick attack?
- Are you extending through the ball to get outside sets to their desired target?
- Are you getting to the ball with your feet in good position?
- Are you getting to target as fast as you can?

Coaches who regularly ask a lot of questions of their setters, on both tactical and technical issues, will see these players develop into steady performers and confident leaders of their teams.

As with all your training, make your setter's individual training gamelike. It's rare in a game that a setter gets to set the ball without having to move first, so no training should be done that allows the setter to just stand and set. Some of these movements might be quite simple (e.g., the front-row setter is ready to block, and the opposing team puts over a free ball, requiring the setter simply to turn around in the target area and face their side of the court), but always require some sort of movement before the setter sets the ball.

Although it's common for coaches to ask a setter in the 5-1 system to make a decision where to set based on what the opposing blockers are doing, some coaches spend little time actually teaching the setter to recognize what's happening on the other side of the court. During practice, work with your setters on noticing what opposing blockers are doing. A setter can be trained to quickly glance over to the other side while still tracking the ball to get a sense of where blockers are positioned.

Coaches expect a lot of their setters in this system, so it's essential that setters are provided opportunities in both team practices and separate training sessions to develop the technical and tactical skills they need to succeed.

6-2 System

EXPLANATION OF TACTIC

In the 6-2 offensive organizational system two players are placed in opposite positions (figure 16.1) within the rotational order and designated as the setters. Each setter sets when he or she is in one of the back-row positions (right back, middle back, or left back). Because setters come from the back row in this system, there are always three front-row attacking options (assuming the quality of the pass or dig allows the setter options on the set). Teams running the 6-2 generally have the back-row setter play defense in the right-back position because this is the closest back-row position to the frontcourt setter's target zone. When a setter rotates to the front row, and is now considered an attacker or blocker, she will usually also play in the right-front position, allowing her to act as the secondary setter should the primary setter in the back row have to dig an attack from the opponents.

Most teams who choose to use the 6-2 system have two reliable setters who also have strong attacking skills. The system is also popular with young teams wanting to work toward improving both their attacking and setting skills. A common rotational order used in the 6-2 is shown in figure 16.1. Notice that the best setter (S1), the best middle hitter (M1), and the

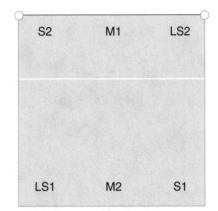

Figure 16.1 Alignment and rotational order in the 6-2 system.

best left-side hitter (L1) form a triangle, giving the setter multiple options. Triangulating these players in this way typically provides for a balanced attack in all six rotations.

PERSONNEL REQUIREMENTS

First and foremost, this system requires two above-average (or better) setters with equal or nearly equal skills. Strong skills in both ball control and movement are critical. If the skills of the two setters are not close to equal, offensive flow will be disrupted as hitters are constantly adjusting to the skill level and different styles of the two setters.

Movement skills are crucial to running the 6-2 effectively. Setters must be efficient when penetrating to the target at the net from the back row. Setters should transition to the net—typically slightly right of center—only after they are sure their backcourt defensive responsibilities have been fulfilled. (How a team should respond when the back-row setter must dig is discussed in the Options section later in the chapter.)

ADVANTAGES AND DISADVANTAGES

Presenting three front-row attackers can cause problems for many opponents, particularly if a defense is relying on a single blocker. If one of the setters is also an effective hitter who will stay in to play across the front row, this system allows for those hitting skills to be used in a way the 5-1 does not allow. Note that the first numeral in this offensive system is 6—which means that all players, including each setter, have opportunities to be a hitter. This makes this system a great choice for aggressive teams with strong hitters.

Additional flexibility in this system is seen in the case where one of the two setters is *not* an effective attacker or blocker. In this case coaches can substitute another player who is a better hitter or blocker in for that setter when she rotates to the front row. The setter goes in again to serve and set from right back. Using two setters reduces the chances that either setter will break down physically because neither must set in all six rotations, another advantage over the 5-1 system.

The 6-2 also compares favorably to the 5-1 in situations in which the back-row setter must dig the first ball, because the second setter (who's in the front row) or the opposite player can set the ball that the back-row setter has dug. In this case the back-row setter purposefully digs to the right-side player, who simply lands from her block, turns and finds the ball, and sets forward to the middle or outside hitter. If the back-row setter has dug a crosscourt shot from the opposing right-side hitter, the right-front player may be covering under the block (if in a player-up defense), so he or she has a little more difficult job to turn, find the ball, get behind it, and still set forward to the middle or outside hitter. In this case it might make more sense for the secondary setter to simply forward-set a back-row attack to her back-row setter in right back.

Another advantage provided by this system is when your setters are also great passers and you need your back-row setter to help get a great pass to get out of a not-so-great rotation. This works especially well if your back-row setter is the left-back player. Have her become the left-back passer while the front-row setter (or opposite) sets the first ball on serve-receive. This is also a great time for the player in right front to attack on the second contact. Once the ball is attacked over to the opponent's side, the primary setter reclaims her back-row setter role.

The most damaging disadvantage of the 6-2 is when a team's two setters have different styles of setting, or when their skills are not evenly matched. For instance, one setter might tend to set a left-side set 3 feet (.9 meter) from the net, whereas the other might set it 4 feet (1.2 meters) from the net. In general, you want your setters to set the same kind of high ball, the same kind of back-set, and so on so that hitters must not constantly be making adjustments.

Differing personalities in your two setters might cause problems, too. If one setter is verbal and aggressive and the other is passive and quiet, hitters will be required to adapt to both styles, which might disrupt a team's rhythm.

The potential advantage of using three front-row attackers is negated when a team lacks basic ball-control skills. The setter needs to have the option to set any one of the three attackers, so all diggers and passers must be able to keep the ball alive for the setter, and all hitters must be able to execute after receiving the set. If all three hitters are not viable options for the setter, one of the prime advantages of the 6-2 system is nullified.

OPTIONS

We have mentioned that when a setter has effective attacking skills that allow her to remain in the front row she will most likely play in the right-front position. This positioning permits her to step back into the setter role if the back-row (primary) setter has made the first dig. This allows for the team to remain "in system," which means that a setter is still running the offense and many options are available as long as the dig is controlled.

If your setter (who's now in the front row after rotating to left front) has dominant attacking skills, he or she might take advantage of these skills and play at left front rather than right front (because there are usually more sets that go to the left side). Making this kind of switch can be especially advantageous if your left-front player is a strong blocker who can make the switch to block effectively on the right side (and who has adequate setting skills if the right-back setter digs) against the opponent's best attacker. The point here is that just because a setter plays right-back defense in a 6-2 system, he or she isn't necessarily limited to playing right-front offense after rotating into the front row. Teams should determine what they are trying to accomplish and deploy their front-row players in such a way to accomplish their objectives.

COACHING POINTS

The 6-2 system presents some challenges for coaches to address. As we mentioned in last chapter's coaching points for the 5-1, training setters separately is important—perhaps even more important for the 6-2 than for the 5-1. Because setters in the 6-2 have major responsibilities aside from setting, including attacking and even possibly primary passing in the serve-receive pattern, these skills will need to be worked on during practice.

Coaches should also monitor how efficiently hitters are performing with both setters. It's quite common for one setter to have a greater assist average than the other, or for hitters primarily hitting off of the same setter to have higher hitting percentages than those hitting off the other setter. This is not always the setter's fault, but statistics sheets taken during practice should be studied so that players are aware of any setter differences that might affect their decisions or duties on the court.

Some people assume that a three-attacker front implies somewhat equal duties and skills among hitters. Coaches and setters must be careful not to adopt this attitude. Yes, more attackers will be involved in this system, but coaches must work with the team's setters to determine who the best hitters are in any given rotation and who should receive the most sets. A case can sometimes be made that any one of a team's hitters could be the primary hitter, but this depends on a team's personnel and varies widely from team to team.

It's easy for coaches to get excited about the many offensive options available in the 6-2 system, especially when their teams have setters capable of setting two or three different types of sets to each position. Be wary, however; just because a setter can set various types of sets to each front-row position, this doesn't mean he or she should. Sometimes the mere sight of three omnipresent front-row attackers is enough to intimidate a defense and give an offense an advantage. In such a case, setters who can set one consistent set to each of the positions will find his or her team enjoying outstanding success, so there's no need to use a complicated offensive system involving various types of sets. A second reason for minimizing the types of sets set to each position is that some hitters lack the necessary skills to attack all types of sets. Again, smart setters know which hitters like to hit which sets and hit them effectively, and will set those strengths.

Begin implementing the 6-2 in simple ways to allow the system to develop from the ground up. For instance, you might first develop your setters' abilities to put up a consistent left-side set, middle set, and right-side set. As you see hitters having success hitting these sets, you can start to use more complicated types of sets and tempos.

A final coaching point regarding the 6-2 system is how this offense might look when run by your team compared to how it looks when run by other teams. If you took video of 100 teams running the 6-2 system, you would see many different offensive options being used, largely because of the far-different skills hitters have from one team to the next. The system allows a lot of flexibility and creativity, so take advantage and modify the system to suit the skills of your team's setters and hitters.

At all levels of volleyball, it is common for coaches to experiment with running individual sets and plays after seeing other teams having success with them—which is fine as long as their teams have the skills and personnel to run those sets and plays effectively. Keep in mind that it's also valuable to create offensive options that have yet to be used by any team. Allowing your setters a role in developing the offense should generate some new options and make setters feel they have some ownership in the offense, which makes it more likely they'll be motivated to make it work.

CHAPTER 17

International 4-2 System

EXPLANATION OF TACTIC

The international 4-2 (I 4-2) is in some ways the simplest offensive organizational system. Yet many teams at all levels have used it with great success. The system is similar to the 6-2 in that it employs two setters who start in opposite positions (figure 17.1), but here setters set when in the front row rather than when in the back row. The term "international" refers to the front-row setter's position when in the front row (right front), which leaves a middle hitter and a left-side hitter to set to. Because the setter is setting from the front row, the I 4-2 looks similar to the 5-1 when that setter is in the front row. Also, because the system uses two setters, many of the same issues arise in this system as arise in the 6-2. In fact, some players and coaches think of the I 4-2 as a combination of the 5-1 and 6-2 offensive systems.

Considering the similarities of the two systems, why do some teams choose the I 4-2 over the 6-2? In general, a team picks the I 4-2 if their setters have relatively weak attacking skills and no players on the bench with strong enough hitting skills to come in and replace them. (Recall that the 6-2 is a good choice only when all three front-row players have good attacking skills.)

As was true for the 6-2, achieving a balanced attack is the objective when determining team positioning; the goal is having no rotations that struggle with getting a side-out. Figure 17.1 illustrates a balanced attack for a team specializing with left-side and middle hitters. Note that the second-best setter (S2) is surrounded by the best left-side hitter and best middle hitter. Assuming the second-best setter will have greater struggles in putting up hittable balls, it's preferable to have your best left side and middle trying to do something with those sets rather than having your second-best players in those positions. Conversely, because the best setter (S1) is surrounded by the second-best middle and left-side hitter, one hopes that the best setter can do something productive when those hitters are struggling to put balls away, especially out of serve reception.

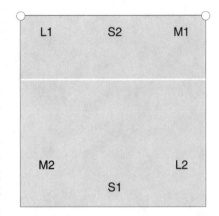

Figure 17.1 Alignment and rotational order in the I 4-2 system.

As your team considers this system, keep in mind that, although simple, with the right personnel you can use the I 4-2 to win a lot of games.

PERSONNEL REQUIREMENTS

As with the 6-2, having two setters with comparable setting skills is critical—and for the same reasons: If the skills of the two setters are not equal or nearly equal, offensive flow will be disrupted as hitters are constantly adjusting to the skill level and different styles of the two setters.

The minimal expectation of any setter is the ability to put up a hittable ball. Beyond that, if setters can isolate hitters in one-on-none or one-on-one situations, or can isolate their best hitters against the opponent's weakest blockers, they have sufficient skills to run the I 4-2.

The setters running the I 4-2 require good movement skills, but they don't have to be as skilled in this area as setters in the 6-2 because defense-to-offense transition in the I 4-2 is much less demanding. Compared to the setters in the 6-2 system, who must move from right back to right front and back again pretty much constantly, the setters in the I 4-2 move much less.

Setters in the I 4-2 system, however, should have stronger blocking skills than those required of setters in the 6-2. Consider that a team running a 6-2 has the option of taking out the setter who has rotated to the front row if the setter has limited blocking skills. In the I 4-2, a team needs a setter who can block effectively against the opponent's (likely) best hitter, because most teams put their best hitter at left front. A team might opt for a switch-blocking strategy (moving a weak-blocking setter to another position so a better blocker goes up against the opponent's best hitter), except that this puts the setter in a tougher position to transition from defense to offense, especially if he or she is now blocking on the left side.

An argument can be made that left-side hitters in an I 4-2 system need to be even more dominant than the left-side attackers in a 6-2 system. Because the setters in an I 4-2 are setting from the front row, opposing teams' blockers can focus more on the left-side hitter, knowing there's not a right-side hitter to be concerned about. Because blockers have fewer front-row attackers to attend to, it's quite possible a well-formed two-player block will almost always be facing the left-side attacker in the I 4-2, which means excellent hitting skills will be required to beat the block. However, if coaches also train middle hitters and setters to run an effective attack from right front behind the setter, teams can neutralize the blockers camping out against their left-side attacker.

Finally, left-handed setters can be a bonus in the I 4-2. Setters who are aggressive hitters with fast arms can contribute as much in this system as the two other hitters on the front row, especially if they're left handed.

ADVANTAGES AND DISADVANTAGES

Advantages of the I 4-2 system begin with the setters. First, out of transition (when opponents are attacking), the right-front setter is (one hopes) already in the general area to which the ball will be dug. If the ball is dug successfully, the setter is saved a significant amount of movement. Second, an inexperienced setter in this system will be mostly setting front sets, because there's no right-side attacker behind her, which is a plus because most beginning setters have difficulty setting back-sets consistently. Third, teams still working on developing ball control can have success running the I 4-2 because setters don't have to travel as far to run down errant passes or digs. This usually translates to more decent swings for the hitters than other systems might allow for teams weak on ball control. Finally, in a case in which your team's two setters are also your best overall players, the I 4-2 allows you to play these players in any back-row defensive position when in the back row and allows them to take swings as a back-row attacker.

The I 4-2 system promotes player development across several areas, allowing many players to work on different skills in various positions. The system tends to make good use of setters who are also skilled at serve reception. Unlike the 6-2 (in which setters are transitioning from back to front in order to set), the I 4-2 frees up your setters to pass from the back row. From the attackers' perspective, the main advantage of the I 4-2 is that most hitters are hitting from their strong side (i.e., right-handed hitters are hitting with the arm closest to the setter). The ball travels a shorter distance from the setter to the right-handed hitter and doesn't have to travel across the hitter's body, because the ball is contacted with the inside arm (closest to the setter), making it easier for hitters to time their attacks.

Finally, the I 4-2 system is advantageous in its simplicity. Younger players can understand and learn the system relatively quickly. However this doesn't mean the system shouldn't be used by higher level teams. Teams with outstanding athletes and excellent ball control can do many things within this system to cause major problems for opponents. One example is to mix things up on offense by having your middle attacker run a multitude of options behind the setter, and hitting some balls off two feet and others off one foot (a slide attack). Or you might put added pressure on blockers by running back-row attacks from between the left-front and middle-front hitters. Another possibility is for setters to jump-set to hitters and jump and attack the second contact as much as possible to give opponents one more element they must defend against.

On the other side, the simplicity of the I 4-2 system can turn into a disadvantage when front-row hitters are having trouble getting kills when the opponent is serving. With only two front-row hitters at any given time, getting a side-out can be difficult if both hitters are struggling. The problem is magnified when a team lacks a back-row attack, severely limiting the options of the setters.

Other disadvantages of the I 4-2 system are common to two-setter systems and were covered last chapter in our discussion of the 6-2. These include problems that arise when a team's two setters are different in skill level, style, preference, tendencies, or personality. See page 145 in chapter 16 for more information.

OPTIONS

Most teams who use the I 4-2 system buy into the specialization benefits the system promotes. However, because this system is simple enough for young teams to use as they learn the game and relatively easy to understand compared to other popular systems, teams should at least consider not specializing in the 4-2 so that young players can learn several skills. For example, it's easy within this system for front-row players (except for the setter) to play both middle and left side. Because the setter is already in the front row, having whoever is in the left-front position in that rotation just stay and play left side and whoever is in the middle-front position stay and play middle front in each rotation is an easy transition for a team to make.

As another way of training skills for beginning players, teams might consider having every player take turns being the setter in the 4-2. If you tried this in a 6-2 or 5-1 system, results might be disastrous because there are significantly more movement demands in the 6-2 and 5-1. So simply, whoever rotates into the right-front position will be the setter for that rotation (sometimes referred to as a 6-6 system). But giving all players the chance to set in the I 4-2 system allows everyone to try running the offense while still providing opportunities for team success.

Also, as a way to confuse and overload an opponent's blockers, consider the occasional use of the backcourt setter in setting the first ball out of serve reception. You wouldn't want to do this regularly, but as long as it's trained in practice this maneuver can be an effective way to keep opponents on their feet because they must deal with three front-row attackers rather than the two they are used to seeing in this system.

Because of its offensive simplicity, the I 4-2 system places a burden on attackers to score points even when formidable blocks are in front of them. This tough challenge doesn't necessarily preclude attackers from having success, however. Although it's tempting for teams to try to create ways to make this simple offensive system more sophisticated, they might consider a tactic that operates within the simplicity of the system. That is, rather than creating complications by adding more types of sets that the setter and hitter need to learn, teams might try having the left-side and middle hitter hit one kind of set effectively to several spots on the opponent's side of the court. For instance, the traditional left front (outside hitter) might hit a ball that's set just inside the left antenna. If a setter can consistently make that set a hittable ball (i.e., not too tight, not too far outside the antenna, and not too low) and give the hitter several options from which to choose, he or she has made this simple system more sophisticated without adding a different kind of set. If this left-side hitter can effectively hit that same set to the deep crosscourt, deep down the line, and at a hard angle, as well as being able to occasionally tip the ball for a point, this will be enough shots to keep the defense guessing what's coming next.

From a middle attacker's perspective, whether the standard set is a quick attack or a slower tempo set (such as a 2), the attacker can develop a number of different shots as well. Because it's believed that most middle hitters tend to hit to left back more than they hit to right back, opposing blockers will try to defend that shot. Most often, if they commit the left-side blocker to help the middle blocker defend that shot, coaches should teach their middle attackers to tip to the left-front position (from where the blocker came), making the ball land just behind the block inside the three-meter line. Most teams will not recover that tip. Continuing to assume the blockers are taking away the crosscourt shot, middle hitters should also learn to turn and hit a deep cut-back shot to the opponent's right back. This neutralizes the block, whether it's a one- or two-player block. An added advantage here is that your middle may force the opponent's setter, who's playing right-back defense, to play the first contact, thus making her unavailable to set the ball. If this occurs, you have taken your opponent out of its system.

Finally, consider that simple systems can be quite effective. Solid ball control, lots of hittable balls for the hitters, above-average hitters who can terminate the ball—this all makes for a sound recipe for success, even when the system being used is one of the easiest to teach, learn, and implement.

COACHING POINTS

Because there's more pressure on the hitters in the I 4-2 system to generate kills against better formed blocks, coaches should consider teaching their setters to jump-set as often as they can to provide a greater opportunity for them to aggressively attack the second ball from a point higher than the floor. This presents opposing defenses with more to think about, which gives the offense an advantage. Consider whether you want to require your setters to become technically sound from the ground before you teach them to jump-set. Coaches tend to be split on this subject. Some begin teaching jump-setting from day one, knowing it's a skill they want their setters to perform, so the sooner they get started the better. If and when you decide to incorporate jump-setting with your setters, be sure their major objective is to set hittable balls—this is always the case, from the ground or the air.

Another point to consider is whether to use the I 4-2 system to teach beginners the game. USA Volleyball encourages coaches to teach players the whole game and not specialize too much too early. Instructing how skills are performed is important, but equally important is to teach why something is done the way it's done. If you have chosen the I 4-2 system for no reason other than its simplicity (which is a fine reason), you have an obligation to teach players the hows and whys of the system. Working within this simple system gives you many opportunities to teach the basics of the game and why we do the things we do. Teach your players why you have your two front-row hitters in front of the setter. Explain the reason for running the I 4-2 rather than the 6-2. Ask them why you teach setters to set one type of hittable ball to the left front and middle front and teach hitters to hit several shots using the same set, as opposed to using a number of different sets. Encourage questions: "Coach, why do we pass and dig to the right of the middle of the court?" Let your players know that no question is a bad question if the answer teaches them something about the game.

The I 4-2 system is a good system for teaching. Trying to think of all the whys of the game when working within a more complicated system, such as the 5-1 or 6-2, is more difficult because more time is spent training the use of those systems, leaving less time to explain the reasons behind them.

Finally, remember that no system guarantees success. Find the system that matches your personnel, and then practice it day in and day out. But even the best-trained teams playing within the system that matches them best will lose matches now and then. More talented teams will win more often than less talented teams, plain and simple, and coaches can't train talent. But don't get caught up in the idea that teams that run complicated systems will win more often than teams that don't. No matter what the system, and certainly with the I 4-2, teams that serve well, pass well, and hit well will have more success than teams that don't. Sell this idea to your team.

© Matt Brown/Icon SMI

Offensive System Drills

The drills contained in this chapter are designed to develop the skills needed to run the offensive systems presented in Part IV. As with previous drill chapters, however, these drills can be used across many systems and strategies in this book. Use the "category" section of each drill to help determine what skills the drills will help with.

Setter Attack and Set

Category: Use with chapters 15 and 17.

Objective: To train setters in recognizing whether a blocker is trying to block the front-row setter's attack or is more focused on stopping the quick attack.

Players Required: 5

Procedure: The setter on team B initiates the drill by performing a full block jump, landing and turning to receive a toss from the tosser. The setter must glance at and be aware of team A's left-front blocker. If the left-front blocker jumps with the setter, the setter should recognize and set the quick attack. If the left-front blocker doesn't jump with the setter, the setter should attack on the second contact. You can run this drill for a set time or require the setter to put away a set number of balls to end the drill.

Variations: Have other players substitute as the left-front blocker to give the setter opportunities to make good decisions with different blockers (and thus different timing). Add a middle blocker who either commits or doesn't commit to the middle hitter; if they commit, the setter should set the left-front attacker.

Common Errors and Corrections: In a drill like this, which is working on eye training, it's likely the setter will make errors in seeing what's happening on the other side of the net. Correcting the error involves the coach focusing on the setter to see when the setter is glancing at the other side, which often can lead to correction of when to look at the opposing team's blockers.

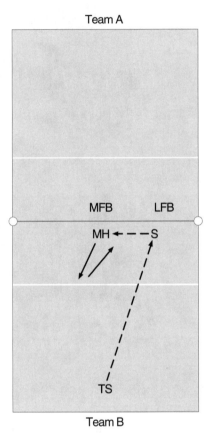

Team A

Team B

Eye Training for the Setter

Category: Use with chapters 15 and 16.

Objective: To train the setter, when coming from the back row, to recognize what the block is trying to take away.

Players Required: 8

Procedure: The setter initiates movement to the net from the right-back defensive position; front-row players transition back from the net to get available to attack. The tosser tosses a ball to the setter, who can set any of the three options. The setter is trying to get hitters a one-on-none or one-on-one situation against opposing blockers. If the setter feels the blockers are cheating away from defending a particular attack, the setter sets to that hitter. Run the drill until the setter gets her hitters hitting against one or zero blocks for a set number of times.

Variation: Instruct blockers to periodically shift in different directions or start in a shifted position, giving the setter opportunities to see where they are defending the attack.

Common Errors and Corrections: Eye training is a difficult skill for setters to master. Many times a setter will glance at the blockers too soon and decide where to set too early. Instruct the setter to glance at the blocker after he or she has penetrated inside the three-meter line on his or her way to the setter target, when it's more likely blockers have begun to shade in the direction they're trying to defend.

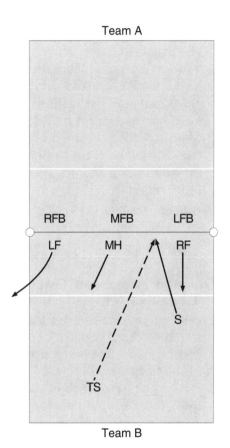

Block-to-Hit Conversion

Category: Use with chapters 6, 7, 8, 9, and 15.

Objective: To give a team who runs a 5-1 the skills necessary to successfully convert from defense when the setter is in the front row.

Players Required: 11

Procedure: The tosser initiates a free ball to team A (team of five), and the ball is played out. Team B (team of six) defends the attack. The rally is played out until termination. Team B must win five rallies before team A wins 10 points. Use a scoring system that gives each team opportunities to win the drill and accomplish the drill's objective.

Variation: Modify the scoring system to make the drill more or less challenging depending on the success of team A.

Common Errors and Corrections: Assuming the focus is on the efficiency of blocker-to-hitter transition, watch for errors in the speed and accuracy of movement from each of the front-row players. Work with players on fast movement away from the net and on establishing desirable starting positions for attackers.

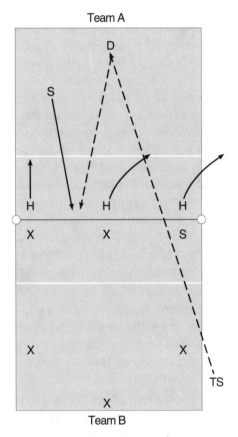

Serve-Receive to Defensive Transition

Category: Use with chapters 2, 3, 4, and 15.

Objective: To give teams using the 5-1 system opportunities to run a serve-receive offense and then transition to defense.

Players Required: 12

Procedure: Team A initiates the serve. The rally is played out until the ball is terminated. Once the ball is terminated, three free balls are introduced by the tosser to team A. Each ball is played out. Once three free balls are played out, team B gets to serve, and the process plays out again. Points are scored as follows: three points for whichever team wins first ball (served ball) and one point for each free ball won (six points per series). Teams play to a set score.

Variation: Substitute free balls for down balls, assuming the players' ball-control skills allow for quality digs.

Common Errors and Corrections: Successful free-ball conversion can be defined as an 80 percent success rate or higher. However, many teams struggle to achieve that rate of success. Ensure that the team receiving the free balls is converting at this rate or higher. An unsuccessful attempt might be due to a poor dig, a nonhittable set, or a nonterminal swing by the attacker.

Setter Back-Row Transition to Quick Attack

Category: Use with chapters 15 and 16.

Objective: To give setters and middle attackers repetitions in running quick attacks with the setter coming in from the back row.

Players Required: 8

Procedure: The middle attacker on side B starts at the net and initiates movement off the net to get into position to hit. The setter releases from back-row position and runs toward the net. The tosser tosses to the setter, requiring the hitter to open up to the ball. The hitter approaches for a quick attack. Alternate setters and middle hitters on side A and B. Run the drill for three minutes or until a set number of attacks are successfully executed.

Variations: If ball control is efficient, a ball can be tossed over the net to a digger who then digs to the setter. The drill can also be run on both sides of the net with middle blockers blocking and transitioning to attack.

Common Errors and Corrections: Watch for errors in middle-hitter timing and spacing between themselves and the setter. The hitter should be jumping about 2 to 3 feet (.6-.9 meter) from the net and about an arm's length from the setter. Pay close attention to this spacing between the setter and hitter, so the setter has room to put the ball between the hitter and the net, and the hitter has room to take a full swing without touching the net.

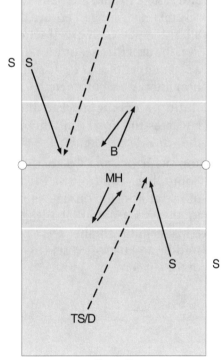

Team A

Team B

Dig, Set, and Quick Attack

Category: Use with chapters 6, 7, 8, 9, 11, 12, 13, 14, and 16.

Objective: To work on running quick attacks from live digs.

Players Required: 11

Procedure: The tosser tosses to the setter on team A, who sets the left-side attacker, who hits the ball crosscourt. The middle-front blocker on team B slides over to block the ball, and then transitions off the net to prepare to attack. The setter releases and transitions to the net and sets a quick attack if the dig is controlled enough. Middle-front blockers, middle-front hitters, and setters should alternate after several repetitions to ensure that all hitters get to hit off all setters. Run the drill for a set time or until a set number of successful transition attacks are completed.

Variation: Move the attack to different areas and don't limit them to the left-side attackers.

Common Errors and Corrections: Some digs won't allow for the quick attack. Encourage setters to always set hittable balls, perhaps including higher sets to the middle and back-row sets to one of the diggers.

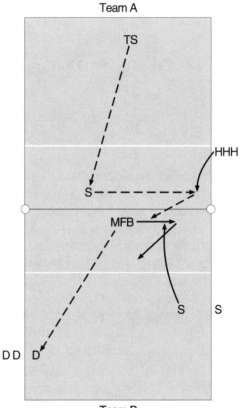

Team A

Team B

Setting Against the Flow

Category: Use with chapters 15, 16, and 17.

Objective: To teach setters to set against the flow, based on where blockers are leaning or moving because of the quality of the pass.

Players Required: 11

Procedure: The tosser on the side of five (side A) initiates a toss to the setter as the left-side hitter transitions off the net (free-ball transition). The setter sets the left-side attacker, who attempts to terminate the ball against team B. If the ball is dug more toward the left side of the net, the setter back-sets to the right-side attacker. This goes against the flow, since if the middle blocker has read the pass quality as poor, he or she will tend to follow the ball into the court toward the left-front attacker. Anticipating this, the setter should set the right-front hitter. If the ball is dug more to the right of center and beyond, the setter runs either a front quick attack or sets the left side.

Variation: Occasionally the setter can set the middle attacker to gain needed repetitions, especially if the dig is perfect.

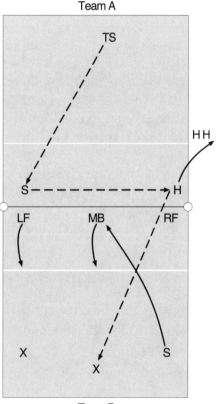

Team A

Team B

Common Errors and Corrections: Note that the setter will sometimes have trouble getting the set out to the left-side and right-side attackers when setting against the flow. When the setter is setting the left side because the dig is right of center, he or she needs to extend fast to get the ball all the way outside for the left-side attacker to hit.

Four vs. Six in a Row

Category: Use with chapters 15 and 16.

Objective: To work on consistently terminating sets from front-row hitting positions.

Players Required: 12

Procedure: A tosser on team A initiates a ball over the net to the digger on team B (team of 5). The ball is played out. Team B's setter sets to hitters in all three front-row positions for three minutes. After three minutes, team A (team of six) must terminate three balls in a row, with one set going to the left side, one to the middle, and one to the right, requiring each hitter to terminate one set.

Variation: If after three minutes you want to focus on a particular attacker, have the setter set the same hitter and require him or her to terminate three consecutive sets.

Common Errors and Corrections: Almost invariably, two of the three attackers will successfully terminate their sets, and the third attacker will fail to do so, causing the drill to continue. If this happens, instruct the setter to set the third hitter first to possibly take some of the pressure off.

Serve-Receive to Defense

Category: Use with chapters 2, 3, 4, 15, 16, and 17.

Objective: To work on the transition to defense.

Players Required: 12

Procedure: One side of six (team A) initiates the ball into play with a serve. The ball is played out. If the team receiving serve (team B) wins the first rally, the tosser initiates a free ball to the serving team. If team B wins the second rally, it scores one point. If the serving team (A) or the team that receives the free ball wins either the first or second rally, no points are scored, and team B rotates and serves, with another free ball tossed to the serving team if the receiving team wins the first rally. Play to a set number of points, depending on how long you want to work on this aspect of the game.

Variation: Instruct servers on each side to serve to specified targets.

Common Errors and Corrections: Because much is being asked of the players in this drill, errors in execution will occur on both sides of the net. Work with both sides, reinforcing what players are doing well and engaging them in solving problems.

Make the Choice

Category: Use with chapters 15 and 17.

Objective: To train the setter to recognize if the block is defending the front-row setter's attack or the middle attack.

Players Required: 6

Procedure: The tosser on team A initiates a free ball to the digger on team B. The left-front blocker for team A either shifts position to defend the quick attack or stays on the setter to defend the setter attack. As the ball is traveling to the setter, the setter glances to see what the left-front blocker is doing. If this blocker has shifted toward the quick-attacker, the setter attacks on the second contact. If the left-side blocker has stayed on the setter, the quick attack is set.

Variation: To give the middle hitter experience in hitting a quick attack when the ball is coming from different directions, move the side B digger around in the backcourt.

Common Errors and Corrections: Expect the setter to make errors in seeing what blockers are doing. Encourage the middle hitter on side B to go for the terminal shot even when facing (possibly) two blockers. If the setter attacks on the second ball and the left-front blocker is defending the quick attack, the setter is expected to terminate the ball.

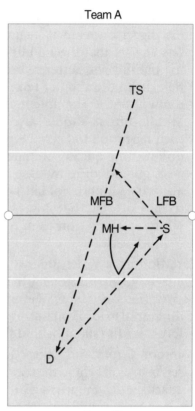

Team A

Team B

Behind the Setter

Category: Use with chapters 15 and 17.

Objective: To help the I 4-2 setter (or the front-row setter in the 5-1) and middle attacker get comfortable in setting and hitting behind the setter.

Players Required: 6

Procedure: The tosser initiates the ball to the digger on team B. Team B's setter sets any set that the middle hitter can hit behind the setter, which can be right behind the setter (zone 7) or all the way out to the antenna (zone 9). Middle hitters should alternate with each repetition to keep the pace of the drill moving quickly. Initiate tosses for a set number of minutes, then require a specified number of kills, either consecutive or total. The middle blocker and left-front blocker on team A are trying to block each set.

Variations: For variety, allow the middle attacker to hit occasionally in front of the setter (i.e., one hit out of every five). The drill can also focus on hitting off of one-foot takeoffs (slide) behind the setter.

Common Errors and Corrections: If the sets being run behind the setter are quick-attack speed, timing issues will arise. Also watch for the middle hitter crowding the net, leaving little room for the setter to put the ball. Observe the hitter to see if appropriate spacing has been established between hitter and setter.

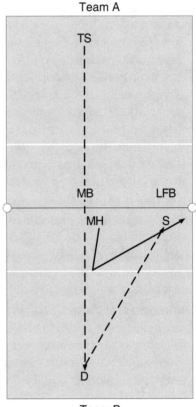

Serve-Receive Transition

Category: Use with chapters 2, 3, 4, 15, and 17.

Objective: To give the setter (at left-front position) repetitions in making what's considered to be the most difficult transition from serve-receive to the target at the net to run the serve-receive offense.

Players Required: 10

Procedure: The server on team A initiates a serve to team B (team of six). Team B's setter transitions to the target area at the net to set any one of the front-row hitters. Setters should alternate each repetition to keep the pace of the drill moving quickly. After a set number of repetitions, require a number of pass-set-kill combinations, either consecutive or total, to end the drill.

Variation: To keep players' interest, introduce a free ball after each served ball and play out.

Common Errors and Corrections: Pay close attention to the quality of the passing and how hittable the sets are. Many teams struggle in getting even an opportunity for a terminal swing. Most errors in passing and setting are results of an individual error usually from reading, anticipating, or timing errors. Observe closely and provide feedback.

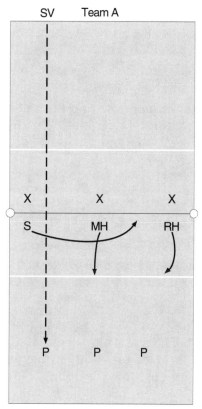

Team B

Transitioning From the Short Serve

Category: Use with chapters 2, 3, 4, 15, 16, and 17.

Objective: To successfully run the serve-receive offense from a short serve.

Players Required: 10

Procedure: Team A's server initiates a short serve to land on or inside the three-meter line. Team B's passers communicate who will pass. Team B's hitters transition, and the setter runs the offense. In each rotation, servers serve for two minutes, and then team B must pass-set-terminate five times to end the drill.

Variation: To keep passers honest, servers should serve occasional deep balls that keep passers deep.

Common Errors and Corrections: When teams serve short, they're trying to disrupt the timing of the opponent's offense. Passers receiving the short serve should pass high enough to give the setter and hitters time to transition to their positions.

Setter Attack to Deep Corner

Category: Use with chapters 15 and 17.

Objective: To train the setter to attack the deep corners on the second contact, which is an area opponents typically leave open.

Players Required: 6

Procedure: The tosser on team A initiates a free ball or down ball to the digger on team B, who digs to the setter. The setter attacks on the second contact (preferably with one hand) and puts the ball either down the line or crosscourt, ensuring the ball lands in the deep corners, 25 to 30 feet (7.6-9.1 meters) back from the net.

Variation: As setters develop attacking skills, work with them on attacking with either hand.

Common Errors and Corrections: Inexperienced setters learning how to attack the second ball deep will make contact at various heights, sometimes below their head and other times too far in front of their bodies. The point of contact should be at the same neutral position each time so the setter's body position looks like she is jump setting until the last second (so opposing blockers can't read if the ball is going to be attacked or set); work with setters on consistency and disguising their attack.

Transition With Setter Dig

Category: Use with chapters 15 and 16.

Objective: To practice transitioning from defense to offense in the 5-1 and 6-2 systems, and reacting to the setter having to dig in the defensive alignment.

Players Required: 12

Procedure: The game begins with the coach, hitting a down ball to team A's back row. When that point ends, the coach feeds a free ball to the losing team's side and it is played out. The coach now begins a second series by initiating a down ball to team B's side, followed by another free ball to the losing team's side. After four balls have been initiated from one sideline, the coach switches to the other sideline and continues this two-ball pattern to allow the defenders to dig balls coming from the opposite angle. A point is awarded to the team that wins both rallies. If each team wins one of the two rallies, then it is called a "wash" and no points are awarded. After predetermined point total or time limit is reached, each team rotates one position.

Variations: If the setter is in the back row, the coach can hit the down ball to that player's area to see how the offense will react to the setter digging the first contact. The emphasis is on quick transition footwork for the front-row players—reading and closing the block then turning and running off the net, and always "getting available" as hitters. For back-row diggers emphasis is on consistently digging the first ball "in system" allowing for a transition set and attack.

Offensive Strategies

CHAPTER
19

Spread Strategy

EXPLANATION OF TACTIC

The spread strategy can be used in any offensive system as long as a team uses a left-front hitter and right-front hitter, both of whom remain close to their respective antennas. The setter sets hitters in all zones along the net, including at the left-side and right-side antenna, thereby spreading the offense all along the net. This system forces opposing blockers to defend the entire net.

If an opponent pinches their outside blockers inside the court 3 to 5 feet (.9-1.5 meters), which is normal if they have responsibility to help defend a middle attack, they'll find it difficult to defend an offense that uses a spread strategy, especially if the offense can also run an effective quick middle attack. Even if the outside blockers aren't pinched in, a spread strategy makes it difficult for middle blockers to get outside to close the block, because they're continually stressed. This allows outside hitters to hit against a one-player block or a poorly formed double-block. In either case, the attacker has the advantage and should be able to put the ball away.

The spread strategy becomes even more effective if a team uses more zones along the net, although doing so requires good ball control, hitters using various approach patterns, and experienced setters who can successfully put sets to many different zones to keep opposing blockers off balance, guessing, and stressed.

To picture how the spread strategy works, you need to understand a net numbering system. The most common numbering system uses nine zones along the net (figure 19.1). As you're facing the net, zone 1 begins at the left antenna and works its way to zone 9 at the right antenna. Each zone is 1 meter (3.2 feet) wide. To give

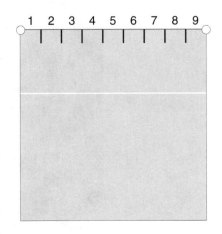

Figure 19.1   Spread strategy net zones.

you a frame of reference, most setters who set from right of center will be in zone 6. Many coaches like the idea of a numbering system for communication purposes and may simplify the nine zones down to as few as three. Even the highest-level teams won't run sets from all nine zones, so simplifying the number system is acceptable and encouraged.

In using the spread strategy, a team gives its hitters many opportunities to hit between blockers who might be jumping at different times and not close together. The tactic of the spread strategy typically decreases the chances of opposing blockers forming well-positioned blocks in order to defend an attack.

PERSONNEL REQUIREMENTS

The personnel needed to run a spread offense is tied to how many zones along the net are to be used with the hitters. If the spread strategy is using only three zones (zone 1 for left-side attackers, zone 5 for middle attackers, and zone 9 for the right-side attackers), then the personnel requirements are minimized. A three-zone spread strategy requires setters to consistently set hittable balls to these three positions, most likely a traditional four set to the left side, a five set to the right side, and preferably a front one set to the middle (these numbers represent how high the set is at its peak). This would be the simplest example of the spread strategy.

Because a key to success when using a spread strategy is being able to run an effective quick attack, you need setters who can set consistent quick sets to attackers. Otherwise your attackers won't be able to beat the blockers to the net, which virtually cripples the strategy. Also, because the ability of a setter to effectively run a middle attack depends on a team's ability to pass and dig well, the spread strategy requires accurate passing. A pass or dig that isn't good enough for the setter to set the middle hitter nullifies a primary purpose of the spread strategy: to get the middle blocker to hesitate before releasing outside so the left- or right-front hitter can beat the block.

Hitters in this strategy must be able to read what kind of blocks they'll face. Being able to recognize if the outside blocker is blocking next to the antenna (blocking the line) and knowing if and when the middle blocker is going to close the block are two examples of the kinds of reads hitters need to make. If the middle blocker can get outside and only partially close the block, the outside hitter has a hole between the blockers through which to attack. The key is for the outside hitter to see the play develop and recognize the options available.

From the middle-hitting perspective, there's a good chance that outside blockers won't try to help block the middle attack, so they start their base position as blockers closer to the outside, where they can at least ensure they'll be able to block their assigned outside hitter. Because the middle attacker is now hitting against one blocker, it becomes critical for the hitter to put the ball away because he or she has a major advantage. It's expected that any hitter attacking against one blocker will win that ball every time.

A spread strategy using more than three zones somewhat alters the personnel required to make it work. Above-average passing and digging skills are still important to ensure the quick-attacker can be set, but even more demands are now placed on the setters. Setters must be able to set a wide variety of set locations and tempos with consistency. This is a lot to ask because many setters have trouble putting up consistently hittable balls to just three zones. Adding another zone or two requires more precision from setters to ensure balls are hittable. Along with being nimble and precise, setters must also be smart. They are running the offense, so they need to understand how a new spread-offense play should be run, in what situations to run it, how often it should be run, and by what hitters.

As for hitting, the more complicated setting scheme will place greater demands on hitters. If your hitters aren't up to the task of hitting a wide range of set locations and tempos, your team is better off sticking to the three-zone spread. All front-row hitters must be able to hit their sets with enough effectiveness that points are scored. Running an additional set (instead of going for the kill) just for the sake of running it doesn't necessarily increase the chance of stressing or overloading your opponent.

ADVANTAGES AND DISADVANTAGES

Whenever an offense forces an opponent to defend the entire net, from antenna to antenna, the offense gains the upper hand. Defending the entire net is difficult no matter how much experience the blocking team has. The spread is especially useful when an offense is considerably shorter than their opponent. Spreading the offense along the net neutralizes the size discrepancy.

Depending on the type of serve-receive and defense a team uses, running the spread offense allows for ease of transition to hitting zones, especially if outside hitters are primary passers who might pass on the outside of a serve-receive pattern. This could be the left-front or right-front passer in the five-player W (figure 2.1, p. 12) or the left-front and right-front passers in the four-player U (figure 3.1, p. 18).

In general, the spread offers more advantages to teams with at least one extremely strong setter and, to a slightly lesser degree, at least one extremely strong hitter. If you're blessed with a team stacked with strong setters, the greater the attraction of using the spread. If your team has both strong setters and strong hitters, your team may be virtually unbeatable using the spread offense.

Disadvantages to the spread arise when a team tries to use more than three zones at the net and it is not experienced or skilled enough to do so. As mentioned, using more than three zones creates pressure for the setter to set hittable balls. Hitters too are more challenged when an offense adds a fourth (or fifth) zone because they are expected to keep up with the setters and handle more difficult sets. Unless you're a team with experienced and intelligent setters and versatile hitters, be cautious about trying to use more than three zones.

OPTIONS

Ideally, the spread strategy pulls outside blockers from their base position out to the edge of the net. Although this makes it easier for the outside blockers to form one-player blocks against outside hitters (because they're closer to the position they want to be blocking from), it also forces the middle blocker to travel a greater distance to close the block. This gives the edge to the attacker, assuming the hitter can effectively hit around a one-player block (which should be a safe assumption to make). Positioning outside hitters closer to their respective antennas is often a response to recognizing that an opponent is comfortable using one blocker to defend the quick attack, which might make for an advantage for the hitting team. If this happens when using the spread strategy, there's no need to adjust your strategy.

However, once opponents begin to defend differently against the spread strategy, teams usually need to adjust their offensive strategy. Because it's assumed that any offense has a hitter who will get more sets than other attackers, defensive teams will begin to overload their blockers to the most likely point of attack. Assuming that the left-side hitter is the hitter getting more sets than others, it's quite common for the middle blocker to cheat a bit or release early in that direction. This movement adjustment by the blocker invites the setter to back-set to the right-side attacker. Figure 19.2a illustrates how far a blocker would have to move to defend the opponent's right-side attack. So while the left-side hitter can still get enough swings to be productive, more responsibility falls to the right-side hitter to become the primary attacker in this situation, capable of putting balls away. A similar expectation occurs if

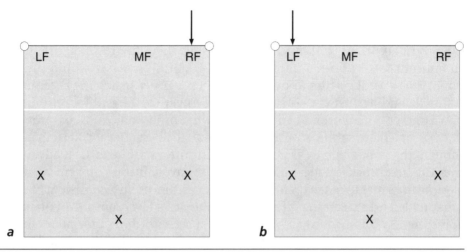

Figure 19.2 Blocking adjustment against the spread strategy when *(a)* the left-side is the dominant attacker and *(b)* when the right-side is the dominant attacker.

the right-side hitter is the likely point of attack. Figure 19.2*b* shows the middle blocker shading toward the right-side attacker, again illustrating how far the blocker will have to travel back to defend the left-side attack.

No doubt, there will be some teams who won't alter their offensive approach no matter what the defense does. In the case where the offensive team is generally more talented and skilled than the defensive team, maintaining the same strategy (until they stop you) is appropriate. Subtle changes to the spread strategy are recommended when the defensive team's adjustments take away options for key hitters, tipping the scales back toward the defensive side of the net.

COACHING POINTS

All players, including hitters, need a general sense of the opponent's strategy in slowing down their offense. They should know the answers to questions such as these:

- Do the blockers start bunched inside or stay outside?
- Do the blockers do any kind of switch blocking, trying to get their best blocker against the best attacker?
- Are the blockers big?
- Do the opposing players take away an area when they block, or are they trying to block every ball?
- Do they always try to get two blockers up on the hitter?

An offensive team that can answer these questions will be able to use the spread strategy more effectively. Once the questions are answered, an offense can adjust accordingly. If blockers start inside, the setter running the spread should put sets to both antennas. Blockers starting outside would provide opportunity for the setter to run sets to various zones inside the antennas. If teams defend against the spread by trying to get their best blocker on your best attacker, setters should check to see what other matchups are provided that might lend to setting someone other than the best attacker. Keep in mind, though, that when all else is equal, the best hitter has the tactical advantage over the best blocker. Bigger blockers might have minimal movement skills, alerting the setter to make them move longer distances on a consistent basis in order to defend against the offense. These are just a few examples of offensive adjustments. Once offensive players have a sense of how they are going to be defended, they can form a better plan for kinds of shots (line, angle, tips, etc.) that will be effective in that situation.

Because there's no doubt that running a spread strategy will require more movement and transition from various players, be sure to practice these movement demands in practice. A primary left-side hitter who's also a primary passer needs lots of reps in passing and then transitioning to the attack area. Practice the skills of passing and hitting together, not separately. As you coordinate the systems of serve-receive, defense, and offense, be sure to require players to perform the movements and skills just as they will perform them in a match.

Because the spread strategy is trying to overload and stress blockers, practice drills should be performed against the block. This will let the offense know the kinds of problems it creates (or doesn't create) for blockers so that it can adjust as necessary.

© Daiju Kitamura/AFLO SPORT/Icon SMI

Fast-Tempo Strategy

EXPLANATION OF TACTIC

The fast-tempo strategy incorporates fast, low-arching quicker sets to various zones along the net. This style of play can be a variation of the spread offense, but the fast-tempo can be employed no matter what offense a team is using. Although big, athletic teams can benefit from using fast-tempo sets, teams that are undersized will likely benefit more in running this offense, which is predicated on faster sets to beat the blockers. This strategy helps to neutralize blockers who are bigger and teams that are overall stronger in blocking. The fast-tempo strategy can be used in all three front-row hitting positions but requires precision from passers, diggers, and setters.

As we saw last chapter, the net can be divided into nine zones (see figure 19.1, p.172), with left front being zone 1 and right front being zone 9. In this numbering system for play sets, the first number is the zone the fast-tempo set is set to and hit from. The second number refers to the height of the set relative to the top of the net. For example, the traditional regular high sets for each position would be a 15 for the left side, a 52 (or 53 for younger teams) for the middle attacker, and a 95 for the right side. This indicates that the 15 is a set hit from left front (zone 1) and at its peak will reach 5 feet (1.5 meters) above the top of the net. The 52, otherwise known as a front two, will be hit from the middle front (zone 5) and rise 2 feet (.6 meter) above the net at its peak. The traditional right-side set, the 95, is in zone 9 (right inside the right antenna) and rises 5 feet (.6 meter) above the top of the net at its peak. In shorthand, this set is often called the five or back five, whereas the 52 set is shortened to just 2. Slow- and fast-tempo sets mean different things to different people, but for our purposes here we'll define a fast-tempo set as one in which the second number is four or lower for the outside attackers. Because a two set for the middle (or a three for younger teams) has been defined as a regular high set, middle-hitter fast-tempo sets will have the number one for the second number in this system. Below are some examples of fast-tempo sets, along with suggestions on which hitter is most likely to hit them. The first three are the quickest tempo sets, one for each of the three front-row attack positions. The next three are sets for the left-side attacker at varying tempos, and the final two are different tempo right-side sets for the right-side or middle attacker to hit.

▶ 51. Otherwise known as the front one or the quick, in this set the hitter is ideally up in the air, presenting a target for the setter *before* the setter touches the ball. This set is usually hit by the middle attacker but can also be hit by the right-side attacker if he or she has the quickness and timing to do so. If the right-side attacker is left handed, the 51 can be a very effective fast-tempo set run in front of the setter.

▶ 31. The tempo of the 31 is the same as for 51; again, the hitter is up in the air presenting a target for the setter before the setter makes contact. The 31 requires more precision than the 51 because the hitter is farther away from the setter. In most cases the middle attacker will hit this set, but it can also be run with the left-side attacker, especially if this hitter presents a big target for the setter while in the air. You'll see very few teams, if any, attempt to run this set with their right-side attacker swinging around in front of the setter. This is only done when the right-side hitter is left-handed and extremely quick.

▶ 71. Also known as the back one or back quick, this fast-tempo set is run right behind the setter, who's setting (assuming a perfect pass or dig) from zone 6. If the right-side hitter is left-handed, this is the hitter who usually hits this set. A right-handed middle attacker might also hit this set, if he or she has the timing and speed to go around behind the setter and get up in the air early, presenting a good and early target, often hitting off of a one-foot slide approach. If in the rare case you have a left-handed middle attacker, you would not want to run the 71 with the hitter making the approach from the middle, because he or she will be moving in the wrong direction.

▶ 14. Some consider the 14 (sometimes abbreviated to 4) to be a high set, but once again you should decide what differentiates a fast-tempo set from a regular-tempo set so that it best meets the needs of your team. The 14 is almost exclusively hit by the left-side attacker. Although not quite as crucial in this set, good timing between the setter and hitter remains important. Though the hitter won't be in the air before the setter sets the ball (as in the 51 for the middle attacker), a left-side attacker will often need to start the approach before the ball gets too far away from the setter after they have released the set. Knowing what kind of tempo to expect for this set allows the hitter to generate speed on the approach, and to jump and swing with a fluid motion. Most hitters begin the approach just after the setter has set the ball. However, quicker athletes might begin a little bit later, and slower athletes a little earlier.

▶ 13. This is a faster-tempo set hit by the left-side attacker that's often used to stress the outside blocker by getting the hitter to the point of attack faster than the blocker can handle. This set also prevents most middle blockers from getting outside to help defend the attack because it is low, quick, and to the antenna. Because this ball gets to its intended target quickly, the hitter usually starts the approach before the setter has set the ball.

▶ 12. This is probably the fastest tempo set your team will run with your left-side attacker. This is a difficult set because the hitter is about halfway through the approach before the ball is set (think alley-oop play in basketball). Because the ball must travel from zone 6 to zone 1 very quickly, the timing challenges for the setter and hitter are significant. This set should be attempted only by high-level teams with setters and outside hitters with a lot of experience and from an on-target pass.

▶ 94. This set is the right-side equivalent of the 14. A key difference is the timing the hitter will have as compared to the 14. Because the 94 travels across three zones (from zone 6 to zone 9), and the 14 travels five zones (from zone 6 to zone 1), the right-side attacker (assuming he or she is right-handed) will need to leave a bit sooner than described in the 14 because the ball is not spending as much time in the air. Right-side attackers who also hit occasionally from the left side will find themselves struggling with timing issues because they're hitting in front of and behind the setter. The 94 can also be hit by the right-handed middle hitter, and is a good play to run when there's a front-row setter and no right-side attacker. This set is often used by the middle to hit a "slide" attack, in which the middle hitter slides by and behind the setter in an approach pattern somewhat parallel to the net and takes off from one foot (like for a lay up in basketball). The one-footed slide takeoff has grown in popularity over the last several years and is a difficult hit to defend because the hitter is often facing outside the court (toward the right sideline), making it tough for the blocker to read the hitter's shoulders, hips, and eyes to get in front of the attacked ball.

▶ 93. Experienced teams with outstanding ball control might use this set with the middle attacker approaching parallel to the net and behind the setter, providing another opportunity for the attacker to jump from one leg. Success with this set requires precision passing and outstanding ball control. The right-side hitter can also hit this from a one-foot approach if they begin their approach from inside the court out toward the antenna, or if they take a straight-in approach inside the sideline toward the net near the right antenna.

These are eight examples of relatively high-risk fast-tempo sets that can be incorporated into a fast-tempo offensive strategy. Of course the more of these options your team chooses to use, the greater the pressure placed on your passers and diggers. When considering incorporating these sets into your offense, keep in mind that you should use them only if needed. If your team is already having success with high-tempo sets, there might be no reason to add these higher-risk fast sets to your offensive arsenal.

PERSONNEL REQUIREMENTS

As mentioned earlier, precise ball control is critical to running these sets successfully. Imagine your left side trying to hit a 13 out of serve-receive, but the pass is low and off to the right side of the court out of bounds. There's no way the set could be run. Again, recall the axiom to never attempt tactically what you can't execute technically.

Much is required of the setter in running these types of sets. Assuming ball control is at a level at which fast-tempo sets are possible, consider waiting until your setter can consistently set a 15, 52, and 95 before adding anything faster. Requiring your setters to set these higher balls consistently well before advancing to faster sets might serve as motivation for them to work hard in the technical aspects of footwork, hand position, and ball release. If setters can't set a consistent high set to each position, they probably won't be able to set fast-tempo sets consistently either.

The same goes for your hitters. Once they are consistently effective at hitting a 15 (left side), a 52 (middle attacker), and a 95 (right side) and can hit a variety of shots (deep angle, deep line, off-speed, etc.) off the traditional high set, they can progress to the faster sets. Of course hitters in all positions must be able to handle the demands of getting off the net quickly to get in position to approach and hit the fast-tempo set. Players with minimal movement skills (slow-twitched athletes) will have a hard time transitioning off the net and getting into position to hit a fast-tempo set.

ADVANTAGES AND DISADVANTAGES

Fast-tempo sets are difficult to defend for both front-row and back-row defenders. Teams that develop the ball control needed to run fast-tempo sets will find themselves hitting quite often against zero- and one-person blocks, giving the offense a clear advantage. Even if there are two blockers, to get a well-formed block up, the blockers must correctly guess where the set is going to go.

A fast-tempo offense is exciting and entertaining, both for players and spectators. If a team has the technical skills they need to run this offense effectively, they can have a lot of fun doing it. Enjoyment is a good motivator, so if teams are having fun in an offensive scheme, they'll likely be more motivated to endure the kind of training fast-tempo plays require. Another advantage is that these plays may give your team the feeling of confidence that comes with having a secret weapon. Often getting to try these plays may be held up to the team as a reward of sorts for achieving goals or for performing well in other areas.

One of the disadvantages of a fast-tempo strategy is that mistakes in timing are crippling. For instance, a left-side hitter who's hitting a 13 set has a much smaller window in which to attack the ball when compared to a traditional high set. The same can be said for the middle hitter hitting the 51 and 31 and the right-side attacker hitting the 71. Even if everything (pass, hitter's transition, setter's transition) is perfect leading up to the setter setting the ball, there's still a chance that the timing of the set and of the hitter's approach won't be in sync, leaving a team scrambling just to get the ball over the net. Also, the faster you run your offense, the more stress you put on your own hitters to transition quicker and possibly father along the net, which could cause some hitter fatigue.

OPTIONS

The game of volleyball should proceed from simple to complex techniques, tactics, and strategies. Diggers must learn the basic dig before working on the diving dig, the sprawling dig, and so on. The principle of simple to complex progression definitely applies to teams wishing to employ a fast-tempo offense. Setters and hitters must become adept at running traditional higher plays and developing excellent ball-control skills before trying to perfect the skills necessary to play the fast-tempo offense.

Many teams attempt a gradual incorporation of fast-tempo sets into their offensive plan. To run even one type of fast-tempo set requires very good passing and digging for the players involved, but there's no requirement that *all* front-row hitters must be involved in fast-tempo strategies. Consider a team that hits traditional high sets with the left- and right-side hitters (15s and higher for the left sides and 95s and higher for the right sides) and uses their middle hitter for the fast-tempo sets. This type of offense can be very effective because the opponent's middle blocker must defend the quick attack and will thus have trouble getting out to block either outside hitter, even though they're hitting a higher set.

Think also about using two of your three front-row hitters in a faster-tempo offense. A team who uses the left-side hitter as its outlet hitter (the hitter who will probably get a traditional high set when the pass or dig doesn't allow other sets) can use its middle-front and right-front attackers for faster-tempo sets. A play within this strategy might be a 15 for the left side, 31 for the middle, and a 71 for the right side. This allows the setter an outlet set if the pass isn't perfect, but also many offensive options when the pass is perfect.

Finally, there will be times when an opponent manages to defend the quick-tempo sets. If this occurs, mix some slower sets into your offense. Good blocking is a matter of reading and timing, so mixing up the timing of your sets might be enough to throw the defense off.

COACHING POINTS

Because the margin of error is quite small when running fast-tempo sets, many gamelike repetitions during practice are necessary. Here are a few elements to consider for front-row hitters hitting fast-tempo sets.

▶ Left-side attackers. Very rarely should left-side attackers begin in the zone from which they want their approach to start. Invariably, a left-side attacker is a primary passer who passes when in the front row. If left-side hitters are running a fast-tempo set out of the serve-receive pattern, they need to work on drills that require them to pass, transition, and then hit, just as they would in a game. Further, if the left side is hitting fast-tempo sets out of their defensive position, he or she should start at the net, block an opposing attacker, then transition off the net to approach for the fast-tempo set, or drop off and dig, then transition to hit.

▶ Middle attackers. These attackers have a wide variety of movement demands to execute before they hit the fast-tempo set. Assuming they're involved in every block (two-blocker system), they will need efficient transition movements from the net after blocking in order to get available to hit. That this transition will have to be worked out as they're moving from the left side, right side, and middle means that progress toward becoming efficient fast-tempo hitters might come slower. Also critical are the movement demands placed on the setter before setting the fast-tempo sets. If the setter is front row and involved with the block, he or she must be required to perform this gamelike movement before she sets the ball. Because it's probable that the middle blocker is involved as well in this blocking situation, forcing both the middle blocker and the setter to block and then transition is a gamelike drill, allowing for more transfer to the game. One of the more advanced elements is the running of a middle quick attack when the pass or dig isn't perfect. Because teams hope that a fast-tempo set can still be used when the ball isn't exactly to target, executing gamelike repetitions under this circumstance is helpful. Although we're not suggesting that you should run a fast-tempo set if the setter is 10 feet (3 meters) off the net, it's possible for a setter who's 2 to 3 feet (.6-.9 meter) off the net to still set the middle hitter a faster-tempo ball—but only if trained and practiced under gamelike conditions.

▶ Right-side attackers. As is true for left-side attackers, right-side attackers might be involved in receiving serve and being required to pass and transition before hitting the fast-tempo sets. Again, the attacker should not start in the same zone that he or she will hit from. Like left-side attackers, the right-side hitter will be involved as a blocker (but probably more often than left-side hitters will because opponents traditionally set more often to their left-side hitters than to their right-side hitters). The right-side blocker, then, should be involved in drills that require them to start at the net, make a block attempt, and then transition off the net to hit the fast-tempo set. There will be times when the right-side blocker will be the off-blocker (when the opponent sets their right-side attacker), so the right-side hitter should begin that movement in a hitting drill from the net, dropping off to dig and then transitioning to hit, so that training is similar to what occurs in real games.

Another coaching consideration relevant to this strategy is the type of defense a team uses, and where that defense places front-row diggers. Say a defense is using a two-blocker system, and the off-blocker pulls into the court close to the net to defend tips. If it's the left-side hitter who's the off-blocker, it will be very difficult for her to move halfway into the court (roughly 5 feet [1.5 meters] from the net) and then try to transition to hit a 13 set. Though it's fun and sometimes quite effective to run these fast-tempo sets, serious consideration must be given to how many of them should be used based on the defensive system your team employs.

Finally, we want to mention the potential offensive benefit to fusing the fast-tempo strategy with the spread strategy. As discussed in chapter 19, the spread strategy uses sets in a minimum of three zones—usually zones 1, 5, and 9—to force blockers to defend the entire net. It's possible for a team with excellent ball-control skills to apply fast-tempo plays within the spread strategy. Fusing the spread and high-tempo strategies can cause major stress for an opposing team's blockers and back-row defenders because they will have to get two blockers up at any point of attack or else resort to commit blocking on one attacker. Training your hitters to each hit and get good at one higher-tempo and one quicker-tempo set in the same zone can cause havoc with the opposing blockers.

©Jim Metzendorf/Icon SMI

Multiple Tempos With Combination Plays Strategy

EXPLANATION OF TACTIC

This strategy involves two hitters hitting from zones close to one another (e.g., a left-side hitter hitting from zone 3 and a middle hitter hitting from zone 5), with the first hitter hitting a faster-tempo set and the second hitter hitting a slower-tempo set. Running the two hitters into two zones side by side is intended to overload the blocker responsible for defending hitters in that area, requiring the blocker to choose which hitter to focus on. Perfectly executed multiple-tempo plays result in a blocker who has no chance to defend one of the attackers. A second possible use is to run two hitters into the same zone, but each hitting different tempo and different height sets to overload the blocker in that zone, causing that blocker to jump with the first hitter, leaving the second hitter in a one-on-one or one-on-none situation.

Say, for example, the middle attacker hits a 51 (first tempo) and the left-front attacker hits a 42 (second tempo) or a 2 set from just left of the middle attacker's left shoulder. If the blocker decides to jump with the 51 (the front quick), and the setter sets the 42, the 42 can still be attacked (despite being slower than the 51) before the blocker has time to land and slide over to defend it. On the other hand, if the blocker opts to defend the 42, the setter should read the blocker's intention and set the faster tempo set to the middle hitter, again leaving no time for the blocker to adjust.

This example illustrates the advantage of running a multiple-tempo combination play. But for the strategy to work, the second tempo set must be run quick enough to prevent the blocker from defending the quick attack and still having time to land, adjust position, and get back up to block the second tempo set. If the second tempo set is run so high that the blocker can adjust to defend it, there's little use in running these sets side by side.

Let's now look at some sample multiple-tempo combination plays and review what the plays are designed to do. Refer back to 19.1 (p. 172) to remind yourself how the numbering system is identified along the net and to chapter 20 (Explanation of Tactic, p. 178) to remind yourself how sets are numbered according to their tempo. In the samples below, the first number refers to the left-side attacker's set, the middle number indicates what the middle attacker will hit, and the third number indicates what the right-side attacker will hit. Note that in every combination play, there's always a higher outlet set, giving the setter an option if the ball isn't accurately directed to target, thus allowing him or her to fulfill a setter's most basic responsibility: giving a hitter an opportunity to hit the ball.

▶ 14-51-42 (figure 21.1). This play is often called the *right X*. The 14 to the left-side hitter represents the outlet set in case the pass or dig isn't perfect. Assuming the 51 is run efficiently, the objective is to overload the middle blocker, who must decide whether to focus on the middle attacker hitting the quick 51 or the right-side attacker coming in front of the setter and around the middle hitter to hit the slower 42. This play is effective if the middle blocker hesitates defending the 51 or jumps to defend the 51 and won't have time to block the 42 if the setter sets that second tempo option.

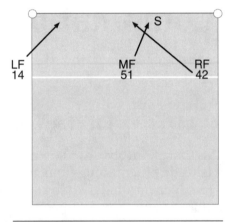

Figure 21.1   14-51-42 (*right X*) positioning.

▶ 42-51-95 (figure 21.2). This play is also called a *tandem*. Here, the 95 is the outlet set to the right-front hitter. Though still trying to overload the middle blocker, this play is also meant to cause the right-side blocker problems by requiring that blocker to follow the left-side hitter into the middle of the court. Ideally, this will cause an uneven and poorly formed block even when two blockers defend the play. Also, if the outside blocker is inexperienced in recognizing this multiple-combination play and hesitates at all, the hitter will have enough time to create an advantage for the offense.

▶ 14-31-52 (figure 21.3). This play is sometimes called the *wide X*. The left-side hitter serves as the outlet hitter. The play is designed to force the middle blocker to choose between defending the 31 (middle hitter) or the 52 (right-side attacker coming to the middle of the court). Even in the blocker's best-case scenario the hitters are provided with a tactical edge. If the middle blocker follows the middle hitter (hitting the 31), and the left-side blocker follows the right-side hitter (hitting the 52), this still creates a one-on-one situation for both hitters.

▶ 52-31-95 (figure 21.4). The right-side hitter is the outlet attacker on the 95 set. This play is designed to cause major confusion between the middle and left-side blockers. Because the middle hitter and left-side hitter are in essence trading places, the two blockers are forced to communicate how they will defend. If the blockers decide to assume responsibility for the hitter who's coming into their zone, hitters should still be able to put the ball away against the single blocker—and there should always be a single blocker on this play because the zones are spread far enough apart. Better yet, if the blockers try to follow the hitter who started in their zone, chances are good that neither blocker will get up on either hitter.

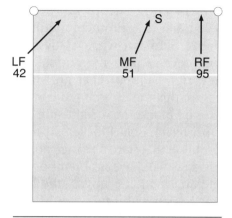

Figure 21.2 42-51-95 (*tandem*) positioning.

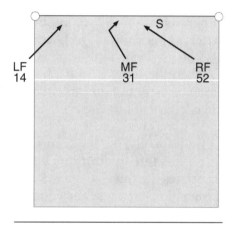

Figure 21.3 14-31-52 (*wide X*) positioning.

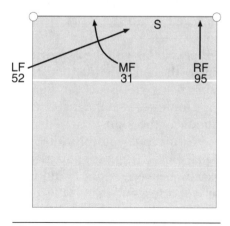

Figure 21.4 52-31-95 (*front X*) positioning.

▶ 14-71-52 (figure 21.5). The left-side hitter is again the outlet hitter on the 14. Similar to what was described in the previous play, the middle attacker and right-side attacker are switching zones, this time hoping to confuse the middle blocker and right-side blocker. Once again, if the blockers try to follow the hitter that started in their zone, both blockers will have problems defending the attack successfully. If the blockers trade responsibilities, the hitter who gets the set will still likely have the advantage over the single blocker.

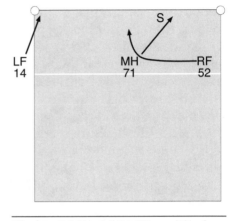

Figure 21.5   14-71-52 positioning.

The previous plays are designed for when the setter is in the back row, either as part of a 6-2 or as one of the three rotations of a 5-1 (in which the setter is a back-row player). However, multiple-tempo combination plays can also be used when the setter is in the front row, usually with a similar result to when the setter is in the back row. As you watch teams play, notice that some of them use multiple-tempo combination plays involving a back-row attacker. The following explanation of back-row attacks should be helpful as these plays are discussed.

Traditionally, the backcourt is divided into either three or four zones. Figure 21.6 illustrates the three-zone back-row attack designations. Because the court is 30 feet (9.1 meters) wide, each zone is 10 feet (3 meters) wide, so each set to the back row would be in the center of that particular zone. Though the terminology can be changed regarding what you call these zones, we'll refer to them as A, pipe, and either C or D, with the A zone being closest to the left sideline, and the C or D zone being closest to the right sideline. Pipe indicates a set that's set exactly in the middle of the court. Figure 21.7 illustrates

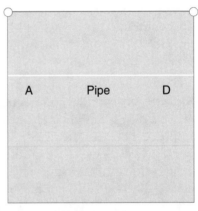

Figure 21.6   The three-zone back-row attack designations.

these four zones. Simply called A B, C, or D, these zones are divided into four equal parts. The pipe is still used in the four-zone system, referring to the area exactly between zones B and C. Many teams call these backcourt zones by school colors and many USA Teams use red, white, blue, and pipe (with blue closest to the right back). For the sake of simplicity here, we'll use the three-zone designations A, pipe, and C.

Now let's look at some multiple-tempo combination plays that can be used when the setter is in the front row. Here the first number indicates what the left-side hitter will hit, the second number indicates what the middle hitter will hit, and the third number indicates what the back-row player will hit. Which back-row player will be the back-row attacker is indicated in parentheses (LB = left back, MB = middle back, and RB = right back).

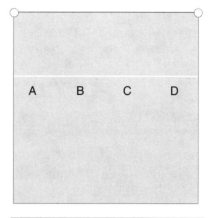

Figure 21.7 The four-zone back-row attack designations.

▶ 14-31-pipe (LB or RB). The left-side hitter is the outlet hitter. Because the middle front is hitting a 31, and either the LB or RB is hitting a pipe, the objective is to make the middle blocker commit to one of these sets. If the blocker commits to the 31, the pipe is wide open to hit, probably with no blocker. If the middle blocker notices the back-row attacker approaching for the pipe and focuses on the back-row hitter, the middle hitter will have a major opening and possibly no block at all.

▶ 14-31-C (RB). The left-side hitter is the outlet. In this combination play, an added dimension is the possibility of the setter attacking the ball on the second contact. The play is designed for a dominant back-row attacker (who's preferably left-handed). In this case, the middle blocker is forced to choose between the 31 and the C from right back. In addition, the left-side blocker must determine if the front-row setter, especially if the setter is jump-setting, is going to attack on the second ball. If the blocker jumps with the setter, the back-row hitter can hit without any block or a late block, depending on how fast the back-row set is run. If the left-side blocker is focused on stopping the back-row attacker, the setter now has a good opportunity to attack for a kill, because likely no block will be up. The setter being able to attack depends on the team's ability to pass and dig well.

▶ 31-94-A (LB). Here the A hitter is probably the outlet hitter (i.e., the one who gets the set if the pass or dig doesn't allow the setter to set a quick-tempo set to the left-side hitter [31] or a relatively fast-tempo set to the right-side hitter [94]). As you visualize this play, it becomes clear that the front-row hitters are vacating the A zone, hoping to free up the A hitter to hit against one blocker, or even no blocker. The A hitter will have to put the ball away against one blocker if the right-side blocker doesn't follow the left-side hitter in. This creates a major problem, however, if the right-side blocker doesn't move in because the middle blocker is now trying to determine if he or she should defend the 31 or follow the middle hitter around to defend the 94, which can be hit by the middle hitter off either a one- or two-foot approach. Regardless of what the right-side blocker does, an opening will be present somewhere, and it will be up to the setter to track what the blockers are doing so he or she can make the best choice on which hitter to set.

PERSONNEL REQUIREMENTS

At this point, it's assumed that you have progressed your hitters and setters from very simple sets that they can execute consistently and are now moving them toward more complex and difficult sets. You have seen that the plays illustrated in the previous section are not the easiest plays to run even in the best of circumstances. Imagine, then, the difficulty of trying to run any of these combination plays when the setter is running all over the court trying to chase down an errant pass or dig.

So, personnel requirement number one is having the passing and digging skills to consistently put the ball to the target, allowing the setter to set any of the options that are a part of the play. Second, a team must be able to run the first tempo set that's part of any combination play. Third, because many of these sets (e.g., 52 for a left-side hitter, 94 for a middle hitter, or 52 for a right-side hitter) require hitters to travel a considerable distance, it's helpful to have athletes who are agile and can cover a lot of ground efficiently and effortlessly. Slow, lumbering hitters will have a difficult time hitting combination sets effectively. However, all hitters should have the capability of running their approach parallel to the net and jumping off of one foot for a slide attack. This style of approach can get the hitter to the ball quicker and is also very hard for blockers to get in front of.

ADVANTAGES AND DISADVANTAGES

The biggest advantage to running multiple-tempo combination plays is the confusion you can cause blockers and backcourt defenders. These plays force blockers to decide which hit to defend because when the plays are run properly they won't be able to defend both. With great passing and digging, setters can set their hitters against zero, one, or poorly formed two-player blocks.

With effective ball-control skills, teams running these plays can have a lot of fun and keep players motivated to develop the passing and digging skills that make these plays work.

Because combination plays require using more types of sets, both from the frontcourt and backcourt, they keep more players involved. Players must stay focused or else risk missing an assignment.

For some teams, a disadvantage of using multiple-tempo combination plays is that players need to be well experienced and also well accomplished in their skills. These plays won't work for all teams. For example, a setter who has previously been required to set only three basic sets (e.g., the 14, 51, and

95) will likely have a tough time adjusting to setting multiple-tempo combinations without a lot of additional practice.

Another possible disadvantage to using these plays is that an offense's tendencies can become predictable. For instance, it will become very clear to an opponent when a team's first tempo sets (13, 31, 51, 71, etc.) are never or rarely set. This allows the opponent's blockers to write off the first tempo attackers and focus on the remaining hitters. Teams need to run the first tempo plays often enough to keep the defense honest and guessing.

OPTIONS

Many of the options open to teams using multiple-tempo combination plays were presented earlier under the explanation of tactics. Here we'll offer just one warning: If running multiple-tempo combination plays is part of a team's regular game plan, this can spell trouble on a night when overall ball control is lacking. Poor ball control means minimal options for the setter in running these plays. Teams should be able to recognize quickly what's happening on the court and adjust their game plans, to match the situation. All teams will have off nights, or nights when important players are in a slump, and on such nights the more complex plays will suffer most. On some nights the best option is probably to keep things simple.

COACHING POINTS

It's never pleasant to inform players that they won't be featured in the multiple-tempo combination plays you have chosen to use, but this is part of a coach's job. Simply put, not every hitter and setter have the skills necessary to be involved in these kinds of plays. As all coaches know, a big part of coaching is diplomacy. If you have hitters adept at hitting only one type of set, use these hitters as much as you can despite not including them in the team's combination plays.

As you begin introducing these plays to your team, progress from simple to complex in two ways. First, advance from what you believe is the simplest combination play for your team to run to the most difficult combination play for your team to run. Second, begin teaching these plays from the easiest ball to handle, which is the free ball. Introducing combination plays for the first time off a down ball or a hard-driven ball will prove frustrating for everyone involved.

Work first on the simplest combination play that begins with a free ball coming to the offensive side. Once basic efficiency has been established in this one play off a free ball, advance to a more difficult ball to handle—the down ball. On the opponent's second or third contact, a player swings at the ball like an attack, but from on the ground rather than jumping. Once a team shows the ability to run this play off a down ball, they can try it on a hard-driven ball that's attacked by the opponent. During this progression a coach will learn if his or her team can be generally capable of running combination plays out of these three situations. In the same way, only allow your team to first run these plays in a game off of a free-ball situation—your team's secret weapon. Then, when comfortable, allow them to run them off of a down-ball transition, then finally off of an attacked-ball transition.

Be cautious in yielding to the temptation of adding more multiple-tempo combination plays to your team's arsenal than you really need. Although these plays are fun and exciting for everyone, it's possible to overwhelm your players with too much to learn. If a team can learn just a few basic combination plays and execute them extremely well, this will nearly guarantee a high level of offensive success.

Finally, because combination plays are designed to stress and overload the defense, blockers should be a part of any drill in which these plays are trained. Although coaches can gain valuable information by watching an offense's effectiveness in running combination plays, they'll learn even more—about both their offenses and their defenses—through observing how blockers respond to the plays.

© Alan Look/Icon SMI

Swing Strategy

EXPLANATION OF TACTIC

Teams use the swing strategy when they want particular players (usually left-side hitters) to receive serve from all six rotations. The swing allows a team's best passers to receive serve as much as possible, including when they're in the three front-row hitting positions. The term "swing" is used because front-row players will generally pass from inside the court and then swing into their front-row hitting positions. The strategy can be used in any kind of serve-receive but is most common in the three- or four-player serve-receive patterns. The simplest form of the swing strategy is to have the hitters receive serve and then quickly move to attack from their usual front-row positions.

Figures 22.1 through 22.6 show a three-player serve-receive with both left-side hitters (LS1 and LS2) as passers in addition to the right-side attacker (OPP) in a 5-1 (one-setter) offense. Refer back to figure 15.1 (p. 138) to see how players are arranged in the rotation in a 5-1 system. In addition, review the material in chapter 15 (Options section) about the overlap rule involving adjacent players. As a reminder, here's a list of players and their adjacents:

- The right back is adjacent to the middle back and right front.
- The middle back is adjacent to the left back, right back, and middle front.
- The left back is adjacent to the middle back and left front.
- The left front is adjacent to the middle front and left back.
- The middle front is adjacent to the left front, right front, and middle back.
- The right front is adjacent to the middle front and right back.

Understanding the overlap rule is necessary as your team manipulates serve-receive patterns within the swing offense.

In figures 22.1 through 22.6 you can see how the swing element is incorporated. Notice for example in figure 22.1 that the best left-side hitter (LS1) is right front, and the opposite (OPP) is left front. Once the opposing team serves, both of these players swing out to their hitting areas. Simply, the opposite player swings outside to hit a left-side attack, and the left-side attacker swings to the right side to hit a right-side attack; then they make their switch to their normal front-row position once the ball enters the opponent's court. This is but one possible option. Figures 22.2 and 22.5 illustrate how the swing strategy is most often executed. Note in these rotations that the left sides (LS1 and LS2) are passing from the left-back position (LS1 in figure 22.5 and LS2 in figure 22.2). Once they pass, they will very likely swing outside to gain an effective approach angle (assuming they're right-handed attackers).

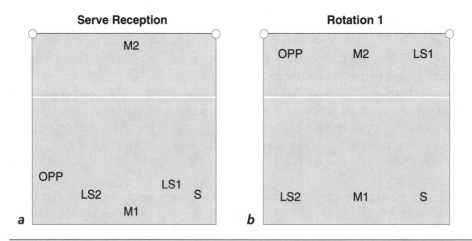

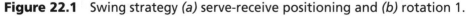

Figure 22.1 Swing strategy *(a)* serve-receive positioning and *(b)* rotation 1.

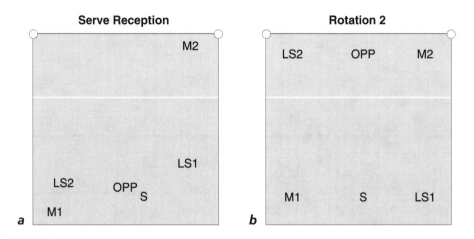

Figure 22.2 Swing strategy *(a)* serve-receive positioning and *(b)* rotation 2.

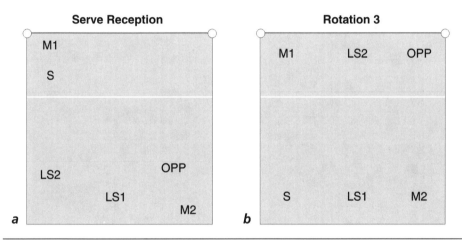

Figure 22.3 Swing strategy *(a)* serve-receive positioning and *(b)* rotation 3.

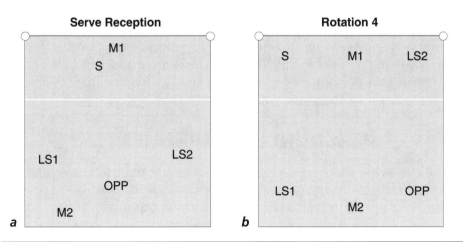

Figure 22.4 Swing strategy *(a)* serve-receive positioning and *(b)* rotation 4.

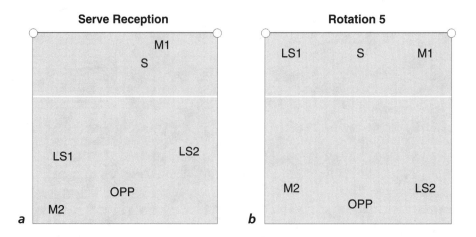

Figure 22.5   Swing strategy *(a)* serve-receive positioning and *(b)* rotation 5.

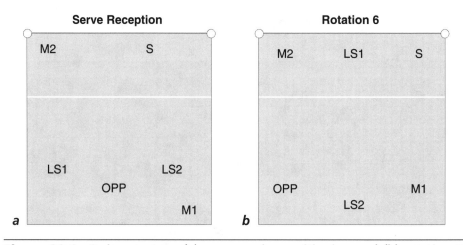

Figure 22.6   Swing strategy *(a)* serve-receive positioning and *(b)* rotation 6.

The primary reason teams choose to use the swing is to allow their best passers to receive serve most often, requiring front-row players to handle primary passing duties and then transition to become attackers. As we move to discussing the personnel needed for this strategy, assume that the left-side passers and opposite are the primary passers in this system.

PERSONNEL REQUIREMENTS

To use the swing strategy just described, in which both left sides and the opposite are the primary passers, your team must have three excellent passers. (Refer to the appendix [p. 235] to review how to rate players in the skill of serve-receive.) Ideally, all three of these passers are at least above a 2.0 average, and preferably at or above 2.5. Because left-side attackers are typically two of the team's best hitters, these players must be able to handle the stress of passing in a three-player serve-receive while being counted on to provide outstanding hitting as well. When opposing teams see that a primary hitter in a team's offense (usually a left-side hitter) is also a primary passer, the servers will serve them a lot of balls, hoping to wear them down physically. This passer must have physical (conditioning), technical (passing technique), and tactical (passing and hitting) skills to respond well to the opponent's tactics. Having said this, it's helpful if these primary passers and key hitters are strong athletes with good jumping abilities. Stronger, quicker, and more explosive athletes will be better equipped to handle the demands of this strategy.

Regardless of the system your team is playing, it's important to have a setter who can set consistent and hittable balls, but this is even more true in the swing strategy. Because greater demands are placed on the players who pass in all six rotations, having consistent sets allows the primary passers/hitters to play at a high level because they know they'll receive a consistently hittable ball. Late in a long match when these primary passers/hitters are getting inconsistent sets, greater stress is placed on them than when they're getting consistently hittable balls each time. Setters must work toward being consistent in their delivery of all sets but perhaps especially when setting to those players who have both hitting and passing responsibilities because in a long match these players will likely become fatigued.

ADVANTAGES AND DISADVANTAGES

One of the main advantages of the swing is that a team's best passers can receive serve in all six rotations, which allows the serve-receive offense to run efficiently. Even great serving teams will have difficulty disadvantaging their opponent when passers are performing at a high level.

The swing offense also allows hitters greater opportunities to hit many types of sets along the net out of serve-receive, which can confuse the defense. This advantage becomes more prominent as hitters develop a greater range of skills and a bigger repertoire of sets. Because front-row passers are passing from back-row positions, the swing strategy can confuse the blockers as to who the front-row hitters are. This gives the offense an advantage because the blockers might be watching the wrong players to get their reads on sets and attacks.

A disadvantage arises when a team is unable to pass well on a given night. Not only does the pass limit what the setter can do, but the front-row players who are primary passers are more likely to be out of position to hit any kind of ball because they are often positioned in the back row to receive serve in the first place. This results in the team providing the opponent a free ball, giving attack advantage back to them.

Of course an injured player is a disadvantage in any system or strategy, but a swing offense might have more trouble adapting to injury than others. Because three of a team's hitters carry a heavy passing and hitting load, keeping these three players healthy is particularly important. If one of these players gets hurt, it's very rare for the sub to come in and perform at the same level. An injury also poses problems on serve-receive because a new player communicates differently from the injured player as part of the serve-receive, resulting in a possible miscommunication among passers.

Another disadvantage involves an opponent who can consistently serve the ball into the last 5 feet (1.5 meters) of the court into all three back-row positions. Teams that can force passers to move backward, especially front-row players, reduce the chances of hitters getting aggressive swings. If a left-front player is passing from the left-back position (figure 22.2) and has to receive serve deep in the corner where M1 is standing, the left front will have difficulty on two fronts. First, he or she may have trouble passing the ball well. Second, even if the pass is perfect, the transition for the left-side player is a significantly longer distance compared to when the ball is served into the middle of the court.

OPTIONS

If you have three great passers, but two are middle blockers and one is a left-side player, it's possible to use the swing strategy with these players as well. Designing serve-receive for two, three, or four passers is encouraged, assuming your team is placing its best passers in the zones that allow them to receive the most serves (while not violating the overlap rule).

As mentioned in the previous section, teams must be ready to adjust to the opponent that can serve consistently to the deep corners. Figure 22.7 illustrates one such adjustment used when an opponent is serving deep crosscourt to the left-side hitter (LS2). In this modified serve-receive pattern, the M1 moves into the serve-receive pattern, allowing the LS2 to move forward. The LS2 now only has responsibility to pass the short crosscourt serve and can focus more on hitting. Of course this adjustment would occur only if the middle hitter has adequate serve-receive skills and you have trained this adjustment in practice.

If a front-row hitter can't get to his or her designated hitting spot, the swing hitters

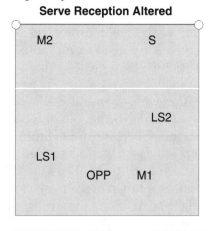

Serve Reception Altered

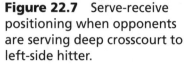

Figure 22.7 Serve-receive positioning when opponents are serving deep crosscourt to left-side hitter.

should hit a set from another spot along the net until they are better able to transition to their designated position. Alternatively, some teams employ a strategy in which swing hitters can hit anywhere along various zones of the net, based in large part on their overall attacking capabilities and what opposing blockers are doing to stop them. It's also possible to incorporate the swing offense with the left-side hitters passing in any one of the passing positions.

COACHING POINTS

A coach will probably know who the team's best passers are, but if there's any doubt, keep statistics (in both games and practices) for every player who passes. You want to be sure to have your three best passers receiving serve as often as possible in this strategy.

In practice, allow plenty of competitive opportunities for primary passers to pass and then transition to hit against well-formed blocks. Depending on who's passing and from where, it might be difficult to run many fast-tempo sets, as described earlier. Consider overloading your primary passers and hitters during practice, forcing them to learn how to be productive against a much bigger block than they'll see in matches. Even consider designing drills in which these players are required to pass and terminate a number of balls against three blockers. If they can have success with this in practice, you know they'll excel against one- and two-player blocks in real games.

Finally, don't underestimate the roles of the nonpassers in the success of a serve-receive. In figures 22.1 through 22.6, you might have noticed that certain players are placed in the corners (to avoid overlap) as part of the serve-receive pattern. It might seem that these players have no useful purpose, but that's not so. Players without passing responsibility should be communicating to teammates before the ball is served, offering suggestions to the passers on what kind of serve is coming and to what spot. Then, after the ball has been contacted by the server, these players call out where the ball is going and whether it's in or out. Be sure to involve your team's nonprimary passers in all serve-receive plays so they have the chance to play the critical roles available to them.

Offensive Strategy Drills

Offensive strategies can often be hard to master. The drills presented in this chapter will help develop the skills needed to implement the strategies contained in Part V. As with other drill chapters in this book, the drills are often useful in developing other skills simultaneously to keep practices as effective as possible.

Exchange Drill

Category: Use with chapters 21 and 22.

Objective: To teach ball control, hitting to zones, and to practice hitting different sets. It can be used as a warm-up or competitive drill.

Players Required: 6

Procedure: The drill starts with hitters digging and passing to the setter, who sets for a swing from crosscourt, right front to right front. After a specified time, the hitters hit down the line, right front to left front, then to the other side of the court, where the swings are crosscourt, left front to left front, and finally down the line, left front to right front.

Variation: This drill can also be a competitive game, with five cooperative rallies over the net then playing the sixth rally out for a point.

Hit the Gap

Category: Use with chapters 19, 20, and 22.

Objective: To teach left-side attackers to hit the gap between the right-side blocker and middle blocker, a gap that's common when teams are using a spread offense.

Players Required: 9

Procedure: The tosser initiates a free ball to diggers on team B, who dig to the setter. The setter sets the left-side attacker only. The left-side attacker looks for a gap between the right-side blocker and middle blocker. If a gap is present, the hitter hits through. If there's no gap, the hitter finds a way to terminate the ball without having to tip. The tosser initiates free balls rapidly for a set number of times. Left-side hitters then terminate a set number of sets.

Variations: Have right-side hitters perform the same drill. Players may also initiate with a down ball then served ball.

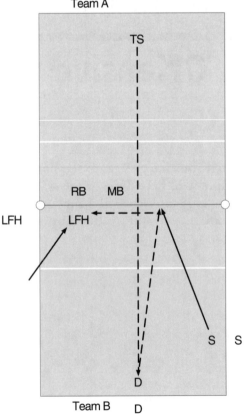

Common Errors and Corrections: Often a gap occurs between the blockers, but the hitter doesn't attack the gap quickly enough. Work with hitters to accelerate quickly so they hit the gap before it closes up. Work with the setter and covering players to verbalize for the attacker (one, two, or no blockers up, or "gap" or "split," etc.).

Watch the Middle Blocker

Category: Use with chapters 19, 20, and 22.

Objective: To teach setters where to set based on where the middle blocker is positioned (because middle blockers tend to shift slightly one direction or the other when facing teams who run the spread strategy).

Players Required: 10

Procedure: The tosser initiates a free or down ball to the digger on team B. The setter penetrates to the net from the right-back position. As the setter transitions to the net, he or she glances at the middle blocker on team A. If the middle blocker is shifted toward the left-side attacker, the setter sets a wide set (zone 9) the right-side hitter. If the middle blocker is shifted toward the right-side hitter, the setter sets a wide set (zone 1) to the left-side hitter. Have setters alternate repetitions for a set amount of time or a set number of successful repetitions to end the drill.

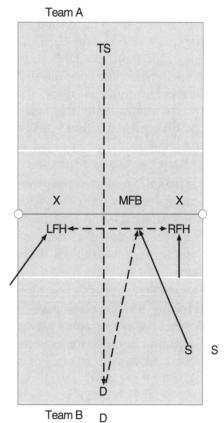

Variations: Incorporate a middle attacker on side B. The drill can be run with a front-row setter and two hitters, setting the middle hitter wide behind the setter if the middle blocker shifts toward the left-front hitter. Another option is to have the middle hitter start closer to the setter, as if he or she is planning to run a 9 set to the right antenna.

Common Errors and Corrections: Setters often glance at the middle blocker too early to get a good read on his or her intentions. Watch the setter carefully to see when he or she is glancing at the middle blocker and have them adjust as necessary. The setter should first eye check the blockers as he or she is penetrating to the setter target at the net, and glance again just as the dig or pass is contacted.

Block, Transition, and Terminate

Category: Use with chapters 13, 19, 20, and 22.

Objective: To train the left-front blocker to transition outside to terminate a set in zone 1 after helping block the opponent's quick attack.

Players Required: 7

Procedure: The tosser initiates a free ball to the digger on team A, who digs to the setter. The setter sets a quick attack to the middle hitter. Immediately after the quick attack has been contacted and blocked by team B, the tosser tosses the ball to the setter on team B, who sets to the left-side attacker in zone 1. Team B's left-front blocker must then help block the quick attack, land, turn, and run to get outside and available to hit. Team A's setter/left-side blocker and middle blocker attempt to block. Repeat for three minutes, with attackers alternating for each repetition, and then have the left-side attacker put a set number of balls away to end the drill.

Variations: The left-side hitter can hit various sets after helping defend the quick attack. The drill can be done with the right-side blocker helping block a 2 set in the middle then transitioning outside for a kill.

Common Errors and Corrections: When left-side blockers are asked to help defend the quick attack, they might simply go through the motions of defending because they're concerned about getting outside to hit. If this occurs, work with left-side blockers to ensure they're actively involved in defending the quick attack. Add that they can only score a point on their attack if they have an adequate block move.

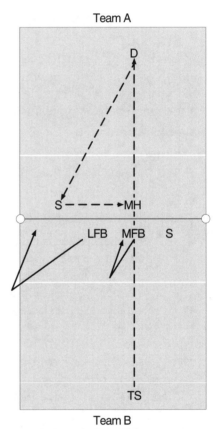

Team A

Team B

Drill the Angle

Category: Use with chapters 19, 21, and 22.

Objective: To teach the right-front blocker to transition off the net and hit the crosscourt shot from zone 9, anticipating a gap between the left-front and middle-front blockers.

Players Required: 6

Procedure: The tosser initiates a free ball to team B's digger. The digger digs to the setter coming up from the back row, as team B's right-front blocker is transitioning off the net. The setter sets the right-side hitter a ball in zone 9, and he or she hits a deep crosscourt shot. Position one or both blockers on team A to block the right-side attack.

Variations: The right-side hitter can hit various shots once they have established efficiency in hitting the angle. Require right-side attacker to approach with a one-foot slide-attack.

Common Errors and Corrections: Because the right-side hitter is being asked to drill the angle, he or she might fail to establish a neutral starting position inside the sideline from which to start their approach. Watch where they begin their approach to ensure the right-side attacker can hit both crosscourt and down the line.

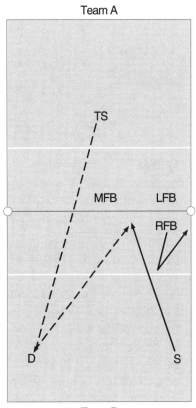

Team A

Team B

Rapid-Fire Spread Sets

Category: Use with chapters 19 and 20.

Objective: To train the setter to be consistent in delivering spread sets to the left-side attacker in zone 1 and the right-side attacker in zone 9.

Players Required: 4

Procedure: The tosser tosses balls rapid fire to the setter, who alternates setting the spread set to the left-side and then the right-side attacker. This drill can be used to condition the setter—tell the tosser to toss balls that make the setters move a lot off or along the net. This is a timed drill so switch the hitters and the setter every 2 to 3 minutes.

Variations: Require the setter to jump-set some or all the tosses. Coaches could also require alternating setters to penetrate from right back to the net each time and then cover the hitter he or she sets to or alternate hitters for each repetition in the same way.

Common Errors and Corrections: The setter is required to set consistent and hittable sets, which is challenging because of the rapid-fire nature of the drill. Watch for breakdowns in the technical aspects of setting and correct them as necessary. Examples might be that the setter does not get squared to the target if running a ball down, causing the set to be delivered too far off or inside, or the setter may not get all the way back to target or defensive base between sets. If this is the case, slow down the tosses slightly and reemphasize beating the ball to the spot.

Continuous Quick Attack

Category: Use with chapters 15, 16, 17, 19, 20, 21, and 22.

Objective: To give setters and middle attackers repetitions of quick attacks to train timing and execution.

Players Required: 8

Procedure: The tosser initiates free balls to any one of the three back-row diggers on team B. Team B's middle-front blocker reads and transitions off the net just before the free ball is contacted by the tosser. The digger digs to the setter, who runs a quick attack with the middle hitter. The middle hitters trade on each repetition to maintain the pace of the drill. The middle-front blocker on team A attempts to block or slow down the quick attack. A new toss is immediately initiated and the drill sequence repeats.

Variation: Although this is a rapid-fire drill, the tosser can alternate the initiation point, location, speed, and height of tosses to make the drill more game-like (variable and random).

Common Errors and Corrections: Watch for errors in timing and spacing between setters and middle hitters. Work with hitters on developing appropriate transition footwork and timing their approaches based on the dig; also watch the speed of the dig and the spacing with the setter.

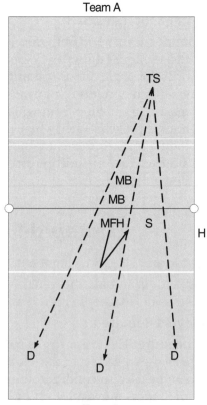

Team A

Team B

Block Out, Hit Quick

Category: Use with chapters 8, 9, 11, 12, 13, 15, 16, 17, 19, 20, 21, and 22.

Objective: To train middle blockers to block outside and quickly transition off the net to terminate quick attacks.

Players Required: 7

Procedure: The tosser initiates a free ball over the net to team A's digger, who digs to the setter. The setter sets the left-side hitter while the setter and middle-front blocker on team A get into position to block. Once the ball is contacted by the hitter, the tosser tosses a ball to the setter on team A's side of the net as the middle hitter transitions off the net to hit the quick attack. Give middle hitters many repetitions with each setter that they'll hit off of in a game. This kind of transition and quick attack requires much rehearsal of timing and spacing.

Variations: Increase the number of free balls introduced to team B. Examples might include blocking once outside, transitioning on a free-ball toss two or three more times, then blocking outside again (maybe to the other outside attacker). The tosser should also move around to initiate the tosses to and from different parts of the court so the digger and middle hitter see balls coming from many different angles. Another option is to have the middle hitter hit a series that involves all of his or her possible quick attacks both in front of and behind the setter.

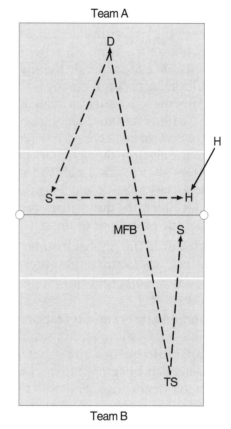

Team A

Team B

Common Errors and Corrections: The most common error is the middle blocker not getting off the net efficiently enough to be a legitimate attacker. Train efficient footwork to allow the blocker to get off the net and into position to initiate a quick attack from the middle.

Right-Side Quick Attack

Category: Use with chapters 11, 12, 15, 16, 17, 19, 20, 21, and 22.

Objective: To give the right-side hitter repetitions in blocking and transitioning off the net to hit a quick attack.

Players Required: 8

Procedure: The tosser initiates a free ball over the net to the digger, who digs to the setter. Team A's setter sets the left-side attacker while the right-front blocker on team B attempts to block. After the block attempt, team B's right-side hitter and middle blocker transition off the net as the setter penetrates to the net from the right-back position. The tosser tosses a ball to the setter, who sets a quick attack to the right-side hitter. The quick attack can be run behind or in front of the setter.

Variations: The right-side hitter can hit other sets besides the quick attack. Require a one-foot slide approach on the quick sets.

Common Errors and Corrections: Right-side hitters hitting quick sets typically hit crosscourt, a shot that will be defended once opponents know the hitter's tendencies. Work with right-side attackers at approaching at an angle to allow them to hit the quick attack either crosscourt or down the line.

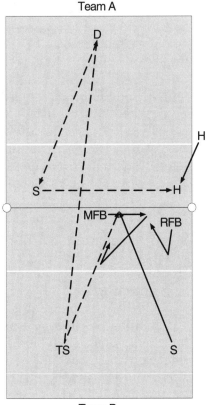

Team A

Team B

Left-Side Quick Attack

Category: Use with chapters 8, 9, 11, 12, 19, 20, 21, and 22.

Objective: To give left-side attackers repetitions in blocking and transitioning off the net to hit a quick attack.

Players Required: 7

Procedure: Team B's left-front blocker starts at the net and then transitions off the net just before the tosser initiates a free ball over the net to team B's digger. The setter sets the left-side attacker whatever type of quick attack is part of the offensive system. Blockers on team A position to block the quick attack. Left-side attackers switch every repetition to maintain the pace of the drill.

Variation: If attackers are experienced enough, have them use a one-footed takeoff with some of the quick attacks.

Common Errors and Corrections: Any time a left-side hitter is hitting a quick attack, timing errors are likely between the hitter and the setter because the left-side hitter is traveling quite a distance to make the attack. Watch and train setters and hitters on timing and spacing.

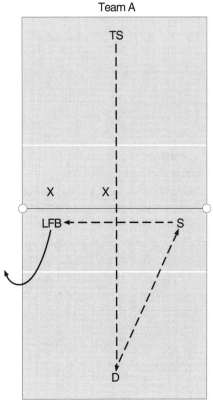

Team A

Team B

Front Row vs. Front Row

Category: Use with chapters 11, 12, 13, 15, 16, 17, 19, 20, and 21.

Objective: To train front-row players in transitioning from blockers to hitters.

Players Required: 8

Procedure: Tossers alternate tossing free balls to the setter on their side of the net. Setters run a fast-tempo offense while the other side attempts to block. Blockers transition quickly off the net after the block attempt to become available to hit. Play a rally score game to 15 points.

Variation: Have tossers vary the initiation point, height, and speed of the toss.

Common Errors and Corrections: In a fast offense, setters are more likely to set unhittable balls because timing is trickier than in a high-set offense. Watch for setters giving hitters an opportunity to terminate the ball at every set. Train consistency through multiple reps.

Hitting the Right X

Category: Use with chapters 15, 16, 20, and 21.

Objective: To give right-side and middle attackers multiple repetitions in hitting the right X.

Players Required: 8

Procedure: The tosser initiates a free ball over the net to the diggers on team B, who dig to target as the setter moves toward the net and blockers transition off the net to become hitters. The setter sets either a 51 (front quick set) for the middle hitter or a 42 (front 2 set) for the right-side hitter swinging around in front of the setter and just past the 51 hitter's shoulder. Have more than one middle attacker and right-side attacker ready to maintain the pace of the drill.

Variation: Incorporate blockers to defend these shots.

Common Errors and Corrections: The most common error with this drill is the setting of the 42, which invariably is too high, giving opposing middle blockers a chance to land from blocking the 51 hitter and still defend it. Work with setters and right-side hitters to establish the appropriate tempo and placement of the 42.

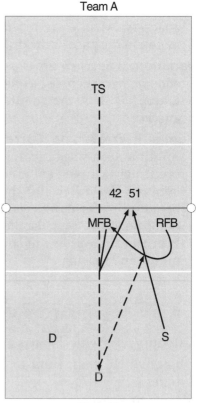

Team A

Team B

Hitting the Wide X

Category: Use with chapters 15, 16, 20, and 21.

Objective: To give the right-side attacker and the middle attacker multiple repetitions hitting the wide X.

Players Required: 8

Procedure: The tosser initiates a free ball over the net to the digger on team B, who digs to target, as the setter moves toward the net and blockers transition off the net to become hitters. The setter either sets a 31 to the middle attacker or a 42 to the right-side attacker. Have more than one middle attacker and right-side attacker ready to maintain speed of the drill.

Variation: Have the tosser initiate free balls from different spots on the court that alter in speed, height, and direction. This drill should incorporate blockers as much as possible so the hitters and setter are able to see if the middle hitter is able to draw the middle blocker with him or her.

Common Errors and Corrections: A common error is for the quick-attacker (31) to crowd the net, which makes him or her less of an option. Also, the right-side attacker sometimes makes his or her move in front of the setter too soon, taking away the deception the play should have. Coaches should ensure that the 31 attacker is jumping 2 to 3 feet (.6-.9 meter) away from the net and that the right-side attacker remains in a neutral position as long as possible before swinging around in front of the setter to attack (disappear-appear concept).

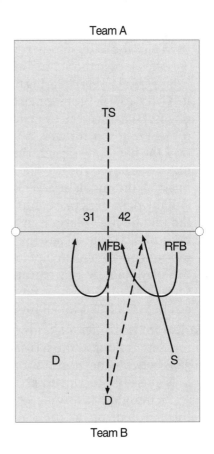

Team A

TS

31 | 42

MFB   RFB

D   S

D

Team B

Multiple Tempo With Back-Row Attack

Category: Use with chapters 15,16,17, 20, and 21.

Objective: To provide repetitions of multiple-tempo attacks using the back-row attacker.

Players Required: 10

Procedure: Team B's front-row players (two plus the setter if front row in the 5-1 offense or in the 4-2 offense; three front-row attackers if playing the setter in a back-row 5-1 rotation or in a 6-2 offense) start on the net and transition off as the tosser initiates a free ball over the net to the digger. The digger digs to the target. The left-side attacker hits a 14, the middle attacker hits a 31, and the right-back player hits a C (or the middle-back player if in a 6-2 or a 5-1 offense with a back-row setter). Blockers on team A attempt to defend this play. Run the play repeatedly for several minutes so tempo and timing can be established for all hitters.

Variation: Use different kinds of back-row sets (as long as the sets are in the gaps between the front-row options). It is possible to run this with the setter in right back so the setter digs the first ball up to the right-front player, who then sets the C to the back-row setter to attack.

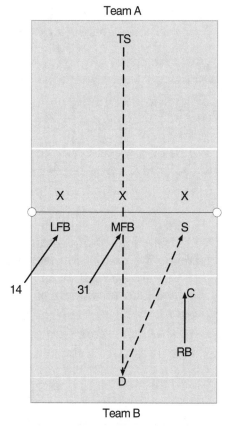

Common Errors and Corrections: In running any combination play, the timing between the setter and all offensive options is critical and the aspect of the play most likely to break down. Observe the synchronization of setter and hitters to ensure the play is running effectively, making it difficult for blockers to block any attack other than the one they have committed to.

Stress the Block

Category: Use with chapters 2, 3, 4, 15, 16, 19, 20, and 21.

Objective: To give setters experience in calling multiple-tempo sets based on the position of the block.

Players Required: 10

Procedure: Blockers on team B begin in base position, which will change about every three plays. The setter on team A, based on how the team B blockers initially position, huddles with the hitters and calls a play meant to counter what the block is trying to defend. The tosser on side B tosses across the net to the digger, who then passes to target, and the called play is run.

Variations: Allow blockers to randomly change their base positions as often as they choose.

Common Errors and Corrections: When setters make a mistake in their call of play, ask them what they saw that made them think the play would work. Often, what they saw is correct, but the play they call doesn't counter what opponents were trying to take away. Explain why a different play would have been a better call.

Pass, Swing, and Hit (Left Side)

Category: Use with chapters 2, 3, 4, 15, 16, 17, 19, and 22.

Objective: To give left-side passers in the front row repetitions receiving serve, and then transitioning to left front to hit the set.

Players Required: 7

Procedure: The team A server initiates a serve to the passer in left back. The passer passes to the setter, then transitions to hit from the left-front position. The setter sets the left-side attacker on team B, who terminates the ball, while blockers try to stop the attack.

Variations: Have the server serve some balls short as well as deep. Add a second passer to practice decision making.

Common Errors and Corrections: Young players often begin their transition to hit before completing the entire task of passing. Instruct passers to finish the pass, and then transition to become a hitter. If they have trouble making that transition, have them pass the ball higher, giving themselves more time to transition.

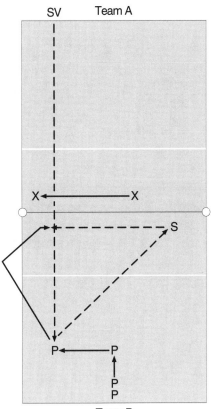

Team B

Pass, Swing, and Hit (Right Side)

Category: Use with chapters 2, 3, 4, 15, 16, 19, and 22.

Objective: To give right-side passers in the front row repetitions receiving serve, and then transitioning to right front to hit the set.

Players Required: 8

Procedure: The server initiates a crosscourt serve to the passer in right back, who passes to the setter. The passer transitions and hits from the right side. The setter sets the right-side attacker, who terminates the ball, while blockers try to stop the attack.

Variations: Instruct the server to mix up serves—short, deep, standing float, jump float, and so on. Add a second passer to practice decision making.

Common Errors and Corrections: When a right-side hitter has passing responsibility, they tend to pass and hit all in one motion, causing timing problems. Instruct players to pass, transition to where they'll start their approach, *stop*, and then time their approach to hit the ball.

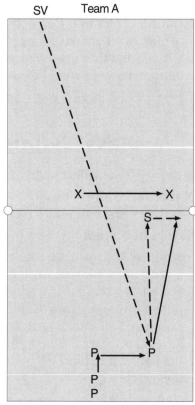

Team B

Stress the Hitter

Category: Use with chapters 15, 16, 17, 19, and 22.

Objective: To overload the left-side attacker by positioning three blockers to try to stop the attack.

Players Required: 8

Procedure: The server initiates a serve to the passer, who passes to the target, then transitions outside to hit from left front. The setter sets the left-side attacker, while the attacker (without tipping), attempts to terminate the ball against three blockers.

Variations: Have servers challenge passers with various types of serves. Add a second passer to practice decision making.

Common Errors and Corrections: Because there are three blockers in position, the most common error is the hitter getting stuff-blocked. Instruct the hitter to hit hard and high off the blockers' hands or to wipe his or her shot off the blocker's outside hand and out of bounds to counter the well-formed block.

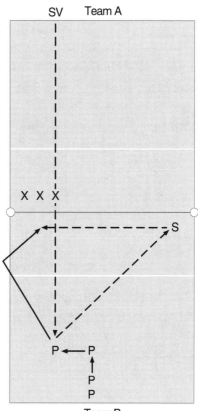

Talk, Transition, and Terminate

Category: Use with chapters 2, 3, 4, 15, 16, 17, 19, 20, 21, and 22.

Objective: To train communication among two front-row hitters (left front and right front) in the primary passing lanes.

Players Required: 9

Procedure: Servers initiate the serve by directing it between the two passers. The passers call and pass the ball, and then transition to their hitting areas. The setter can set to either hitter. Run the drill a set number of minutes, and then require a set number of kills to end the drill.

Variation: Have the server serve short balls between the passers, requiring them to communicate about who will receive the serve.

Common Errors and Corrections: Poor communication is the common error in this drill. Instruct passers to call for balls as early as they can and then to go for the pass aggressively. If both players call for the ball, remind them that the one with the best chance of making a good pass should call the ball and receive the serve. The passers must respect each other's abilities and responsibilities and not try to take every ball.

Hitter vs. Hitter

Category: Use with chapters 2, 3, 4, 8, 9, 15, 16, 17, 19, and 22.

Objective: To create gamelike competition between the primary passers/hitters.

Players Required: 6

Procedure: Servers alternate serving to the primary passers, who pass, transition, and hit. The first passer/hitter who successfully terminates 10 balls against a single blocker wins the contest.

Variation: Challenge particular passers with the type of serve they have the greatest trouble receiving.

Common Errors and Corrections: Achieving overall consistency is the biggest challenge in this drill. Leave passers alone as they strive for consistency in passing and terminating a set, then give positive feedback or instruction after the contest is over.

Ball, Setter, Ball, Hitter

Category: Use with all chapters.

Objective: To practice serve-receive and defensive strategies, as well as blocking patterns and offensive tactics.

Players Required: 12

Procedure: This is a six-on-six, two-ball wash drill. The game begins with a serve and after the point is played out, the coach hits a down ball to the receiving team. If one side wins both rallies, they get a point. Hitters rotate after each two-ball series. When one side wins three points they win the mini-game, the middle hitters sub in and switch sides, and both teams rotate to begin the series again.

Variations: Make the nonwinning side stay in that same rotation until it wins and rotate. Have the front row switch with the back row on its side rather than just rotate when it wins.

Common Errors and Corrections: Setters and teams may try to get to fancy with their plays and not achieve the success they need to win the rallies and thus rotate. A good philosophy especially when in a difficult rotation, is "simpler is better." Teams should go with what will work to get them the win in that difficult situation. Allow your setter to run the serve-receive pattern so if he or she finds the team stuck in a bad rotation, he or she has the option of changing the pattern to give the opposing server and defense a different look or alter their serving and defending strategy. Some teams will practice changing things up if they have been aced or produced poor passes that didn't allow good swings two or three times in a row. Whatever your team decides to do, make sure it has had time to think about and rehearse those possibilities in practice.

Systems, Strategies, and the Team

© Kin Man Hui/San Antonio Express-News/ZUMA Press/Icon SMI

Practicing Team Tactics

If you have read the previous 23 chapters, you now understand the different types of defensive and offensive systems and the pros and cons they bring to your team. As you prepare for a match and are assessing your current team in light of what you have read, you might make some unexpected discoveries. You might realize, for instance, that your upcoming opponent's left-side attacker's tendencies and your own players' skills call for a player-back defense. However, when you turn your attention to your opponent's tendencies from the right side, and again consider the skill level of your own personnel, you might determine that a player-up defense appears to make more sense. So, what do you do?

Such dilemmas are common at all levels of volleyball and typically require some creative problem solving. Coaches should not be afraid to think out of the box or to be as creative on designing defenses as they are in creating their offense. So, one solution to the scenario just described would be to develop a hybrid defense of your own creation that makes best use of your team's strengths while exploiting the weaknesses of your opponent. How is such a defense created? How does a team play both a player-back defense *and* a player-up defense? The answer is by alternating defenses based on the rotation you are in or the hitters you face in each rotation, and subbing as necessary to have your best defense on the court at any given time in response to the offensive maneuvers of your opponent. Such an adjustment is the kind of team tactic that coaches need to make, sometimes well before a match begins and other times on the fly. Either way, the adjustment won't work unless your team has trained for the possibility during practice. Using practice sessions to prepare for as many of the possible situations your team might encounter on the volleyball court significantly increases the chances of success in matches. Of course teams will fare far better when their coaches have strong knowledge both about the systems they have chosen for their team (based on player personnel) and on how to run an efficient and effective practice that allows for growth in individual skills while training tactics that make the team better as a whole.

So, when it comes to developing practice sessions that make the absolute best use of a team's time, where does a coach start? First, based on assessments of individual players' skills and on how these players come together as a team, the coach makes a list of objectives. These might include such items as "improve individual hitting," "teach and train team serve-receive," and "sharpen free ball transition." Once a team's most significant problem areas have been determined and objectives listed to address them, the coach is ready to design (or borrow or modify) efficient and effective drills that focus on helping the team meet its objectives.

ELEMENTS OF SUCCESSFUL DRILLS

The most useful drills are gamelike, fun, and competitive. They should include all players, whenever possible, whether in six-on-six or smaller groups rotating into the drill. All players need a role to play in each drill to stay engaged and learning. Good drills also allow opportunities for coaches to give feedback to individual players without stopping the drill for everyone.

1. Drills must be gamelike. In fact, changing your language from "drill" to "game" will help coaches in designing them as needed to mimic the situations teams will see in the competition. A gamelike drill requires players to perform movements and skills just as they would execute them in a live game. Common features of gamelike drills include the following:

- They require players to perform movements that occur before the ball is contacted, such as a front-row hitter starting at the net and then making the transition off the net to become available to hit.
- They require players to perform movements that occur after the ball is contacted, such as a server running to his or her defensive base position after making the serve.
- They introduce the ball into a game in a way that simulates how it will be done in an actual competitive match. For example, if a team is working

on defense-to-offense transition, the ball should be attacked by a live attacker rather than by a player or coach standing on a box or platform.

- They continue until a natural conclusion. As a minimum, play a rally until it reaches its natural conclusion on one side of the net. If working on serve-receive, the natural conclusion on one side of the net would be to pass, set, and attack, which puts the ball over to the opponents. Even better is to play the rally until it reaches its natural conclusion completely, meaning in the pass-set-hit game just mentioned there would be a blocker and possibly diggers who would play the ball out.

2. They must be fun. If the games you design are enjoyable, players will be more motivated to run them and thereby improve.

3. They must be competitive. There are many ways that games can be scored to introduce a competitive element. Based on your objectives for a particular practice session, be creative with how you score your games so that players have opportunities to win.

4. They should allow opportunities for coaches to stop an individual player for feedback without significantly interrupting others in the game.

5. They should provide opportunities for all players to get touches and show improvement. Typically, getting lots of repetitions is a key to improvement. Create gamelike drills that provide many contacts for all players.

MAKING THE BEST USE OF PRACTICE TIME

There's much debate over how much time should be spent on the individual skills of the game versus time spent on team skills, such as team serve-receive, backcourt defense, and so on. One prevalent thought is that regardless of the level they are coaching, coaches should spend time in each practice on individual serving, individual passing, and, to a lesser extent, individual attacking. Whether you're coaching high levels or beginning levels, practicing serving and passing will enhance your team's chances of success.

You'll need to consider how much time to spend practicing team systems such as team serve-receive, backcourt defense, blocking systems, free-ball and down-ball transition, and defense-to-offense transition after an opponent has hit a hard-driven ball to your side. Obviously, along with individual skills, team skills and systems must be practiced extensively. A common theory is to elevate the importance of team serve-receive as compared to the other systems. Before the advent of rally scoring, when teams could only score if they served, many coaches and players thought a team had to have a good side-out system (team serve-receive and attack). Interestingly, even with the prevalence of rally scoring, coaches continue to believe much practice time should be spent working on team serve-receive, especially because effective team serve-receive and team offense can result in a point.

POSITIVE ERRORS VERSUS NEGATIVE ERRORS

Regardless of how much practice time your team spends on individual skills compared to team skills, a key element to consider during practice sessions relates to errors. We understand that our players, no matter how experienced or how well trained, are going to make errors. One factor that separates good players from great players and good teams from great teams is the number of positive errors a player or team makes compared to the number of negative errors. Great players and great teams make far fewer negative errors than good teams. Good teams make more positive errors than negative errors.

Obviously a passer who can't pass the ball perfectly is going to try to make more positive errors than negative errors. Here are some examples of positive and negative errors within the context of serve-receive. Note in each scenario the distinct benefit of the positive error (though still an error) over the negative error.

1. When receiving serve, pass the serve too far off the net (positive error) rather than too close or over the net (negative error). If a passer finds he or she can't pass a ball perfectly to target, then attention is turned to making a positive error, which in this case is keeping the ball on his or her side of the net to give the setter opportunity to put up a hittable ball for the attacker. In contrast, a serve that's passed over the net puts the passer's team immediately on defense, with no chance to terminate an attack and making it harder for his or her team to score.

2. Pass or dig the ball too high (positive error) rather than too low (negative error). The ball that's passed too high presents some challenges for the setter, but it still gives him or her a chance to set the ball to a hitter. A ball that's passed too low gives the setter little time to put up a hittable ball, making it more likely that the opponent will get a free ball or a down ball.

3. In most cases, pass or dig the ball too far right of center (positive error) rather than too far left of center (negative error). Because most offenses have their setter to the right of center, passing too far to the right still gives the setter a chance to front-set to an attacker rather than back-setting from an awkward position.

Though these three examples are all within a particular offensive context, positive and negative errors occur in every aspect of the game, on both offense and defense. In one more example, a serve that goes over the net but out would be considered a positive serving error, versus a serve into the net (negative error). It would be a positive error to serve out because it still gives the opponent's passers an opportunity to have to play the ball and perhaps make an error in judgment, whereas serving in the net doesn't even require a decision on their part. If a team can execute perfectly, that's great, but when they can't, making a significantly higher number of positive errors over negative errors will still give the team a good chance for overall success.

RANDOM AND VARIABLE PRACTICE

Another principle important to discuss relative to practicing team tactics is random and variable practice. Volleyball is played in a very random and variable way, and it's rare that a player gets to perform the same skill twice in a row or under the exact same conditions. A server must hit to different targets, run into the court, and become a back-row digger. A hitter who hits a ball over the net (to various targets) that's kept in play must become a blocker before he or she gets an opportunity to hit again. A digger who just made a backcourt dig, this time off the opponent's crosscourt attack, and is also a team's primary back-row hitting option must transition to get available to hit the back-row attack.

All of these examples illustrate the unique randomness and variability of volleyball. If we adhere to the principle of practicing like the game is played, then drills in practice should take on more random and variable characteristics. For instance, a drill that's focused on individual passing should require the passer to pass balls (from many angles) and then transition to their next responsibility (whether it's hitting, hitter coverage, or some other responsibility). A drill that focuses on hitting should require the hitter to also perform the skill of blocking afterward, or digging before hitting. This way, players develop the ability to remember how a skill is performed, even in the midst of having to do something else. Research clearly indicates that one of the keys to successful execution lies in athletes' abilities to retrieve the motor program that allowed the skill (or a similar skill) to be executed. The forearm passer who simply passes the exact same ball from the same angle, speed, and trajectory repeatedly without having to do anything else will not get the necessary repetitions in retrieving the motor program of passing. For this too happen, the passer must pass and then perform some other skill (and it might just be a movement rather than an additional contact of the ball) and then come back to pass again (from a slightly different angle), requiring them to retrieve the motor program that allowed for the successful pass. Though there is some benefit to practicing in blocked formats (the opposite of random practice), especially for the young or beginning performer who's learning a new skill or motor program, teams that practice primarily in random and variable environments tend to produce more effective players. The difference is between players who can perform the skills of the game and players who can adapt to and *play* the game.

WHOLE PRACTICE VERSUS PART PRACTICE

Whole practice is performing an individual skill or movement in its entirety, whereas part practice is practicing something less than the whole skill. An example of whole skill practice is the hitter who transitions, approaches, and hits a ball that is set to him or her. Part practice in the skill of hitting indicates that something less than the whole skill has been performed. In this case, maybe the hitter transitions off the net and approaches, but doesn't hit the ball. A blocker blocking against a coach who's on a platform is practicing this skill in part, rather than whole, because he or she isn't required to watch the hitter (read and anticipate) and learn what the hitter might be doing based on the speed of the approach or the angle being taken to the net, and so on.

There's much debate over the value of whole practice over part practice. Many successful teams incorporate part practice as a key element of team training; others practice only or mainly in whole practice mode, requiring players to perform skills in their entirety. One thing is generally agreed on: If you choose to practice some skills in part, keep the parts (or "progressions") to a minimum. Advance players to practicing the whole skill as quickly as possible. Also generally agreed on is that if a coach is having trouble deciding which type of training (whole or part) to incorporate in practice sessions, he or she should choose whole practice.

Part practice is also more acceptable and useful in training individual players who may be having trouble executing a portion of a skill. However, a few part-skill repetitions and then back to the whole skill repetitions is the best way to get players to integrate use of that whole-skill in a game. After all, in a match players aren't allowed to perform just part of the skill—they must perform the whole skill. The only exception to the above is if there is a safety issue, such as when teaching players emergency retrieval skills such as rolling or diving. For these skills you may want to break them down into parts that can be safely practiced.

Other factors come into play regarding this issue. One, players who leave the sport of volleyball tend to do so for one primary reason: lack of fun. Coaches who are coaching younger teams, whose players are trying to figure out where volleyball fits into their lives, should keep this in mind and practice the game in whole, knowing that whole practice is much more fun than part practice. Though practicing in part might provide a sense that the skill is being developed efficiently, the movements required to successfully generate a skill are so interrelated that they should be practiced as a whole. Two things highlight this point. If coaches agree that a hitter wants to hit the ball hard (requiring a fast arm swing) and feel that a fast and strong approach is necessary to generate a fast arm swing, what would be the motivation to practice the footwork and arm swing separately? Further, even if the approach and arm swing were practiced together, why would a player not be allowed to hit the ball so they can have an opportunity to get feedback produced by the entire skill?

As you determine where you fall on the "whole versus part" practice debate, keep in mind these three primary goals, which we want to occur regardless of who we are coaching:

- Learn both individual and team skills.
- Have fun.
- Skills learned in practice transfer to matches.

SCORING SYSTEMS

Another consideration related to practicing team tactics is the development of scoring systems to determine if improvement in areas of weakness can be evaluated. Though books suggest a myriad of ways of scoring drills to determine if objectives are being met, coaches can and should create scoring systems to fit their particular needs. Scoring systems need not be too complicated or cumbersome. Determining if objectives are being met can be relatively easy. Say for example that your outside hitters need to attain 10 kills for every 2 hitting errors they make in order to reach a particular objective. Quite simply then, the scoring system would chart how many kills a player gets and how many errors are committed. If the player reaches 8 kills but has already committed 2 errors, the standard has not been met. At that point, a coach can determine what should happen, such as requiring the player to repeat the drill.

From a team drill perspective, coaches can develop scoring systems that fit the needs of their teams. For instance, in a six-on-six game, when one side is working on team serve-receive and a group of servers are working on serving aggressively enough to score an ace, you might make this game a contest between servers and passers. The passers try to get a set number of perfect passes before the servers get a set number of service aces. Whoever reaches their stated goal first receives a reward (e.g., no responsibility to help take down the net after practice). All coaches need to do here is determine what ratio of perfect passes and service aces is most appropriate.

WRAPPING UP

You now know how to develop objectives for practice; how to run a gamelike drill; how to determine how much time to spend on individual versus team skills; how to develop scoring systems; and the value of random practice and whole practice. Your objectives are stated, and your practice is planned.

Now let's assume that part of your practice is being spent on team skills. Does this require that your drill must contain six players on each side? Many coaches would say yes, but in fact the answer is no. Say for example you are working on team serve-receive. Your minimum requirement is to have one server on the other side of the net plus however many players you incorporate into your team serve-reception pattern. You're not concerned with team serve-reception offense but only with serve-reception accuracy. So you create a game that involves the number of passers you will incorporate in the game and one server. If you have the luxury of having more than one court, this drill could be copied on court number two, giving players more opportunities to respond. Even with only one court, you can have passers and servers on each side of the net, once again providing many quality repetitions.

Another example is a coach who wants to work on team backcourt defense and transition (being able to successfully dig the ball and attack effectively against live blockers). This type of gamelike drill at a minimum needs only three front-row blockers on one side and six players on the other side to work on team defense and transition. Although there are no backcourt defenders on the side with the three players, a coach will be able to chart whether the team is achieving the objective of effectively digging and attacking from an opponent's attack.

These two examples illustrate that the majority of drills you run, whether they are meant to develop individual or team skills or systems, can be performed with fewer than 12 players, often far fewer, so don't feel you need to be able to form two complete teams in order to run effective drills as part of a successful practice.

Finally, always emphasize to your players or teammates that no practices are going to be perfect. Sometimes it takes a long time for things to click. During the course of any drill or practice session, less-than-perfect situations will occur. Errant passes and digs, a set that's too tight, or diggers faced with digging a ball when their front-row teammates have failed to put up a block are all examples of teams being "out of system." Players and coaches alike need to understand that every team, no matter how good they are, will face many circumstances in which they are out of system. No team is immune.

Coaches should work with their teams to create advantages for themselves and their team even when out of their primary system. For example, on the errant pass or dig, the setter should still work at putting up a hittable set to the attacker. Getting a swing from the attacker in this situation can still provide opportunities to win the rally via a terminal attack. The setter who puts up a tight set should still encourage the hitter to be as aggressive as the situation allows. Maybe the hitter can hit with a half-speed arm swing or strategically place an off-speed shot in the deep corner (because defenses tend to creep up and in when they see a tight set on the opposing side of the net). The digger trying to dig a ball when the blockers have failed in their responsibility should work hard at digging a settable ball (dig as high as necessary, giving the setter time to get under the ball to set). The more effective teams are in staying aggressive, rather than becoming frustrated, when temporarily out of system, the more opportunities they have of creating a successful play. The reality is that coaches must plan for their teams to be out of system and must devise ways to practice best solutions to specific out-of-system situations, so players will all still be comfortable being aggressive on offense—out of system, but not out of sync.

© Imaginechina/Icon SMI

Match Coaching Tactics

Your team has learned the strategies, been rehearsed in the offensive and defensive systems, and trained hard to prepare for competition. Now you need to make sure that everything comes together as you get ready for the matches that will test the cohesiveness and strength of your volleyball team. In this chapter we'll review many issues for players and coaches to think about as they prepare for, play in, and reflect on matches. We'll divide our discussion into three parts—player preparation, match preparation, and postmatch—as we progress through a team's match-day considerations.

PLAYER PREPARATION

As match time approaches, teams need to do what it takes to get all players in optimal physical and mental condition for competition. This includes

- reviewing goals,
- preparing players based on their individual needs,
- reminding players what to focus on,
- talking to the setter,

- expressing confidence,
- reviewing opponent's tendencies, and
- leaving time for warming up.

1. Review goals: We discussed in chapter 24 how to develop scoring systems that determine if individual objectives are being met. The same scoring system objectives used in practice can be used to determine individual and team goals that need to be attained to better the team's chance of success. Knowing that every opposing team wants to win as badly as yours does, your team should try to determine which goals must be reached to give your team opportunities to win. As coaches work with their teams, trends develop that inform the coach of the standards of performance that must be reached to increase chances of winning matches. These goals might concern number of aces per game, number of unforced errors per game, hitting percentages, and so on. Though some goals will likely remain constant regardless of the opponent, others will change based on the competition. For example, if you're playing an opponent that's weak in receiving serve, the goal set for number of aces will probably be higher than average. In any case, a team's goals should be specific, measurable, and attainable. Don't make "winning" a goal, and don't make "playing well" a goal. Winning might not be realistically attainable against some opponents, and playing well isn't specific enough and can't be measured. Coaches should give their teams a role in helping identify and formulate team performance goals, with your guidance, as this creates team buy in to team goals.

2. Prepare players based on their individual needs: Some players need to be psyched up for a match, and others need to be calmed down. Coaches and teammates can acquire this kind of information in several ways, including via direct observation during practice and games. Notice how a player responds when playing against either a poor opponent or an opponent that your team hasn't defeated in a while. Against poor opponents, players may tend to take performance for granted, become overconfident, or get sloppy. Against a stronger opponent, players might tend to mope or give up on balls they should pursue. If you're a coach, be aware of what's happening in the everyday lives of your players. If you're a player, get to know your teammates well enough to know how to help them get ready for a match. Forming bonds off the court will lead to greater team unity on the court. If players can each think of their own emotional readiness scale, they should strive to each be at about a seven or eight out of ten to be prepared mentally and emotionally to compete, rather than at nine or ten, which may be too hyped up to perform well, or at four to six which may not be ready enough.

3. Remind players what to focus on: Every player has his or her own role on the team. The right-side blocker blocking against the opponent's best attacker needs to focus primarily on blocking. In most systems, the weakest passer will receive the majority of the opponent's serves, so he or she needs to focus on serve-receive. If you're a coach, also determine what your team's collective area of focus should be, based on the opponent, and then identify what individual players' primary tasks will be. Players might need to have more than one area of focus. For instance, an outside hitter who needs to be an effective terminal attacker and also an efficient passer in team serve-receive needs to focus on both these major areas, but in proper sequence.

4. Talk to your setter: Ask questions to ensure your setters know how the offensive plan is to be carried out. The setter is the one responsible for running the offense on the floor and likely requires extra time prematch to clarify his or her match duties. Regardless of what the offensive strategy might be (running quick attacks, setting the right side, etc.), a brief prematch setter-coach conversation to ensure the game plan is understood is time well spent.

5. Express confidence: Competition can make some players question their ability to do the job required to win. Counter doubts by expressing confidence in your team's ability to execute the game plan. Even if the opposing team has higher-skilled personnel, express to your players, or teammates, that they are prepared and can have success. Recognize the challenge ahead of you, but don't dwell on the opponent. Instead, focus on your team's preparedness and abilities to achieve the goals and objectives they have established.

6. Review your opponent's tendencies: What does your opponent do after a time-out? Who is its go-to hitter? What do the players like to do in transition? If you have this information, you can adjust your game plan accordingly. Of course you need to be sure that all players are aware of any adjustments your team will make in light of an opponent's tendencies. Once you feel your team has a good understanding of an opponent's tendencies, check them by asking questions. If, for instance, you know that after a time-out your opponent likes to set the right-side attacker, ask your players what they are expecting.

7. Leave time for warm-up: Because of all they try to fit in during a prematch routine, many teams don't leave enough time for adequate warm-up. Raising body temperature, loosening muscles, and getting repetitions on the ball all require time. Most teams devote 30 to 40 minutes to warming up before a match. Warm-up methods vary widely from team to team, but every warm-up should include

- enough activity to raise the core body temperature;
- active and dynamic stretching; and
- ball touches.

The first two of these elements will prepare players for the movements and demands of the game, and the third will get players mentally loose and ready to play their best volleyball. Following the established prematch routine also helps put players in a calm, confident state of readiness for the competition.

MATCH PREPARATION

After a successful prematch routine, your team should be both physically and mentally ready to step onto the court. Once the match is about to begin, coaches, and to a lesser extent players, have several things to think about before the first serve is contacted. These include

- starting positions,
- time-outs, and
- substitution patterns.

Once the match is underway, adjustments nearly always must be made based on your team's performance and the abilities and tactics of your opponent.

1. Starting positions: Before a match begins a coach must submit a lineup to the scorekeeper to indicate who will start in each position. Decisions on starting positions are generally based on basic volleyball strategies and individual team tactics, including those that follow.

- Put the best server in right back or right front. If your team is serving first in the game, start in a rotation that places your best server in right back, making him or her the first server of the game. If your opponents serve first, start your best server in right front so he or she will be the first server upon rotating when it's your team's turn to serve.

- The best blocker blocks against the opponent's best attacker. Assuming you have information on how your opponents will start, start in a rotation where your team's best blocker faces your opponent's best attacker for the most rotations possible. If the opposing team's best attacker starts in the left front, start your best blocker either in left back or left front so he or she can block against the best attacker the majority of the time he or she is in the front row.

- Use your most effective rotation. Instead of starting your players in specific positions to match up against an opponent, place your players in what has been your most effective rotation. Your most effective rotation is typically the one in which your team scores the most points. (You can get this information from official score sheets after matches have ended. Simply add the number of points your team scores for each rotation and subtract the number of points lost.)

- Put the best hitter in left front. Start your best hitter in left front to give him or her the most opportunities to hit. If your best hitter is your only legitimate offensive option, this tactic is particularly recommended. It gets tricky if your best hitter in left front is part of the rotation that allows the most points. In such a case, the coach should make the decision he or she is comfortable with, knowing it could go either way.

2. Time-outs: Coaches need a time-out plan so they can communicate and share information with their teams as efficiently as possible in the limited time allowed them. How best to spend this time will vary from team to team; the important thing is not to waste any precious seconds. In a 30-second time-out, for example, coaches might choose to talk for 10 seconds, give the players 10 seconds to talk, and then devote the last 10 seconds to water breaks and maybe one-on-one quick pep talks between coaches and individual players. Some coaches like to ask guided questions of their players during time-outs to keep players focused and help them learn lessons that will help them not only in the current match but in future matches as well. Remember that every match is not only an opportunity to earn another victory but also a chance for instruction that will carry over to the next match. It is smart for coaches to include time-outs in practice to train making the best use of time-outs during matches. Regardless of how you construct your team's time-outs, be sure that you have specific objectives for those time-outs, and that they are met. Finally, coaches should have a protocol guiding when to use their time-outs. For instance, How many consecutive points will you allow an opponent to score before calling a time-out? Should you save your time-outs for late in the game? Would you ever call a time-out when your team is serving? Early in the game?

3. Substitution patterns: With so many teams specializing these days, most teams have predetermined substitutions, such as a back-row player going in for a front-row specialist. Though having a predetermined subbing pattern is sound strategy, coaches should also consider substitutions that allow certain game-time objectives to be met. For instance, you might have a player (not a predetermined sub) come off the bench to serve a jump serve in the hopes of catching an opponent off guard. Another player might be a blocking specialist coming in at the end of a game, especially if you know where the opposing setter is going to set the ball. Trust your instincts. Not everything has to be by the book. There will be many times when a substitution that isn't predetermined makes sense from a technical and tactical standpoint.

4. Game and match adjustments: Every team encounters scenarios that require rethinking the original game plan. Adjustments might be based on an opponent's unexpected tactics, or on the performance of your own team. Say you're playing against a familiar team who always starts in the same rotation with the same players (e.g., the best outside hitter starts in left front). You want to get your best blocker in a starting position that allows her to block against their best attacker. You line up in game one assuming your opponent will start its best outside hitter in left front, only to discover that she's starting in right back. This means your best blocker won't be blocking against their best attacker. Such surprises happen all the time at all levels of play. Once you see that the opponent is using an unfamiliar rotation, express confidence to your team that they'll still be able to execute a large part of the game plan.

And whoever ends up in the position to block against the opponent's best attacker should have a brief moment with the coach to be reminded what that hitter's tendencies are.

On the other side, there will be times when your team does something that wasn't planned for. For instance, say one of your outside hitters isn't a key part of your offensive game plan (the setter has better-skilled hitters to give more sets to). But as the match progresses, this hitter turns out to have a hot hand and is having the hitting match of his or her life. Of course you advise your setter to adjust to feed the hot hitter. Regardless of the reasons, a team that can make adjustments in the middle of a game or match will generally have more success than an opponent that can't.

Though we have recommended that coaches trust their instincts when making adjustments, it's also critical that any adjustment has been rehearsed and trained in practice. Anticipate in practices the adjustments that might have to be made against an opponent, and allow time to train these adjustments.

POSTMATCH

The match is over. Your team has either won or lost. Players either played well, did not play well, or somewhere in between. Regardless of the level at which your team plays, it's critical for the coach to address the team following a match to deal with some or all of the following issues.

1. Determine if objectives were met: For instance, if a prematch objective was to serve two aces per game, did that in fact happen? (You might need to get the official score sheet or your statistical work sheets before talking stats to the team.)

2. Ask your players how they felt about meeting their prematch expectations: For instance, if players knew they needed to be aggressive in attacking the ball, ask them for their opinions on how they thought they did. You can ask them to grade their performance, individually and as a team, using scales such as 1-10 points or A-B-C-D-F.

3. Ask players how they feel overall about the match: What did the team do well? What areas need to be improved? The same scales as above can be used to rate their performance and set goals for future practices and matches.

4. State what you felt were key elements to the match: If your team won the match and played well, be sure to tell players specifically what they did well. If your team lost and didn't play well, suggest one or two areas for improvement to be practiced before the next match.

5. Be positive: If your team wins, it's easy to be positive in your postmatch talk. But recognize that some matches aren't going to go your way. There will be times when your team doesn't play well and you have to dwell somewhat on the negatives in order for the team to recognize areas that need improvement, but don't let the negatives overtake the positives. Be sure to give your team members at least one positive to take away with them. There's always something positive to say, even after the worst of losses. Don't let your players hang their heads. Buck them up, get back to practice, and make sure everyone is ready for the match ahead.

Appendix:
The Ranking System

For many teams, passes are ranked using a 3-point system. A 3 pass indicates a perfect pass to the desired target, high enough to make every option available to the setter who will determine who to set. A 2 pass is a ball passed high enough and close enough to target (although not perfect) that the setter can get to it and have most of the offensive options in that rotation available. In many cases, a 2 pass gives the setter the option of setting any hitter except for the hitter who might be hitting a quick attack (usually a middle hitter). A 1 pass is a ball that usually causes a team to scramble to keep the ball in play, often resulting in giving the opponents an overpass or free ball (a ball that's not attacked). Further, a 1 pass may also be one that's errant enough that the designated setter isn't able to retrieve it, making it necessary for someone else to assist the setter by handling the second contact. Finally, a 0 pass is a service ace by the opponent. This serve is not returned because it has either hit the floor untouched or is passed so errantly that no one can retrieve it (e.g., the pass that goes into the stands or out of the field of play, such as behind the team bench). It's a common benchmark that if specializing primary passers, then each of them should be passing above a 2.0 average, and ideally closer to a 2.5. To calculate a passer's passing average, you would need to chart each pass for each individual passer. This can be done by rotation, by area of the court passing from, or overall. To come up with this number you would multiply each 0 pass by 0 points, each 1 pass by 1 point, each 2 pass by 2 points, and each 3 pass by 3 points. Once you have these points, you divide that number by the total number of passing attempts, giving you a number between 0 and 3 (see table). This may be one way to actually determine which passers should become primary passers and also verify that you have the correct passers passing most of the served balls.

Computing Passing Scores

Player number	PASSING RATING				Total points	Total attempts	Rating
	0	1	2	3			
12	/	///	//	/////	22	11	2.0
7		/	////	///	18	8	2.25
2	///	///	//////	/////	25	15	1.67
5			///	//	12	5	2.4

Total points = number of 1 passes × 0; number of 1 passes × 1; number of 2 passes × 2; number of 3 passes × 3. Passing rating = number of points divided by passing attempts.

About USA Volleyball

Founded in 1928, USA Volleyball is a Colorado incorporated nonprofit organization recognized by the United States Olympic Committee (USOC) and the Federation Internationale de Volleyball (FIVB) as the National Governing Body for the sport of Volleyball in the United States. USA Volleyball's primary duties, obligations, and responsibilities are to

- be the expert authority for the sport in the United States and a leader in the world;
- train and field teams to compete in and win medals at the Olympic Games and the Pan American Games;
- prepare athletes and coaches for sustained competitive success in all international competitions;
- develop and promote the sport at all levels for athletes, coaches, officials, and other participants;
- increase awareness of, and interest in, the sport among the media and the general public; and
- govern the sport in conformance with the Olympic Sports Act in a fair and reasonable manner.

USA Volleyball is responsible for both the Olympic disciplines of indoor volleyball and beach volleyball. USA Volleyball has over 240,000 registered members, 12,000 teams, and 5,000 clubs nationwide. With an annual budget in excess of $11 million dollars, USA Volleyball supports the USA men's and women's senior national team programs, youth and junior national teams, national championship events, coaching education and certification programs, grassroots development, and programs for the disabled and Paralympic Teams. USA Volleyball has a rich tradition of success as evidenced by winning an Olympic medal in every Games since 1984 and capturing numerous World Cup, World Championship and Continental Championship titles.

Stu Sherman, associate director of development at Graceland University in Lamoni, Iowa, wrote *Volleyball Systems & Strategies*. He coached collegiate-level volleyball teams from 1986 to 2004. His teams twice took runner-up and once won the National Championship at the National Intramural-Recreation Sports Association (NIRSA) National Collegiate Club National Championship. Stu has been a USA Volleyball Coaching Accreditation Program (CAP) Cadre member since 1994. He conducts coaching workshops all across the United States and in 1998 was named USA Volleyball Outstanding Clinician and Best Clinician for Iowa Region of USA Volleyball. Stu would like to dedicate this book to his son, Sterling, who has put up with him for the better part of 17 years. Sterling has been his son, his sidekick, and his right arm. He is simply a young man who has provided him much laughter, support, and friendship. While sometimes he has to be the hard-nosed dad as he tries to guide him into adulthood, he is extremely blessed to have him in his life. Sterling, you're the best.

Diana Cole, director of Coaching Education Programs at USA Volleyball, assisted in the development and writing of *Volleyball Systems & Strategies* and oversaw much of the DVD production. Diana is a USA Volleyball Coaching Accreditation Program (CAP) Cadre member and Level III accredited coach, traveling several times a year to both teach and administrate at various coaching courses around the USA. Her background includes coaching stints at several high school teams, collegiate programs, as well as USA Volleyball Junior Club teams. She has also participated in clinics and camps from the under 12's to collegiate levels.